Praise for *Deconstructing Undecidability*

"*Deconstructing Undecidability* offers a welcome contribution to the literature on Derrida and religion. Where some interpreters associate deconstruction with an indeterminate openness, Michael Oliver shows that Derrida sees the act of decision as problematic but unavoidable. Drawing on Derrida, Oliver argues that theological debates over liberation and divine election must reckon with the need for discernment. With sensitivity and insight, Oliver offers an account of the struggle for justice that attends to its persistent ambiguity." —David Newheiser, Australian Catholic University

"Michael Oliver examines the power of the theme of exclusion in determining the critical analyses and constructive remedies of certain progressive theologies—most specifically, postmodern and liberationist—alongside the theme's slippery, challenging complexity. He exposes a deconstructive-like double bind: the tendency to isolate and demonize exclusion as the source of all bad religion, theology, and ethics and the simultaneous inability to provide a theo-ethical remedy that does not itself participate in some form of exclusion. In doing so, Oliver brings to light a difficult truth that has not always been sufficiently addressed in our best progressive theologies, thereby offering progressive theologies an invitation to be more self-aware, transparent, and self-critical, toward the hoped for outcome of becoming even more viable and more compelling." —Chris Boesel, Drew University

Deconstructing Undecidability

Deconstructing Undecidability

Derrida, Justice, and Religious Discourse

Michael Oliver

LEXINGTON BOOKS/FORTRESS ACADEMIC
Lanham • Boulder • New York • London

Published by Lexington Books/Fortress Academic
Lexington Books is an imprint of The Rowman & Littlefield Publishing Group, Inc.
4501 Forbes Boulevard, Suite 200, Lanham, Maryland 20706
www.rowman.com

6 Tinworth Street, London SE11 5AL

Copyright © 2020 by The Rowman & Littlefield Publishing Group, Inc.

All rights reserved. No part of this book may be reproduced in any form or by any electronic or mechanical means, including information storage and retrieval systems, without written permission from the publisher, except by a reviewer who may quote passages in a review.

British Library Cataloguing in Publication Information Available

Library of Congress Cataloging-in-Publication Data

ISBN 9781978704381 (cloth)
ISBN 9781978704404 (pbk)
ISBN 9781978704398 (electronic)

*For my sons, Trace and William,
in an attempt to start a new tradition.*

Contents

Acknowledgments	ix
Introduction: How to Avoid Decisions: Denials	1

Part I: Deconstructing Undecidability

1	Religion *sans* Exclusivity, "Perhaps"	17
2	Rereading Undecidability: An Appreciation for the Aporetic Double-Bind	41

Part II: Justifying Decisions

3	The Injustice of Exclusivity	77
4	The Injustice of Indecision	119

Part III: Deconstructing Divine Undecidability

5	Un/Avoidable Divine Decision	157
6	Un/Avoidable Human Decisions about Divine Decision	181

Conclusion: The Decision Maker That Therefore I Am	209
Bibliography	229
Index	237
About the Author	241

Acknowledgments

I would like to begin by acknowledging, and thanking, the editors and staff at Lexington Books/Fortress Academic and Rowman and Littlefield for their assistance throughout this entire process, especially Gayla Freeman, Neil Elliott, and Lisa Dammeyer.

This project, in its various stages, was not only completed in the midst of a great cloud of witnesses, past and present, but deeply influenced by their presence and voices. At its earliest stages, the seeds for the thoughts and ideas about the issues engaged here were planted during my time as a graduate student at Drew University, where I had the distinct pleasure of working with—and learning from—many brilliant scholars and teachers. This includes, most especially, Ada Maria Isasi-Díaz, Otto Maduro, Traci West, Laurel Kearns, Melanie Johnson-DeBaufre, Nancy Lynne Westfield, Robert S. Corrington, Kate M. Ott, Virginia Burrus, Stephen Moore, Hyo-Dong Lee, Althea Spencer-Miller, and Gary Simpson. Any sound, theo-ethical instincts that I possess have their fingerprints all over them. At the top of that list is Chris Boesel, my doctoral advisor and dissertation committee chair, who not only taught me how to read (with and against) Derrida, but also whose rigorous pursuit of perfection fueled my own, consistently refining and sharpening my thoughts and words in every stage of the thesis-writing process, and helped me tap into a potential that I did not know existed. Additionally, our similar approach, sensibilities, and ethical desires with regard to these issues and ideas helped me find my own voice in the midst of these discourses. I also want to especially thank Catherine Keller, whose voice in my head always urged me to consider an-other approach, an alternative position, a different way, urging me to a novelty I could not envision on my own. Her continued support, encouragement, and availability has been an invaluable resource throughout this journey.

Thank you to all my students, who I can only hope learned as much from me as I did from them. As a lecturer and adjunct professor at Drew, Rutgers, Seton Hall, Caldwell, Monmouth, and Raritan Valley, these students helped me think even harder and deeper about these issues, endured my tirades and antics, and who were helping me write and rewrite this project, even when they did not realize it. At Oxford, I have had the pleasure of working with many brilliant young minds, at the undergraduate and postgraduate level. In countless tutorials, supervisions, seminars, lectures, discussions, or classes, I was invigorated to push further and deeper into these issues and questions. This is especially the case for the inaugural run of the undergraduate Liberation Theology and Its Legacy class, who read through versions of this manuscript in conversation with the rich liberation theological tradition and offered honest, substantive, and insightful feedback. The postgraduate seminar for first-year masters students (newly named Figures and Themes in Modern Theology) also provided fertile ground for continuing to wrestle with, think through, and continually hone my thoughts. The students at St. Benet's Hall—Lorenzo Baldwin, Pablo Garcia-Moreno Dora, Natasha Frank, Inès Bonneau, Henri du Périer, Henry Martin, Ned Seagrim, Martha Harlan, Serena Reeve-Tucker, Leone Astolfi, Charlie Pozniak—will always have a special place in my heart; I appreciated your sincere interest in hearing about this project. Thank you, and the fellows—Mary Marshall, Brian Klug, Louise Nelstrop, Susan Doran, Nicholas Waghorn, Fr. Oswald McBride—for making St. Benet's feel like home. My only wish is that I had more time to work with and learn from Werner Jeanrond before he moved on to Oslo, who has been a source of continued inspiration and support.

I also want to thank all my colleagues, staff, and friends at Oxford for helping me to feel welcome and get situated across the pond. Special thanks to Graham Ward, who has mentored me through the early-career process, been a continuous sounding board and source of wisdom, and helped me navigate these often mysterious waters. The administrative staff at the Faculty of Theology and Religion has been incredibly supportive, especially Fran Roach who has always kept me on my toes. I am also grateful to the Patristics and Modern Theology research seminar for inviting me to give a version of Chapter 5 and generating a very lively conversation indeed. My research assistants have been particularly helpful in the final stages of this project, which includes Nikolaas Deketelaere's proofreading and helping me not lose sight of the importance of con/text(s), and Stefano Salemi's assistance with indexing. I am especially thankful for the friendships I have made at Oxford and the outlets they provided for reassurance. Best wishes to my old office mate, Darren Sarisky, heading down under—thanks for the sound advice and input you offered. And most especially for Dafydd Daniel, who has become not only a dear friend and close confidant, but also someone I could always turn to for honest feedback, an encouraging pep-talk, or some hearty laughs and a bout of blowing off steam—all of which were integral to this entire process.

Personally, no endeavor worthy of such effort can be accomplished without the love, support, and encouragement of family and friends. Heartfelt thanks and love to *la mia famiglia*, my sons, mother, brother, sister (in-law), father, aunts, and cousins who always supported and encouraged me, even when they could not understand. This book is dedicated to my sons, Trace and William, who never cease to make me proud to be their father. My brother, Sean Parello, has always been a healthy counterweight to my tendency to drift off too far, grounding me when I needed it most. I am thankful for his help with the cover art; but even when it wasn't directly about the content or this process, our conversations and discussions were always feeding into my own thoughts about this. A special thanks to those family members who are no longer with us, whose memory and presence in my life has shaped me into the person I am: Joseph Fiorellino, Chandler Oliver, Thomas Parello, Salvatore Parello, Audrey Parello, Andrea Fotia-Brown, and Angelina Fiorellino; even though they are not present to share this with me, they are forever in my heart. Thanks to all my friends who never let me lose touch with the "real world," especially Thomas Meredith and Vincent Imbrosciano, whose friendships are invaluable to me, and who each provided precious insight based on their unique worldviews. I feel fortunate to have had access to immense wisdom and counsel throughout various stages of this process, and I am thankful for the particular presence of Damian Elias and William Noble.

Above all, I am especially grateful for my partner, Kim Scobie, who has supported, encouraged, and loved me through this process from its very beginning, even when it might not always have been clear to her how or to what extent. The cover image is an apt analogy not only for the argument put forward here about the impossibility and inescapability of decision manifested in the palette, but also a metaphor for her gift to me without even trying.

Introduction

How to Avoid Decisions: Denials

> *If there were a devil, he would not be the one who decided against God, but he, that in all eternity, did not decide.*
>
> —Martin Buber, *I and Thou*

Over the past few decades there appears to be an increased awareness and avoidance of what Jacques Derrida has referred to as "the decision that *cuts*, that divides"—in other words, an increased hypersensitivity and allergy to the necessary exclusion inherent in every choice.[1] This is especially the case in discourses that seeks to achieve or is concerned about social justice, where exclusion and division are identified as that which is the source of injustice, or at least that which prevents or obstructs justice. Relatedly, theological and religious discourses that are aware of the perpetuation of unjust status quos have become increasingly keen to identify how exclusion "names what permeates a good many of sins we commit against our neighbors."[2] As a result, over the last few decades we find a sustained analysis and critique of religion's problematic exclusivity and a focus on the "struggle to do away with faith structures of exclusion" that continue to privilege white, male, heteronormative, Western, Eurocentric, anthropocentric images, symbols, and perspectives to the exclusion of all others.[3] Christian theologians are becoming more aware that "exclusivistic claims for 'one and only'" no longer seem tenable given the reality of, and growing appreciation for, present-day religious pluralism.[4] As Martin Hägglund puts it, there is a growing consensus that "'good' religion . . . welcomes others and 'bad' religion . . . excludes," and thus the focus has been on avoiding or remedying exclusion as much as possible.[5] Such an awareness of the problem of exclusion and division has made the notion of decision even more problematic, especially when one recognizes the inherent exclusive and divisive nature of decisions and choices.

Against the backdrop of this awareness and recognition, this book is an attempt to dive deeper into the problem of decisions that cut, divide, and exclude. While genuinely affirming the desire to avoid exclusivity, and by extension, decisions that cut or divide, this book critically examines the problematic nature of decision and the ways in which we have attempted to avoid such, with an eye toward gaining a clearer understanding of the problem. In fact, it is the affirmation of this problematic predicament that is this book's primary motivation, such that the goal is to demonstrate how the problem of exclusive decisions is more complex, and thus more problematic, than it initially appears. Simply put, this book argues for the necessity of reckoning with difficult decision(s), even if/when such decisions are exclusive and problematic, because they are inescapable. In fact, one only ever mistakenly inhabits the illusory position of "indecision," i.e., standing outside the decision point, as a reflection of power and privilege. In order to demonstrate this point, I will examine two particular instances in which the problem—and ensuing dynamic—plays out: first, in discourses where a pursuit of justice or liberation from systemic oppression is a primary concern; and second, in theological understandings and negotiations of divine decision. Ultimately, this book aims to gain a greater appreciation for the complexity of the problem of decision—in the contexts of justice work and theological understandings of divine decision—and an acknowledgment of the reality of having to reckon with such difficult decisions as a more responsible approach. A more thorough analysis of the problem of difficult, divisive decisions deconstructs any remedy, revealing an aporetic double-bind, and the rupture of the impossible necessity, and necessary impossibility. The goal is not intended to render the problem unproblematic, nor to make a case *for* any particular, exclusive decision (divine or human), but to raise the stakes about just how problematic they are by revealing the limits of any attempt to remedy the problem. Critically engaging decisions and our desire to avoid them is therefore needed in order to be more rigorous and transparent about identifying and engaging the depth of the problem, in all its complexity and thorniness.

The deconstructive analysis that I will put forward in this book is, in effect, another way to approach the foregoing consensus regarding the problem of decision. In fact, it is an attempt to get at the root of the problem by using the very discourse that has become associated with this consensus. As we will see, undecidability—a term often associated with deconstruction—has become uncritically (and as I will argue, mistakenly) associated with the desire to avoid decisions that cut, divide, and exclude. However, part of the aim of this book is to reveal the *deconstruction* of any such notion of undecidability. Deconstructing undecidability, therefore, means deconstructing the notion that there is a way to escape the double-bind of decisions that cut, divide, and exclude, even while acknowledging that the latter are thoroughly problematic. The end result of such a process leaves us in a position wherein we must discern (i.e., perceive, recognize, detect) decisions that are difficult (i.e., that cut, divide, and exclude). Discerning difficult decisions, which was an alternate title for the book, means discerning between difficult options or choices, even, and especially, when one recognizes the problematic nature of doing so. Discerning difficult decisions also means recognizing and acknowledging the necessity of having to do so, because there is no avoiding the cut of the decision that we have begun to recognize as so problematic. Given the etymology of discern, deriving from the Latin *discernere* meaning "to divide or separate," there is ample reason to stick with the language of discerning difficult decisions, especially when such difficulty arises because of the way we have become more aware of how decisions divide and separate. Nevertheless, the argument of this book remains fixed on pointing to the deconstruction of any safe remedy to the problem of such difficult decisions, such that our discernment becomes much sharper and more difficult. In so doing, we should come to recognize, acknowledge, and take responsibility for the difficult decisions we inevitably make and must continue to make, which, in turn, only raises the stakes and exacerbates previous diagnoses of the problem.

As quoted above, Martin Buber writes: "If there were a devil, he would not be the one who decided against God, but he, that in all eternity, did not decide."[6] In contemporary, progressive discourses the conclusion is that the "devil" is the decision that cuts, divides, or excludes. And while I affirm the inherently problematic nature of such, this book also identifies a concern about the illusion of any way to escape, avoid, or remedy the problem. In the midst of a consensus about the devil of such exclusive decisions—again, a consensus of which I am admittedly a part of—I am attempting to reveal *another* devil, the one that Buber gestures toward in this quotation. A devil that might actually be more pernicious, precisely because it is more insidious. It is the devil of indecision, the devil who does *not* decide—and worse, the devil that deceives us into believing that not deciding is the solution. Perhaps the devil is not only in the details, or the decision, but also in the enticing temptation and deception of indecision. Moreover, as I will go on to argue, indecision is devilish because it is illusory. The temptation of avoiding the difficult decision is perhaps so tempting because it is only an illusion. There is no safe space of indecision that we can retreat to in the midst of such difficult, divisive decisions.

Emilie Townes also sketches quite clearly, and poetically, a way to frame this engagement with the devil of in/decision. She writes:

> Evil does not . . . come in pristine forms. Like goodness, it is messy and rather confusing. Writers often appreciate this more than ethicists I think. And so I engage these writers as mentors and guides. Yet, like mentors and guides, they can only go so far and then I must make the journey on my own. I attempt to provide a set of lenses for examining and understanding the structural nature of evil. In the process, imagination, memory, and history dance through my analysis as Macbeth's three witches—"Fair is foul, and foul is fair."[7]

This book is an attempt to highlight how the evils—or devils—of exclusive, problematic decisions do not come in "pristine forms," and, consequently, that any attempts to critically engage this predicament will always be "messy and rather confusing." More specifically, I aim to explore a depth and complexity to the problem, i.e., its "evil-ness," in order to uncover its messiness. My concern is that if and when we identify decisions that divide as "the problem" we might rest assured that we have accurately identified the entirety of the problem and have begun our good, responsible work of solving or avoiding this problem. But the problem might not lend itself to such a simple analysis, identification, and remedy. It is much thornier, complicated—i.e., more *problematic*—than that. In each of the specific contexts that we will explore, any analysis, identification, and supposed remedy might actually reveal that it has always already been navigating some version of the problem itself. Thus, like Townes, we are left with the realization that "I must make the journey on my own," choosing between various versions of an inescapable problem, discerning difficult decisions. As we dance through these murky, dangerous waters in the subsequent pages, we might begin to recognize, along with Townes and Macbeth's three witches, the ways in which "fair is foul and foul is fair." What was once simply the problem that we must avoid, now becomes much more complicated. What was once fair—*avoiding* decisions that exclude—is now foul; and what was once foul—decisions that exclude—is, in a limited way, somehow fair. This messy and confusing predicament is precisely where this book intends to lead us, with the aim of providing "a set of lenses for examining and understanding the structural nature of evil." In other words, the aim is a renewed understanding of an undecidability that does not mean indecision and in no way provides a solution to the problem, because there is an evilness to indecision as well. Rather, deconstructing undecidability helps us discern, i.e., acknowledge, the inescapability of such difficult decisions.

In "How to Avoid Speaking: Denials," when Derrida finally comes to grips with the realization that he must finally "stop deferring" and "try to explain [himself] directly on the subject, and at last speak of 'negative theology,'" he begins by asking: "How is it possible to avoid speaking about negative theology?" After years of deferring direct engagement with the topic of negative theology, he finally addresses it explicitly. In so doing, however, he realizes that negative theology by definition is a discourse that is predicated on *unsaying* and *avoiding* speaking. Thus he finds himself strangely asking: "How, if one speaks of it, to avoid speaking of it? How not to speak of it?"[8] Derrida realizes that perhaps he was unable to avoid negative theology all along, that he can no longer defer, because in not speaking (about negative theology), was he not always already engaging in some sort of negative theological mode of discourse (about negative theology)? "Is there ever anything other than a 'negative theology' of negative theology?"[9] This book intends to place us at this very intersection with regard to the topic of decision; *Deconstructing Undecidability* could also be called *How to Avoid Deciding: Denials*, insinuating a Derridean denial of the "how to avoid." Its goal is to lead us to an analogous insight, where we, like Derrida, come to a similar realization with the problem of decision, that we were never able to avoid it in the first place, that we have always already been in its midst.[10] Derrida reminds, and performs, the deconstructive predicament that I will try to reenact: an inability to find safe ground or escape the problem, especially one that we would like to avoid. The aim of this book is to try to confront us with the reality of a denial, that to avoid decision as a way of avoiding its dangers—or worse, to think we have succeeded in doing so—is impossible. So how to avoid deciding? Perhaps it is time we stopped deferring.

AVOIDING DECISIONS THAT EXCLUDE

The desire to avoid decisions that cut or divide echoes a larger, more widespread consensus in the contemporary, academic study of religion about the problematic nature of exclusion. Theologians and scholars of religion have reckoned with the problem of exclusivity and attempted to reconceive, if not purge, the exclusive elements of religion. As I have suggested, part of the reason that exclusion is such a primary concern—for which the goal is to remove or limit Christian theology's exclusive elements—is an ethical awareness of the perpetuation of unjust status quos, where we have recognized the tendency to privilege white, male, Western, Eurocentric, anthropocentric, heteronormative images, symbols, and perspectives to the exclusion of all others. Engaging this particular aspect of the sociopolitical problem of decisions that cut, divide, and exclude will be the focus of Part II.

There is also a deeper theological and religious, although not unrelated, aspect to the identification of exclusion as problematic, which we will explore more in depth in Part III. In one of the landmark works in the dawning of modern theology, Immanuel Kant zeroes in on the problem of exclusivity in religion: "far from establishing an age suited to the achievement of the *church universal* . . . Judaism rather excluded the whole human race from its communion, a people especially chosen by Jehovah himself, hostile to all other peoples and hence treated with hostility by all of them."[11] For Kant, it is the Jewish theological notion of chosenness that is problematic for a modern, universal religion because of the former's inherent exclusivity. Of course, for Kant, the universal religion within the bounds of reason that he envisions is indeed Christianity, as we can only "begin the universal history of the Church . . . from the origin of Christianity, which, as a total abandonment of the Judaism in which it originated, grounded on an entirely new principle, effected a total revolution in doctrines of faith."[12] Apart from the glaring Christian supersessionism and disturbing anti-Semitism, Kant's point about the problematic nature of exclusivity in religion has been almost universally accepted and confirmed in modern (and "postmodern") Christian theologies.[13] A thoroughly modern, universal religion must begin with a "total abandonment" of exclusive doctrines and dogmas, and because a notion of divine decision represents the problem *par excellence*, it should be one of the first to go.[14] In the wake of modernity, a sustained analysis and critique of religion's problematic exclusivity has continued, across various theological discourses, even if the goal is no longer to establish a "universal religion." Even when we have come to recognize the limits of any kind of Kantian, Hegelian, or modern notion of universality, there is a still an acute concern about vestiges of exclusivity; in fact, more recent discourses are keen to point out the inherent exclusivity of modern universality itself, highlighting "how modernity's internal dynamics and factors operate 'discursive[ly to exclude].'"[15] This consensus about the problematic nature of exclusivity makes our exploration of the problem of divine decision pertinent and relevant for contemporary theological discourse.

The issue of exclusion as rationale for contemporary attempts to avoid decisions that cut or divide is the backdrop to the argument of this book. Although the primary focus is decision, in each of the subsequent chapters we will explore the way that an identification of a problematic exclusivity is always lurking behind the desire to avoid difficult decisions. Throughout our exploration, I will continually affirm the problem of exclusivity as inherently problematic. The goal, however, will be to dive further into the problem by focusing more precisely on the unavoidability of (some form of) the problem, urging us to continue to confront more honestly the reality of such inescapable difficult decisions.

PART ONE: DECONSTRUCTING UNDECIDABILITY

We will begin by examining a kind of structural inescapability at play in decisions through a particular reading of the work of Jacques Derrida. As such, Part I will set the table for our further exploration by providing the theoretical framework throughout this book. The result of this exploration will be a deconstruction of any attempt to avoid decisions that cut or divide. Thus, for those (of us) who recognize the problem of exclusive decisions the task shifts from avoiding such to discerning between *which* problematic decisions. Moreover, a greater appreciation for the tension of the Derridean "aporia" of *impossibility* and *inescapability* sheds light on the problematic relationship one always already inhabits with regard to decision. In Part I we explore how a more thorough understanding of the precarious predicament we inevitably inhabit will help us to discern the difficult decisions that are always problematic. Such deconstructive insight should therefore shift our emphasis from attempting to avoid problematic decisions, to discerning between various forms of them, because they are inescapable. In so doing, Part I reveals the deconstruction of undecidability as any kind of way out through the illusion of indecision, or a deconstructing undecidability that forces us to more honestly confront its difficult reality.

Part I not only lays the theoretical foundation for the argument of the book, but advances theo-ethical engagements with Derrida. Much of this discourse has emphasized the movement toward avoiding, limiting, or remedying the problem of exclusion (and by extension, decision), epitomized in the work of John D. Caputo. In Chapter 1, we begin by exploring Caputo's work, focusing on his strident critique of exclusivity. Caputo's work sheds a bright spotlight on the problem of decisions that cut, divide, and exclude. In Chapter 2, I critically analyze Caputo's reading with a sharper focus on the deconstructive "aporia" that further complicates the situation by revealing the impossibility of avoiding some form of the problem (of exclusivity, decision). In my analysis, any reading of deconstruction that overemphasizes (a certain kind of) impossibility, at the expense of inescapability, collapses the aporetic tension in the deconstructive double-bind. Critically analyzing Caputo's reading of impossibility in Derrida's work not only advances the insights of Caputo regarding the problem of decision, but also highlights a predicament in which there is no solution or remedy that is not also itself a problem, emphasizing the inescapability of difficult decision(s), or the impossibility of avoiding or remedying such. A renewed understanding of impossibility with regard to decision helps us recognize and appreciate the aporetic tension of the "impossible decision," such that in the face of the "undecidable" one is "still obligated ... to give [oneself] up to the impossible decision ... for only a decision is just."[16] Rather than attempting to avoid decisions that cut, divide, and exclude, a more thorough analysis of the problem reveals a predicament wherein there is no remedy that is not itself also poisonous, where in/decision more accurately captures this problematic predicament.

Having established the theoretical framework for engaging the problem of decision(s) through a reading of Derrida in Part I, the remainder of the book seeks to illustrate the structural dynamic at work in the aporia of inescapable, impossible decision(s) by taking a look at two particular contexts in which this plays out: discourses pursuing justice and theological engagements with divine decision. The move to contextualize the discussion about the structural nature of decision continues to follow the Derridean theoretical framework. As Derrida continually maintains, deconstruction is only ever encountered in con/text(s); it is parasitic, it is, i.e., it only exists, in con/texts: *"il n'y a pas de hors-texte."*[17] If deconstruction "'is' only what it does," then the deconstructive aporia of decision—its inescapability and impossibility—only exists, can only be encountered, in specific, particular con/texts.[18] Thus my attempt to tease out the aporetic tension of deconstructing undecidability can only be fully understood in the contexts themselves.

PART TWO: JUSTIFYING DECISION(S)

In Part II we explore the first context: discourses where a pursuit of justice or liberation from systemic oppression is a primary concern. Here my analysis will both build upon the Derridean insight of inescapable decision established in Part I, as well as add a further element to the analysis: the way in which power and privilege distorts an appreciation of such a predicament, leading to the illusion of a place of indecision.

Early liberationist work emerged in response to the material oppression, marginalization, and exclusion of certain groups, peoples, identities. In order to remedy said exclusion, this work recognized the need for exclusive preference, choice, or decision for those oppressed and excluded, often cast in terms of "the divine preferential option" in theological discourses.[19] In subsequent decades, however, there has been an increased awareness of the limits of such earlier approaches, including critiques of how exclusive preference for *one* oppressed group (or *one* form of justice) has resulted in the further exclusion of *other* oppressed groups (or *other* injustices). In Chapter 3 we will explore these critiques that focused on how such preference or choice was based on "limited understandings of oppression, and especially of the multilayered nature of oppression," which, in turn, have "created new exclusions . . . through a narrow understanding of contexts."[20] Alternatively, more recent work in the fields of women's and gender studies, critical race theories, and other liberation discourses has identified intersectionality, hybridity, and multiple sites of oppression and privilege that complicate the articulation of experience or identity in monolithic, homogenous categories, upon which such choice or preference could be made. In contemporary liberative discourses preference, choice, and decision *for* particular oppressed groups or forms of injustice is considered problematic because such thick and totalizing categories obscure a much more complex and multilayered picture of identities, groups, and experiences.

Building on the argument of Part I, however, Chapter 4 will argue for the inescapability of such problematic decisions, and a more precarious predicament wherein there is no safe place to stand outside or beyond, as we are always already in the midst of difficult decisions. Furthermore, one only ever mistakenly inhabits the illusory position of "indecision," i.e., standing outside the decision point, as a reflection of power and privilege. Drawing on further insights in women's and gender studies as well as critical race theories about how privilege is defined as the ability to exist—or believe one exists—outside or beyond gendered, raced, sexualized identity markers, Chapter 4 argues that one's mistaken belief that they could avoid the difficult decision reflects such privilege.

While this book appreciates the importance and necessity of more recent work in liberation discourses, the core argument of Part II seeks to further the conversation through an appreciation of the inescapability of making limited, difficult decisions for particular forms of justice for persons or groups. Again, drawing on the foundation of Part I, Part II seeks to explore the relevance of Derrida's reflections on justice and the necessity of decision where he writes: "No justice is exercised, no justice is rendered, no justice becomes effective . . . without a decision that cuts and divides."[21] While current conversations about the complexity of experience and identity acknowledge blind spots in early liberationist work that perpetuated injustice, more recent discussions might also be subject to a mistaken belief that one could avoid difficult decision(s). Given all that we have learned over the past few decades of work in this field—about issues of identity, intersectionality, continued marginalization and exclusion, etc.—I double-back toward some of this earlier work, in order to continue to advance the conversation. I am particularly interested in the way such important moves and progress in these discourses might have unintended, deleterious effects on the pursuit of justice that are worth considering. More specifically, how they might fund a move *away* from important, necessary, inescapable decision points. Even more specifically, I am seeking to dispel the illusion of a safe ground that one might retreat to, with regard to problematic, messy, complicated, and difficult decisions. And my argument is that the illusion, the mistaken belief that one could safely avoid difficult decisions, is a product of power and privilege, which leads one to assume a "non-position" or a state of indecision. Simply put, power and privilege can blind us into thinking that we are outside, above, or beyond the decision point, such that we might be able to avoid the difficult decision in the context of social justice work.

PART THREE: DECONSTRUCTING DIVINE UNDECIDABILITY

Finally, we turn to another contemporary context wherein the dynamic of difficult decision(s) plays out: theological negotiations of divine decision. Traditionally understood as "divine election," this theological notion has always been considered inherently problematic; even John Calvin himself—the preeminent figure in the history of the doctrine—referred to the doctrine of divine election as the *decretum horribile*.[22] In contemporary, progressive religious contexts, one of the most pervasive critiques of divine decision is its inherent exclusivity. Whether in terms of predestination where some are eternally chosen and others are not for eternal salvation (or some are chosen for salvation and others are chosen for damnation), or even in more broader understandings of divine decision, the critique of divine decision's inherent exclusivity is one of the reasons many avoid such a theological notion. Contemporary theologians do not "spend time and energy re-discovering this doctrine," but rather are tempted to "deposit it on the dumping ground of those theological doctrines that have proved to be destructive,"[23] which might explain why there is a dearth of progressive, contemporary theological voices explicitly engaging this topic.

Chapter 5 revisits divine decision in an attempt to discover a deeper complexity to the problem by uncovering the issues that arise with the attempt to avoid, remedy, or escape it. Simply put, if the remedy to the problem of divine decision is that the theologian decides the kind of God who decides (or not), or the content of such a decision, then said remedy is trafficking in the very thing it has attempted to avoid or remedy, namely, exclusive election, choice, decision. In so doing, divinity has been reduced to an object of human (theological) decision, which is problematic for those with a theological commitment to a divine reality beyond, apart from, or at least not beholden to the control of the human being. Even if one does not hold a theological commitment to such a divine reality, there might still be an expressed ethical concern about human mastery and control over divinity, wherein it is the human who can declare who or what God is or does, as "when an embodied creaturely reality identifies itself with and so presumes to grasp and control an infinite mystery."[24]

At the same time, the situation is no less problematic for the theologian who chooses to confess, declare, or include some notion of divine decision, as we will explore in Chapter 6. The theologian who chooses to endorse a notion of divine decision must also acknowledge the impossibility of not collapsing it into merely human decision, which is the very thing he/she is trying to avoid, because there is no avoiding the human aspect of deciding—i.e., choosing to confess such. Building again on earlier Derridean analysis, Part III presents the aporetic double-bind of an impossibility for the human theologian to confess or include divine decision, yet also an impossibility to avoid or exclude some form of it. In short, it highlights a predicament wherein the theologian cannot avoid the problem, but must discern between various forms of it, revealing the inescapability of difficult decision(s). Thus, deconstructing undecidability in this context means confronting this double-bind with regard to divine decision—an inability to stand on safe ground when navigating the dilemma it poses. Similar to the argument in Part II, the illusion of indecision reflects an issue of power. In this case, the inescapable issue that both sides are trying to navigate is too much power in the hands of the human theologian, which leads one to believe that they can safely avoid the predicament of the difficult decision.

CONCLUSION:
THE DECISION MAKER THAT THEREFORE I AM

In both of the above contexts examined, this book argues that power distorts one's relationship to the impossibility and inescapability of decision. On the one hand, in the context of justice pursuits, one believes that they could safely avoid the cut of the decision of which a particular form of injustice takes priority, as a reflection of power and privilege to mistakenly stand outside, above, or beyond the decision point. On the other hand, in the context of theological negotiations of divine decision, one believes that they can avoid the cut of the decision by deciding, implicitly, if and what kind of a divine decision has been made, as a reflection of too much power in the hands of the human theologian to mistakenly stand outside, above, or beyond the decision point. While it may appear at first glance that I am arguing in two competing directions—*for* making decisions in one context and *against* making decisions in the other—in fact, the structure of the argument is intended to highlight an aporetic double-bind that inhabits each context, and the argument in these two particular discourses reflects the way that each has tried to escape the double-bind by collapsing the tension on one side or the other. This book argues is that there is no (one) answer or approach to the predicament; moreover, the book attempts to reveal the deconstruction of any such approach or response that would relax the tension, in either direction. In so doing, it urges those concerned about these issues to acknowledge, own, and claim responsibility for the decisions we inevitably engage in. Again, the argument in each discourse is radically contextual; *both* contexts have attempted to avoid the decision in seemingly different ways that nonetheless reflect a structural similarity of attempting to escape the double-bind; and as I will argue, the illusion of power is the culprit in both.

In the concluding chapter, I must enter into these contexts myself and stake my own difficult decision(s). If the argument of this book has led us to the acknowledgment of the inescapability of the predicament, then this analysis must also acknowledge my own presence in these contexts—otherwise such an analysis will be subject to my own critique, as the argument of the book could be read as a way of standing outside the problem, merely pointing out the ways in which it is problematic. In so doing, I would also mistakenly assume a non-position, or an illusory position of indecision, with regard to these issues, as a reflection of my own power and privilege. In the context of decisions for particular forms of justice, this predicament is extremely pertinent, as my identity and experience as an over-educated, white, Western, cisgender, heterosexual male affords me a host of privileges and power. Thus, I must always consider and acknowledge my own identity, social location, and experience. How is it always "gendering" or "whitening" or "straightening" what I am hearing, seeing, responding to, agreeing/disagreeing with? In what ways is it leading me to mistakenly inhabit some kind of a presumed "objective," higher plane, outside or beyond the decision point, wherein I merely critique, analyze, and judge limited, difficult decisions? While I cannot make ultimate, once-for-all decisions about the complexity of such matters—and I am not advocating for this at all throughout the book—I must also be careful not to slip into the illusion that I can avoid making difficult decisions myself, in particular moments, that will always be limited and problematic. In order to sketch this problem out, I close by drawing on contemporary examples because again, this dynamic is only ever encountered in concrete contexts. In so doing, I risk staking a decision regarding complicated issues of identity and justice, inhabiting the precarious position of discerning and deciding, and thus leaving myself open to critique because such will always be limited and problematic. Similarly, in the theological context of divine decision, I risk staking a difficult decision on the issue of divine decision, even as I recognize the problematic nature of such. I draw on Derrida's reflections on exposure in *The Animal That Therefore I Am* to elicit the nakedness we experience in the call to decide, closing the book by illustrating this predicament and giving the reader an example of deconstructing undecidability, discerning and confronting limited, problematic, and difficult decision(s).

NOTES

1. Jacques Derrida, "Force of Law: The 'Mystical Foundation of Authority,'" in *Deconstruction and the Possibility of Justice*, eds. Drucilla Cornell et al. (New York: Routledge, 1992), 24.

2. Miroslav Volf, *Exclusion and Embrace: A Theological Exploration of Identity, Otherness, and Reconciliation* (Nashville: Abingdon, 1996), 72.

3. Ada Maria Isasi-Díaz, *Mujerista Theology: A Theology for the Twenty-First Century* (Maryknoll, NY: Orbis, 1996), 65–66.

4. S. Mark Heim, "Differential Pluralism and Trinitarian Theologies of Religion," in *Divine Multiplicity: Trinities, Diversities, and the Nature of Relation*, eds. Chris Boesel and S. Wesley Ariarajah (New York: Fordham, 2014), 122.

5. Martin Hägglund, "The Radical Evil of Deconstruction: A Reply to John Caputo," *Journal for Cultural and Religious Theory* 11, no. 2 (Spring 2011): 127.

6. Martin Buber, *I and Thou*, trans. Walter Kaufman (New York: Touchstone, Simon & Schuster, 1996), 101.

7. Emilie M. Townes, *Womanist Ethics and the Cultural Production of Evil* (New York: Palgrave Macmillan, 2006), 9.

8. Jacques Derrida, "How to Avoid Speaking: Denials," in *Derrida and Negative Theology*, ed. Harold G. Coward and Toby Foshay (Albany: State University of New York Press, 1992), 82.

9. Ibid., 83.

10. Derrida performs the "always already" in the postscript to this engagement with negative theology, where he begins the essay with an ellipsis (". . ."). See: *Sauf le nom (Post-Scriptum)* in *On the Name*, ed. Thomas Dutoit, trans. David Wood, John P. Leavey, Jr., and Ian McLeod (Stanford, CA: Stanford University Press, 1993).

11. Immanuel Kant, "Religion within the Boundaries of Mere Reason," in *Religion and Rational Theology*, ed. Allen W Wood, trans. George Di Giovanni (Cambridge: Cambridge University Press, 1996), 155.

12. Ibid., 156.

13. For an in-depth analysis of a pernicious and recurring anti-Semitism at work in modern Christian theologies, especially as a reaction to the exclusivity of Judaism, see: Chris Boesel, *Risking Proclamation, Respecting Difference: Christian Faith, Imperialistic Discourse, and Abraham* (Eugene, OR: Cascade Books, 2008). For an in-depth analysis of a pernicious and recurring anti-Semitism at work in modernity more broadly (beginning with Kant), and its wide-spreading racial implications, see: J. Kameron Carter, *Race: A Theological Account* (Oxford: Oxford University Press, 2008).

14. For Kant, this would also include an abandonment of all doctrines and dogmas that necessarily conflict with practical reason and human freedom.

15. J. Kameron Carter, *Race: A Theological Account* (Oxford: Oxford University Press, 2008), 45.

16. Derrida, "Force of Law," 28.

17. Jacques Derrida, *Of Grammatology*, trans. Gayatri Chakravorty Spivak, Corrected edition (Baltimore: Johns Hopkins University Press, 1998), 158.

18. Jacques Derrida, "Afterword: Toward an Ethic of Discussion," in *Limited Inc*, ed. Gerald Graff, trans. Jeffrey Mehlman and Samuel Weber (Evanston, IL: Northwestern University Press, 1988), 141.

19. See: Gustavo Gutiérrez, *A Theology of Liberation: History, Politics, and Salvation*, Revised (Maryknoll, NY: Orbis Books, 1988).

20. Angie Pears, *Doing Contextual Theology* (London: Routledge, 2010), 170.

21. Derrida, "Force of Law," 28.

22. John Calvin, *Institutes of the Christian Religion*, trans. John Allen, vol. 2 (Philadelphia: Presbyterian Board of Christian Education, 1936), 207.

23. Margit Ernst-Habib, "'Chosen by Grace': Reconsidering the Doctrine of Predestination," in *Feminist and Womanist Essays in Reformed Dogmatics*, ed. Amy Plantinga Pauw and Serene Jones (Louisville, KY: Westminster John Knox Press, 2006), 80.

24. Chris Boesel and Catherine Keller, eds., *Apophatic Bodies: Negative Theology, Incarnation, and Relationality* (New York: Fordham University Press, 2009), 4.

Part I

Deconstructing Undecidability

Chapter One

Religion *sans* Exclusivity, "Perhaps"

> Deconstruction saves . . . theology from closure. Closure spells trouble . . . closure spells exclusion, exclusiveness; closure spills blood, doctrinal, confessional, theological, political, institutional blood, and eventually, it never fails, real blood.
>
> —John D. Caputo, *The Prayers and Tears of Jacques Derrida*

The goal of Part I is straightforward, despite its inability to be boiled down to a single purpose—as Derrida says, there is "always more than one."[1] This twofold, intertwined purpose is to critically advance current readings of Derrida in order to offer a fresh understanding of undecidability and the necessity of having to confront difficult decisions. Lurking behind the desire to avoid such decisions is the perennial problem of exclusivity, as I have argued. The work of John D. Caputo, one of the foremost theological interpreters of Derrida, has shone a bright spotlight on the problem of exclusivity in religion. Not only has Caputo's work been regarded as the gold standard for bridging the gap between Derrida and religion, but it also addresses head-on the problematic aspects of religion and justice, emphasizing the movement toward avoiding, limiting, or remedying the problem of exclusion. Consequently, we will therefore begin, in this chapter, by exploring a reading of deconstruction as it relates to undecidability and such difficult decisions, by way of Caputo, as a way of setting the backdrop for the next chapter. Caputo's reading of deconstruction highlights the limits of any decision, because of how they cut and divide, and the way in which deconstruction reveals how being decisive and definitive is thoroughly problematic. The primary goal of Part I is to glean insights from Caputo's groundbreaking work, while also critically analyzing it, in order to bring into sharper focus the deconstructive aporia that further complicates the situation. In Chapter 2, I will offer an alternative reading of "impossibility" in Derrida's work, highlighting a predicament in which there is no solution or remedy that is not also itself problematic, emphasizing the inescapability of difficult decision(s), or the impossibility of avoiding or remedying such. Chapter 2 thus aims to reveal the problem of indecision: that in the face of an acknowledgment of the exclusivity and impossibility of decisions, we still must decide. In the end, the goal of Part I is to demonstrate that "deconstructing undecidability" means an undecidability that resists collapse into indecision—as much as it resists the collapse into any absolute, definitive decision. Highlighting the deconstructive, aporetic tension between indecision and decision reveals that any point of indecision will be as subject to deconstruction as any decision. Caputo has deftly demonstrated the latter clearly and convincingly, so much so that deconstruction has come to be associated with this movement and critique. And while Caputo gestures toward the former, there is a need to demonstrate as clearly and convincingly as he has the simultaneous deconstruction of any point of indecision, lest undecidability becomes too readily collapsed into indecision.

As Walter Lowe acknowledges: "the puzzling situation in which we find ourselves . . . is precisely where deconstruction intends to place us. Indeed the process of situating us at this difficult intersection, and keeping us there, is a good deal of what deconstruction is about."[2] Standing at this intersection, I am suggesting that the way forward includes continuing to confront difficult decisions, and, in so doing, ask how we might critically advance previous attempts to navigate this thorny dilemma, recognizing the limits of each and every attempt, and never resting assured that we have safely avoided the pitfalls. A recognition of the limits of every attempt will include those that are decisive (as Caputo points out) as well as those that lead to indecision.

One way to frame the argument of Part I is an attempt to continue the trajectory Caputo outlines in his early work on radical hermeneutics, where he frames the project as a kind of "radical thinking which is suspicious of the easy way out."[3] Such is my suspicion as well. It was this kind of hermeneutics of suspicion that drove me to first reexamine the perennial problem of divisive decisions and the desires for avoiding them, and my suspicion has only heightened the more intently I think about it. My conclusion is that when one believes they have safely avoided the treacherousness of problematic decisions, they have taken the "easy way out." As Catherine Keller puts it: "When we think we've finally *got* it, have we already lost it?"[4] For those who are genuine in their concern about the issues raised here, the way forward begins by recognizing that there is no certain destination, no pure solution, no assured stance to take, no safe ground to inhabit. To the extent that the argument of Part I will succeed, it will not show us *the* way forward, but "raise the question . . . and let it hang there and resist the temptation" to answer it definitively, but rather try to maintain the courage to remain "intent on keeping the question . . . open."[5] Letting it remain "open," however, must not be understood as collapsing into indecision—as I will argue. Thus, the goal is to maintain as sharp a focus as we can on this predicament, resisting the temptation to relax the tension of the aporia in either direction. In Part I, that predicament remains in the abstract and only be-comes—i.e., can be realized—in particular, concrete contexts, which will be the focus of the following chapters where I will identify the problem of in/decision in theo-ethical pursuits of justice and negotiations of divine decision.

CAPUTO'S EARLY WORK: A STRIDENT CRITIQUE OF EXCLUSIVITY

In order to accomplish the goal of Part I, which is to advance readings of Derrida in a way that heightens our vigilance with regard to discerning difficult decisions, it is appropriate to begin by engaging Caputo's work. The corpus of Caputo's theo-ethical reading of Derrida, from his early work on "religion without religion" (a phrase that Derrida originally coined) to his later "weak theology" and "theology of perhaps," has been accepted as one of the foremost theological and ethical interpretations of Derrida and deconstruction. It is difficult to pick up any work on the relationship between Derrida and religion over the last twenty years—especially those written in English—and not spot Caputo's influence on it. In his reading and deployment of deconstruction, we will find perhaps the harshest critique of exclusivity, as Caputo appears to identify exclusion as *the* problem within and for religion and justice. As such, engaging his work will help situate my overall argument by highlighting the problematic nature of decisions that cut, divide, and exclude. I will go on to argue in the next chapter, however, that deconstruction reveals that the problem of indecision is *just as* problematic.

Caputo's early work on the intersection of deconstruction and religion not only represents a unique approach in the midst of a sorted discourse, but also paved the way for continued engagement between Derrida and religion for future work.[6] Though deconstruction was initially presumed to be hostile to religion or theology, several significant religious or theological engagements with deconstruction emerged in the 1980s.[7] The Anglophone theological reception of deconstruction took on several forms, ranging from its earliest engagements with the "death of God" theologians like Thomas Altizer[8] and Mark C. Taylor who argued that "deconstruction is the 'hermeneutic' of the death of God,"[9] to more confessional engagements by "Radical Orthodoxy" theologians who argued that only orthodox Christian doctrine can do justice to the implications of deconstruction.[10] Of course, in the midst of these two polarizing approaches, there were several other significant theological engagements with Derrida and deconstruction in the ensuing decade.[11]

But in terms of the relationship between Derrida and religion, no one attempted to follow Derrida as closely as Caputo, who in his early work acknowledged and affirmed a desire to fully realize the religious implications of deconstruction. It is Caputo's stated desire to stick as closely to Derrida as possible that makes our critical engagement with his work on the topic of decision so important. Especially in *The Prayers and Tears of Jacques Derrida: Religion without Religion*, Caputo declares at the outset that the goal of this work is "to understand the 'religion' of Jacques Derrida."[12] What separates Caputo's work with Derrida and religion from other, prior engagements is the admission of the latter that theology and religion is distinct from deconstruction, and therefore will need to "break ranks" at some point. Caputo, on the other hand, so closely tries to follow—and even mimic—Derrida in *Prayers and Tears* that it becomes difficult to discern the difference between the theological argument Caputo is presenting and Derrida himself—or for that matter, between Derrida, deconstruction, and the "religion without religion" that Caputo teases out. This is no accident, as Caputo is explicit that he is in fact trying to highlight a certain kind of religiosity at the heart of deconstruction. In *Prayers and Tears* Caputo intentionally plays with religious concepts so as to trouble any distinction between Derrida, deconstruction, and Derrida's religion, such that we continually hear Caputo talk about "Jacques' religion," deconstruction being a religious movement, etc.[13] In fact, Caputo draws heavily on *Circumfession* (though not to the exclusion of other Derridean texts), an autobiographical reflection where Derrida explores his own religiosity, mimicking Augustine's *Confessions* as Derrida discusses his own religion (being Jewish), growing up in north Africa, and his mother (and her death).[14]

Consequently, what we get in Caputo's *Prayers and Tears* is a sustained reflection on Derrida and religion, Derrida's religion, or deconstructive religion—what Caputo will eventually coin as, in short, "religion without religion."[15] Caputo goes so far as to declare that the "religious-ness" of Derrida is not external or foreign to deconstruction, but part of the very thing that stirs the deconstructive movement. Caputo underscores Derrida's statement about his own Judaism in *Circumfession*, where Derrida laments: "that's what my readers won't have understood about me," resulting in being read "less and less well over almost twenty years, like my religion about which nobody understands anything."[16] For Caputo, this means that what we have not yet understood about deconstruction, which causes us to read Derrida less and less well, is its religiosity. Caputo talks about deconstruction being set in motion by a kind of religious aspiration, that which "the plodding language of the tradition (which deconstruction has rightly made questionable)," would have called "a movement of 'transcendence.'"[17]

Caputo's early reference in *Prayers and Tears* to the religiosity of deconstruction, as distinct from traditional understandings of religion, signals the direction in which Caputo's reading of Derrida on religion leads. Caputo's point that deconstruction is set in motion by an overarching aspiration means not only that deconstruction is motivated by a religious sentiment or dynamic, but that the direction is toward a certain understanding of the "impossible." According to Caputo, "justice"—which he will also link to religion—is always aspired for, because it can never be attained; in fact, any attempt to name it already betrays the aspiration, which is why Caputo even critiques the "plodding language of the tradition" that attempts to name such a movement as "transcendence." We should also note the close relationship this religious aspiration has with justice, where Caputo calls it a religious or prophetic aspiration, referencing the Judeo-Christian tradition in which the prophet was considered the mouthpiece of God who demanded justice and spoke truth to unjust powers. What we will find in Caputo's "religion without religion" is the preeminent critique of the problem of exclusion because it represents all that Caputo believes "deconstruction has rightly made questionable," namely determinate dogmas or doctrines that exclude. These are problematic, for Caputo, on two fronts: first, because by their very nature dogmas and doctrines confess, declare, name something definitive about God, denying what Caputo understands as the impossibility deconstruction highlights; second, anything that is exclusive is inherently problematic or unjust.

In order to fully understand the implications of Caputo's critique of exclusion—and how that might apply to our understanding of decisions that cut or divide—let us begin by unpacking how Caputo defines religion, especially how it relates to his deployment of Derrida's "religion without religion." Caputo attempts to clarify: "By religion I mean a pact with the impossible, a covenant with the unrepresentable, a promise made by the *tout autre* with its people."[18] For Caputo, religion (without religion) is about a structural experience of the *impossible*; and as we will see, he understands this deconstructive, structural impossibility as a calling, weeping, waiting, praying for the impossible. Again, Caputo's definition of religion stems from his stated attempt to follow Derrida as closely as possible, so it also follows that this understanding of impossibility will take on a particular emphasis. Derrida's so-called "turn to the ethical" in his later writings often coincided with his so-called "turn to religion," where Derrida engages such religious concepts, terms, and ideas as "apocalyptic," "apophatic," "messianic," and "faith."[19] However, just as Derrida's so-called ethical turn did not constitute a significant shift from the earlier structural work of deconstruction in language and communication (according to more contemporary interpreters), for Caputo, Derrida's engagement with religion also only further illustrates the implications of deconstruction, especially as it relates to language, speech, and all forms of communication.[20]

The religious terms Derrida engages are only used to reveal a general, structural experience of *all* discourse, language, and communication. In Derrida's later work that explicitly engages religious themes, we discover that: "apocalyptic" unveils repetition and response that is indicative of all language;[21] every form of language is "apophatic" (in a sense) because of an inability of language to capture its referent;[22] the "messianic" is a structure of the to-come (that can and will never be present), which can relate to religion but also justice;[23] "faith" is the condition of all language because language is built on a promise;[24] and "fidelity" is absolute or infinite duty.[25] In other words, these religious terms, concepts, and themes become evacuated of their particular, religious content so that they express a general, structural experience that deconstruction reveals, e.g., faith becomes a movement concerned with the impossible, not a particular belief. Thus religion, as Derrida says in *The Gift of Death*, is a "religion *without* religion." Discussing the history of European responsibility, which he argues is tied to religion, Derrida notes that the connection between religion and responsibility is structural, not particularly related to religion per se, and certainly not married to Christianity—it is about a larger movement that the religious points to, but cannot fully capture.

In his discussion of Christian themes, Derrida suggests that they are linked, "internally and necessarily," by "a logic that at bottom . . . has no need of *the event of a revelation or the revelation of an event*." In other words, such logic "needs to think the possibility of such an event but not the event itself." This "major point of difference" allows religious discourse to develop "without reference to religion as institutional dogma," leading to an unfolding of "the possibility and essence of the religious that doesn't amount to an article of faith . . . a *thinking* that 'repeats' the *possibility* of religion without religion."[26] Characteristically clear and unclear at the same time, Derrida is suggesting the *movement* (i.e., the general, structural dynamic) of religion is the focus, not religion itself, and that there is a major difference between the "possibility" of what religion aims for and institutional dogmas, doctrines, and articles of faith. Caputo fully develops this notion in *Prayers and Tears* to underscore how religion itself—as determinate, institutionalized, dogmatic, historical, etc.—often obstructs this kind of movement and aspiration for the impossible. While deconstruction "repeats the structure of religious experience," it does so "*sans* the concrete historical religions," thus "nondogmatically" repeating religiousness or the "religious structure of experience."[27] Caputo performs this repetition by structuring *Prayers and Tears* according to these religious categories: the apophatic, the apocalyptic, and the messianic—Chapters 1 through 3, respectively. There are, therefore, two primary aspects to Caputo's "religion without religion" that are important for us to keep in mind: (a) religion as the aspiration or movement toward the impossible, that (b) is necessarily *sans* (i.e., without) determinate, historical religions, dogmas, and doctrines.

In order to understand why the *sans* is important for Caputo, and more importantly how that is related to the problem of decision, let us continue unpacking his emphasis on the impossible in his reading of deconstruction and how that leads Caputo to privilege open-endedness over closure. Again, in the opening pages of *Prayers and Tears*, Caputo sketches the movement of deconstruction toward this impossibility and the implications for religion (without religion). He talks about deconstruction being stirred "with a passion for the impossible . . . called forth in response to the unrepresentable . . . provoked by the promise, impregnated by the impossible, hoping in a certain messianic promise of the impossible." Deconstruction is not only "moved" by such a provocation and call, but "has always been moving"—in fact, "it gives words to a movement that has always been at work." It settles "into the crevices and interstices of the present . . . against the complacency of the present, against the pleasure the present takes in itself, in order to prevent it from closing in on itself, from collapsing into self-identity." "For in deconstruction," Caputo argues, "such closure would be the height of injustice."[28]

For Caputo, if deconstruction is a movement toward the impossible—that which is always to come that will shatter horizons, that which is unforeseeable and unimaginable—then anything that declares presence interrupts this, putting a stop to this movement, and is thus considered to be "the height of injustice." Its injustice stems—at least in part—from what Caputo believes to be a betrayal of the deconstructive movement. Derrida's early work in deconstruction has shown that Western philosophy (and, of course, religion) has been built on a metaphysics of presence that strives for, but never attains (even when it supposes it has), that which is originary and present. Therefore, in Caputo's reading, declaring presence prematurely—as he believes definitive forms of religion and justice do—is considered "unjust" because it mistakenly assumes a presence that is, though it never can be, fully present, while also denigrating absence, which it can never escape. For Caputo, this deconstructive critique of a metaphysics of presence in Derrida's early work is corroborated by Derrida's later work on religion and justice, where Caputo sees a similar deconstructive critique of any notion of arrival, because justice is always on the horizon, never present, always to come. Thus, in Caputo's understanding, the call to justice (like religion) is a call to this impossibility, beyond present systems and instantiations of justice, which are always incomplete, lacking, and therefore, simply put, unjust. And since closure, answers, and arrival signal the end of waiting—or presence—we must infinitely forestall any such possibilities.

Throughout *Prayers and Tears*, Caputo continues to emphasize this deconstructive impossibility, highlighting and unpacking its implications for religion and justice, by exploring some significant Derridean engagements with religion. In his section on "The Apocalyptic," Caputo highlights the impossibility of deconstructive justice by concentrating on the "to come" that appears in Derrida's writings. Here Caputo strongly argues that deconstruction has become a meditation and prayer for what is coming: "Everything in deconstruction turns on the constellation of *venir* and *à venir, viens* and *invention, l'avenir* and *événement*."[29] This "coming," or call "to come" is the central focus of this section, where the "one" who comes is referred to as "the just one."[30] For Caputo, the justice that is called for in the *viens* is always to come, on the horizon, because all present forms of justice will always be limited and subject to deconstruction. The question this raises, however, is just what kind of justice this is referring to—a point that will be taken up more acutely in Part II as we explore the relationship between justice and decision.

As he transitions to the following section, "The Messianic," we find some guidance to help us decipher what Caputo might mean by justice. Beginning with Derrida's 1989 lecture "The Force of Law: The 'Mystical Foundation of Authority,'" Caputo cites Derrida's hesitation to link justice with a "messianic promise" similar to a "regulative idea." Derrida resists any notion of a horizon that sets limits and defines expectations in advance.[31] Similar to Derrida's musings on messianicity in *Specters of Marx*, this kind of restriction is antithetical to "the messianic" whose very purpose is to "shatter horizons." This leads Caputo to conclude that "the movement of justice is a movement beyond the hinges and fixed junctures of the law." Openness, rather than closure, seems to be integral to the kind of justice at work in the messianic, keeping things "sufficiently dis-lodged and open-ended."[32]

All throughout *Prayers and Tears* Caputo continually emphasizes that closure is to be avoided in the pursuit of justice. In fact, the call for justice is *in itself* a call for openness, expectation, and waiting that can only be thwarted by closure. For Caputo, the passion for the impossible—which is what religion and justice is defined as—precludes closure, for any closing would always be too soon. The *à venir* must remain in a state of expectation and therefore requires a continual "posture of expectancy" for that "which is always and structurally to come."[33] This is because "the one who is coming, the just one, the *tout autre*, can never be present."[34] It is the very essence of the *tout autre*, or "wholly other," that "what is coming be unknown, not merely factually unknown but structurally unknowable."[35] Thus to cease to wait, to enclose, to declare or even *know* what is to come, for Caputo, is considered to be "the height of injustice" in deconstruction.[36]

Caputo's exploration of Derridean engagements with religious themes in the section on "The Apophatic" most clearly demonstrates how deconstruction helps apophatic theology resist such a desire to "know," which means encapsulating, naming, disclosing the secret, or answering the question. The Christian apophatic tradition is ripe for deconstructive engagement (as we will explore in Part III), because of its desire and refusal to name or declare anything positive about God. However, as Derrida notes in "*Différance*," although apophatic (or negative) theology gestures toward the impossible and unknowable, Derrida believes apophatic theology does ultimately refer to an ineffable, hyper-essential being—something Derrida claims is unsustainable according to deconstruction. For Caputo then, Derrida therefore sets theology free from its unjust ways because even though the apophatic theologian claims unknowing, deep down he or she *knows* what they are referring to. And for Derrida, even if said theologian claims the inability to name God, he or she ultimately has a referent in mind. Caputo embraces Derrida's critique and concludes that "negative theology drops anchor, hits bottom, lodges itself securely in pure presence and the transcendental signified," thus closing the circle and cutting off justice.[37] For Caputo, deconstruction therefore "saves negative theology from closure," which is the height of injustice: "Closure spells trouble . . . closure spells exclusion, exclusiveness; closure spills blood, doctrinal, confessional, theological, political, institutional blood, and eventually, it never fails, real blood."[38]

It is at this point that we see most clearly not only the connection between religion and justice for Caputo, but a better sense of how that relates to the problem of decision. As we have seen, Caputo's religious understanding of deconstruction is closely tied to, if not indistinguishable from, a particular understanding of justice. But here we begin to see that religion's association with justice has something to do with the ethical problem of exclusion, which means that Caputo's understanding of religion (and justice) implies an identification of exclusion as problematic. His identification with religion as a passion for the impossible *must* mean a religion that resists closure in order to escape injustice because, for Caputo: (a) closure would assume presence, and would therefore betray the deconstructive movement; and (b) because "closure spells exclusion," which "spells trouble" and "spills blood," it is therefore unethical/unjust. Thus Caputo continually highlights closure as problematic precisely because of its exclusionary nature. And here we can recognize a strong resonance with the contemporary, progressive theological landscape that was briefly surveyed in the introduction: exclusion is that which is (ethically) problematic, i.e., "the problem," and thus should be avoided. Therefore, if Caputo can show that religion (or justice) is exclusive, then it is unjust. Seen the other way around, for Caputo religion (traditionally understood) is unjust because of closure, and closure is ethically problematic because it excludes.

The same applies for justice—any justice that is exclusive is necessarily (and assumingly) unjust, which is why the key to understanding Caputo's notion of justice is openness. It is a justice that cannot be named, made present or known. Justice of this sort must be awaited, it is always to come. Yet he also says that it will surprise us (if/when it comes), because it is unimaginable, unforeseeable, and unbelievable. Therefore, a "religion without religion" that is just entails waiting and expecting something new "to come." And since closure, answers, and arrival signal the end of waiting—or presence—we must infinitely forestall any such possibilities.

Attempting to make things a bit more concrete, Caputo addresses the exclusion of real-life "others" in his chapter on "Circumcision," making connections between Derrida's Judaism and the politics that cut, divide, and exclude. Caputo highlights the machinations of "strong nation-states" that legislate "powerful immigration policies" based on a certain "rhetoric of nationalism, the politics of place, the metaphysics of native land and native tongue" that fund and perpetuate a problematic exclusivity. The work of deconstruction, Caputo argues, helps mitigate against the wide-ranging ethical dangers of closure, including a collapse into a system of sameness that results in an "identity that nation-states build to defend themselves against the stranger, against Jews and Arabs and immigrants . . . against all the others, all the other others, all of whom, according to an impossible formula, a formula of the impossible, are wholly other."[39] Caputo's point is that keeping the system open is intended to break the cycle of sameness that excludes all others based on racial, ethnic, religious, or national identities. And his political point is (still) as accurate as it is valid, especially in the current political climate in the United States and around the world, where the stranger, immigrant, other are (still) being targeted by nation-states under the guise of defense. According to Caputo, deconstruction aids us in the process of resisting exclusionary politics by allowing the *tout autre* to remain "wholly other" in order to respect the difference, unlike a kind of Hegelian *Aufhebung* that collapses into a unifying system of sameness. The "whole point" of deconstruction, Caputo reminds us, is "to keep the system open." If deconstruction truly is an endless "play of differences," then Caputo argues that "its burning passion" is to prevent or forestall any "regathering and reassembling in a systematic whole with infinite warrant." For Caputo, such openness resists the exclusivity of closure, because the *tout autre* would be destroyed if made present.[40]

As is evident, for Caputo, keeping the system open, i.e., intentionally resisting or avoiding closure, is the best way to reduce violence, to work toward and to call for, what names "justice." Thus, any closing, prohibiting, excluding, or regathering, especially when connected with power, is to be avoided, and, again, that deconstruction allows or aids us in that process. In Caputo's reading of Derrida, any closure would prevent the invention of the *tout-autre*, would be too early or soon and would forestall the coming of justice. Consequently, justice is not when things are nailed down, pinned in place, or inscribed, but rather when they are allowed to unsettle, slip loose, twist free, leak and run off, exceed or overflow.[41] What this amounts to, for Caputo, is a call for justice—and a religion that is ethically viable—that directs us outward, beyond the present (system, answer, order, *decision*, etc.), where we pray, weep, wait, and hope for the impossible.

Caputo's definition of religion and understanding of justice, combined with his attempt to align himself as closely as possible with Derrida regarding these ideas, leads him to present "religion *without* religion": a religion *sans* determinate doctrines, institutions, practices, etc., because of the way the latter excludes. This is the conclusion Caputo reaches in *Prayers and Tears* and he continues along these same lines in *The Weakness of God: A Theology of the Event*, where Caputo takes up the "theological" implications of "religion without religion" a bit more explicitly.[42] He begins by describing the nature of God and the task of theology: "[T]he name of God is an event, or rather it *harbors* an event, and . . . theology is the hermeneutics of that event, its task being to release what is happening in that name, to set it free, to give it its own head, and thereby to head off the forces that would prevent this event."[43] In an attempt to construct a theology of the event, Caputo employs eight descriptors to define what he means by "event": uncontainability, translatability, deliteralization, excess, evil, beyond Being, truth, and time. Through each of these descriptors, Caputo shows how the event continually evokes a sense of rupture, in-breaking, surprising, overflowing, releasing. "There is always something uncontainable and unconditional about an event,"[44] Caputo argues, something that betrays any attempt to name it completely, which means that "the name can never be taken with literal force, as if it held the event tightly within its grip, as if it circumscribed it and literally named it, as if a concept (*Begriff*) were anything more than a temporary stop and imperfect hold on an event."[45] Thus theology should recognize that "an event cannot be held captive by a confessional faith or creedal formula," which is why Caputo contends that theology's task is to release and set free, rather than foreclose or hold captive.[46]

What we find in Caputo's work is an emphasis on a certain kind of impossibility that deconstruction reveals and a concomitant attempt to satisfy or appease this deconstructive impossibility by holding out as long as possible. The eventive nature of God's name, and theology as the hermeneutics that releases and sets it free, is aimed at not allowing theology to do what it has always done (or tried to do): to name and declare, which means to forestall and close, and, ultimately, exclude. As a result, Caputo refuses to endorse any notion of religion or justice that can be subject to a kind of deconstructive critique that presumably announces "No!" at every attempt to name, declare, systematize, etc. In so doing, he represents a strident critique of anything that excludes.

It is not difficult to see how this identification of closure and exclusivity as problematic relates to the issue of decisions that cut or divide. Caputo is certainly wary of, and cogently highlighting the limits of, any decision that would claim presence, be final or absolute, because of the betrayal of the deconstructive impossibility. Caputo finds in Derrida a "prophetic passion" that bears witness to the biblical prophets' call for justice against the unjust present orders. This call for justice, as we have seen, is a call to keep the system open, to avoid making the *tout autre* present.[47] What impels this prophetic passion is outside cognition, unknowable, and unpresentable, something "that emerges in our prayers and tears," evoking and provoking them, seeking us out before we seek it or even know it, disturbing and transforming us.[48] This call for justice is a call beyond the present system(s) and what Caputo believes impassions both Derrida and the prophets. Any decision would seemingly betray this movement, especially if and when it is based on a regulative idea, something I could claim to know or name, some explanatory principle.

GOD, "PERHAPS": A MORE DECISIVE LOOK AT IN/DECISION

While Caputo's earlier work gestures toward the problem of decision, obliquely highlighting the structural limits of such and its implications, one of Caputo's most recent works deals more explicitly with the issue of undecidability and is thus most pertinent to our discussion. In *The Insistence of God: A Theology of Perhaps*, Caputo both builds upon his earlier work—which includes highlighting the problem of decision—but also acknowledges, at times, that indecision is also problematic. In fact, when read a certain way, much of Caputo's theology can be read to support the necessity of decisiveness.

In *The Insistence of God* we certainly find the culmination of Caputo's earlier work that identified the problems of limited, dogmatic, doctrinal religion and theology. Here Caputo attempts to further distance his weak theology of the event from strong theology, by drawing on a theological notion of "perhaps." Caputo insists: "One must, it is absolutely necessary, always say 'perhaps' for God: God, perhaps (*peut-être*). Whenever and wherever there is a chance for the event, that is God, perhaps."[49] In contrast to traditionally "strong theology" that employs "omni-nouns and hyper verbs" to establish power and presence, "weak theology . . . is content with a little adverb like 'perhaps,'" which interrupts and intercepts, disrupts and deflects.[50] In a theology of "perhaps," Caputo continues his critique of definitive claims about God, because of how they collapse divinity into "something I have added to my repertoire, brought within the horizon of my experience, knowledge, belief, identification, and expectation."[51] Rather, Caputo proposes a more open-ended notion of divinity, a theology of "perhaps" that appreciates the surprise of the event that will always shatter horizons and expectations.

We will explore the relationship between Caputo's critique of definitive claims about God more fully in Part III, discussing how that relates to decisions about divine decision(s). But our present focus is the structural nature of decision more generally and how Caputo's reading of Derrida relates to that. In the opening pages of *The Insistence of God*, Caputo admits there is every reason to fear "this one small word, 'perhaps.'" While we expect philosophers and theologians to be the ones we turn to in order to help us decide, "'perhaps' is the language of indecision and the suspension of judgment."[52] Drawing on the vagueness and evasiveness of "perhaps," Caputo is pushing theologians and philosophers to wrestle with the implications of deconstruction that always refuses to allow us to say anything definite. And "with a little adverb like 'perhaps,'" Caputo continues to shake the foundation of the business as usual approach of philosophy and theology that has always strived for absolutes.[53]

When read alongside his earlier work, it is clear that Caputo's focus and goal is to highlight the deconstruction of assurance, purity, knowledge, and presence and to point out the ethical consequences associated with philosophy and religion's desire for such, namely how it leads to shutting down, foreclosing, excluding. Because of this inherent and deeply imbedded desire, Caputo acknowledges that saying "perhaps" will always carry a risk and exposure by abandoning the shield of safety provided by presence, principles, actuality, predictability, etc.[54] Whenever we say "perhaps" it will always sound "like the soul of indecision, like a lame excuse for an answer, a refusal to take a stand," and Caputo admits that this can sound risky for those who desire the safety of answers and stances. "Perhaps" will always expose us to the best and worst, which is why he continually refers to our perpetual "fear of one small word."[55]

Despite, or possibly even because of, such a risk, Caputo urges us to reconsider this one small word, because for Caputo the concern about closure is greater than the risk associated with the loss of assurance and certainty. "Perhaps" is worth the risk because it prevents the kind of closure Caputo has always been concerned about and from allowing the present to become identical with itself. It leaves us—or reveals to us how we are always already—structurally exposed to the future of to-come (*à venir*).[56] Given his theological understanding of God as event, the "perhaps" leaves us exposed—for better or worse—to the open-endedness of the future, the event that is always to-come. But "perhaps" also gives us access to something else, something other than what surety and certainty can provide. In his estimation, those who insist on certainty and surety "seize upon the actual and close off an obscure but fertile event."[57] And for Caputo, "perhaps" is the only way to say yes, *oui oui*, to the future and the fertility of this event. In fact, Caputo argues that there is a false sense of security in doctrines, dogmas, orthodoxies, institutions, and definitive decisions, all of which he calls "closed circles, whose seeming decisiveness is, in fact, a way of avoiding responsibility, in full flight from a deeper and more unnerving responsibility."[58] Thus Caputo maintains that "perhaps" requires greater rigor, responsibility, and resolution because it disrupts and unsettles any notion of certainty and assurance.

While Caputo is clear that his emphasis on uncertainty and indecision might lead some to read him as suggesting a "play it safe" or "stay out of it" approach, he maintains that part of the deconstructive methodology he is pursuing is a resistance to the binaries that make such a reading possible. Caputo insists that his goal is not to offer some kind of "safe middle ground that would maintain a strategic neutrality," but rather his approach "belongs to a different register altogether."[59] Speaking more directly about how this relates to decision and the safety of indecision, he clarifies: "'Perhaps' is not the safety of indecision but a radical risk, for nothing guarantees that things will turn out well." It is not, he argues, a "paralysis," but rather what he describes as "the fluid milieu of undecidability in which every radical decision is made."[60] Caputo admits that it may seem like this approach signifies a simple lack of purpose or "sounds like mere propositional indecisiveness, maybe this or maybe that, who knows which?" But he maintains that the "perhaps" is not merely a refusal to answer, but rather the very "depths of responsibility, a recognition of the extent to which the question exceeds us and puts us into question."[61]

Such a recognition of the depths of responsibility and being put into question is the entry point for my argument in this book, and a point that I will clarify in the following chapter: a deconstructive denial of any mistaken assumption that there is a safe approach to the problem of decision, what Caputo refers to as "a retreat to the safety of indecision" or a "safe middle ground that would maintain strategic neutrality." Caputo's emphasis on the rigor, responsibility, and resolution that the "perhaps" offers is precisely what this book is after with regard to gaining clarity on the problem of decision—and it is where we are most in agreement. The uncertainty of the "perhaps" certainly heightens responsibility with regard to the issue of decision. My concern, however, is the way in which this might inevitably lead to a privileging of indecision, which can vitiate such rigor, responsibility, and resolution by similarly offering a false sense of safety or security. Caputo is clear that this is not what he is suggesting and in fact emphasizes repeatedly the risk associated with perhaps. But Caputo's main focus is on pointing out the risk of the perhaps as it relates to deconstructing any definitive decision or decisiveness; in other words, regarding undecidability, he emphasizes the point that any decision will be subject to deconstruction. The whole point of my argument, however, will be to push just as hard in the other direction, highlighting the deconstructive risk that necessarily accompanies any suggestion of the safety of the indecisive; in other words, pointing out how undecidability also deconstructs indecision. While Caputo acknowledges *this* risk, he is more focused on pointing out the riskiness, and advantages, of the "perhaps" for those who desire the safety of the decision. Put another way, while Caputo is nervous about the false sense of security and safety definitive decisions seem to offer, I am *also* nervous about a similarly false sense of security and safety indecision seems to offer.

Continuing the trajectory set forth in his earlier theological work about the eventive nature of God, Caputo continually maintains that these events "happen" and "get themselves said and done, in the middle voice, in and under many names."[62] His understanding of the weakness of God means that God is not the one who acts because God is "not an agent who does things or fails to"; but rather we are the agents who act or fail to. What is most theologically important for Caputo is what gets done "under the name of what is called for in the name of God."[63] So rather than speak about God as if we were referring to some being or agent who says or does things, for Caputo God *is* what is done in and under the name of God. Thus we, as creaturely agents, will be the only ones "able to determine whether God exists"—that is whether what is done in the name of "God" is actually God or not. And this is only done after the fact, when it can be determined "whether this name will have brought justice or shame or have made no difference at all."[64] This is where the "perhaps" is most felt because "it all depends, perhaps, *peut-être*."[65] Sometimes, in fact most times, what is done in the name of God is not very God-like at all. However, this is God's *insistence*, an insistence that calls for existence in what gets done in the name of God. For Caputo, the insistence of God "means that God calls for a response." But, at the same time, since God is not an agent or being "who 'does' things like call," such calling always "takes place in the middle voice."[66]

My focus here is less concerned with Caputo's theological, metaphysical, or ontological understanding of God, which we will explore more fully in Chapter 5, but more with the emphasis on human responsibility that it entails. For Caputo, the weakness of God imposes responsibility upon us to respond to the call issued in the name of God: "When God calls, we are put in the accusative, put on the spot, made responsible."[67] In other words, God's weakness is made strong in our response to the event because the insistence of God "urgently requires our assistance, the assistance that translates God's insistence into existence."[68] And because God's insistence is "a call for a response, a call for existence," this means that the responsibility is on us to answer and respond—in fact, it is a *response-ability*, Caputo admits, to decide. Discussing the eventive nature of God as it relates to such a decision, Caputo writes: "*The event is not the decisiveness of the decision, but the insistence of what calls for existence in a decision.*"[69] Again, we can spot Caputo's nervousness with what he refers to as the decisiveness of the decision, i.e., a definitive, once for all decision. While I have not been suggesting that the decisiveness of the decision is what matters, I have been suggesting—and will continue to argue more explicitly—for the necessity and inescapability of a decision point. And even though it is couched in a perpetual concern about too much emphasis on the "decisiveness of the decision," Caputo does seem to acknowledge the significance of the decision, especially when he points out that the insistence of God calls for existence in a decision. In the following chapter I will highlight a concern that the decision point gets muted in all this discussion about the limits of any definitive decision or concern about the danger of decisiveness. And again, I agree about the reason for such concern. I will simply suggest that we do not forget that in the face of the undecidable, we still must decide. And there are moments Caputo acknowledges the necessity of decision, or comes close to it, when he discusses God's insistence as invoking "the depths of human responsibility," as the ones who are called to respond to an event, which precedes and provokes them.[70] And this responsibility (or response-ability), I will argue, is the decision point; and it is a point that will become more concrete in Part II, when we more explicitly discuss matters of social justice.

In his theology of "perhaps," Caputo continually talks about how "God needs our help," "God needs our response to be God," and how the insistence of God means that God's existence, in insistence, depends upon creaturely agency and action because "God depends on the response."[71] Though Caputo doesn't frame it in this particular way, my reading of Caputo in the next chapter is an attempt to critically advance his insights by building upon this notion, wherein the response includes recognizing the need to discern and *make* difficult decisions—in other words, a necessity to *decide*. And that includes decisions that close, cut or divide, exclude. For Caputo, the "whether or not" of the "perhaps" of God will be determined "by our response" and by decision. So while I might not entirely endorse Caputo's reading of deconstruction or theological understanding of God (and will highlight some issues to consider with regard to such more directly in Chapter 5), there is a resonance between Caputo's emphasis on the necessity of human action and decision and my own insistence on the need for an appreciation of undecidability that recognizes the need for discerning and deciding—a point that will become clearer in the next chapter. Moreover, Caputo's recognition of the precariousness of such decisions also resonates with my own argument because the very reason for avoiding exclusive decisions is our awareness of the difficulty in choosing and deciding, an acknowledgment of the lack of security of a good result or outcome, especially when the stakes are so high. I will not suggest we ignore this good conscience or theo-ethical sensibility, but point out that in the midst of this difficulty, we also need to decide. Anyone can decide when ignorant of the consequences and implications, and Derrida would be quick to point out that this is not, in fact, a decision at all. But to decide in the midst of this awareness, without the lack of security or assurance, is the only decision that is real. And my point is to hold our feet to the fire to recognize the inescapability of these kinds of real decisions. Caputo argues that "the name of God is the name of undecidability itself"; I agree, it is important to clarify, however, just what we mean by undecidability.[72] And to do that, we will turn to a more focused reading of Derrida on the matter of decision in Chapter 2.

THE PHARMACOLOGICAL TENSION OF UNDECIDABILITY

Caputo's recognition of the problem of indecision is not just apparent in *The Insistence of God* either. He hints at it all throughout his writings. However, given his focus on the strident critique and analysis of the problematic nature of closure that deconstruction highlights, there is a necessity to build upon that and also acknowledge—through a similar strident critique and analysis—the problematic nature of indecision, critically advancing these insights as a return to the deconstructive aporia that resists indecision *as much as* any definitive decisiveness. So when Caputo says that "*différance* has not come to bring peace but the two-edged sword of undecidability," there is a need to clarify just what undecidability means.[73] Surely *différance* cannot settle disputes; but this should not merely be read as keeping things open or retreating to a space of indecision, as if that could settle anything either. There is a danger that this book seeks to highlight, and it is a danger that can be fueled by a misunderstanding of undecidability, which is why the goal of Part I—as I will go on to demonstrate more fully in Chapter 2—is to offer a rereading of undecidability, critically advancing previous interpretations of deconstruction and the "ghost of the undecidable."[74] Caputo's work has achieved significant advances in recognizing the ways in which *différance* deconstructs the desire for the transcendental, for power, presence, and purity. But if deconstruction has taught us anything, we must allow *différance* to keep our feet to the fire, and recognize the way in which undecidability is not (merely) indecision.

In *Prayers and Tears* Caputo writes: "Everything about deconstruction requires that we let the *tout autre* tremble in undecidability, in an endless, open-ended, indeterminable, undecidable *translatability*, or *substitutability*, or *exemplarity*." As I will go on to show, this kind of open-ended undecidability must not be understood as a perpetual indecision, a decision that avoids closure, or worse, a safe place of indecisiveness that escapes the deconstructive, aporetic double-bind that always puts us into question.[75] Deconstruction reveals an undecidability that means an impossible decision wherein we must decide. Once again, Caputo does gesture toward this, as he goes on to add that the point of undecidability "is not to let us all hang out to dry, twisting slowly in the winds of indecision," affirming that there comes a point where "each of us must decide for herself what is what." So while he acknowledges that "undecidability is not apathy and impassivity," this aspect of the deconstructive double-bind needs to be teased out, highlighted, and acknowledged *as much as* Caputo's emphasis on how undecidability deconstructs any definitive decision.[76] In the next chapter I will try to double-down on "impossibility," arguing that it is both impossible to decide and yet impossible to avoid deciding.

Caputo maintains that undecidability does not lead to "a bottomless pit down which every decision is dropped never to be heard from again," but rather it constitutes "the haze of indefiniteness with which decision must daily cope, the gluey, glassy *glas* which conditions even very ordinary decisions, in which the urgency and passion of decision are nourished."[77] These are the passages—which are there in Caputo—that need to be teased out. They are lurking in the shadows, and it is the aim of this book to bring them out as a way of offering a corrective to the risk of misreading what undecidability means. The openness of *différance* has been felt; but now we need to feel its closure. We have, perhaps, moved too far in the direction of an undecidability that makes one comfortable with indefiniteness, and the indefiniteness was never intended to do that. Caputo has always maintained that the task, goal, and aim of his engagement with deconstruction was always to raise the stakes, to make things more difficult. He suggests that groping and wrestling with undecidability is the difficult and responsible approach, as opposed to the easy and irresponsible approach of nihilism or apathy.[78] It is these moments in Caputo, where he wants to draw out the difficult and denounce any easy way out, where I agree with him most. My hope is to lead us further into the troubled waters of undecidability, into the madness of the decision point where every decision is both impossible *and* inescapable, to a recognition of undecidability that appreciates the impossibility of decision and the unavoidability of it. While Caputo is right to acknowledge that deconstruction "is an exploration of as many 'instants' of undecidability as it has time (as it is given time) to study," and tends to suggest a kind of permanence to undecidability because it always "precedes, follows, and permeates the decision" as the "first, last, and always." He also clarifies that in the midst of such undecidability, "decisions must be made and indecision broken."[79] My goal is to build upon this analysis of undecidability, to flesh it out and unpack the implications of it, to emphasize that in the midst of undecidability "decisions must be made and indecision broken." It is an attempt to reengage the "perhaps" and clarify that it is not—and perhaps was never intended to be understood as—mere indecisiveness, and to point out the deconstruction of any resolution to the predicament of undecidability that leaves us feeling safe or secure. Although there are these moments in Caputo where he acknowledges this, his main point of emphasis is the problematic nature of closure, division, and exclusion, suggesting a privileging of openness.

Caputo actually directly addresses a similar contention about his privileging of openness to closure in his response to papers delivered on his work with Derrida and religion, that were later published in a series of essays entitled, *Religion with/out Religion: The Prayers and Tears of John D. Caputo*.[80] In particular, the three opening essays of this work express a similar concern about the implications of Caputo's emphasis on the impossibility of justice and religion. In Jeffrey Dudiak's essay, *"Bienvenue*—Just a Moment," Dudiak poignantly asks how a structurally future justice, one that is always coming but never arriving, relates to justice here-and-now? How, for instance, do these abstract notions of justice relate to more concrete and particular—albeit modest—acts of justice? How does the justice that is to come relate to "concrete acts of justice in lived time" where "virtue is required" *here-and-now*, "that is, bread and cold water for the beggars, the poor, the widows, orphans and strangers, concrete justice, today, in the present time, in the ordinary lived time of hunger and thirst"?[81] Dudiak challenges Caputo to think of justice more humbly, in momentary acts of love, e.g., in "cups of cold water" here-and-now, because Caputo's emphasis on impossibility seems to minimize—if not outright denounce—such. In the second and third essays, Ronald Kuipers and Shane Cudney challenge Caputo from a more religious perspective, maintaining that Caputo is overly negative toward concrete religious communities in his early work in *Prayers and Tears* and arguing that Caputo's understanding and emphasis on impossibility denigrates and dishonors concrete, historical, and particular religions, writing them off as "essentially poisonous."[82] They ask whether or not all communities are essentially "violent" according to deconstruction, and how such a focus privileges the abstract and universal.

Fortunately, this compilation includes Caputo's response to each of the essays and critiques. Caputo frankly admits that there is credibility to the claim that he overemphasizes a certain understanding of "impossibility" in *Prayers and Tears*. In response to Dudiak, Caputo clarifies that the messianic justice of the "to come" should not result in resignation or the negation of our demand for immediate justice. In fact, Caputo argues that there are not two times, but one, where the messianic breaks into the present and requires justice here-and-now. It is the messianic demand for justice now that constitutes the present as lived time. Caputo maintains that the "to-come does not consign us to despair" but actually is intended to intensify "the demands of the moment, injecting the life of justice into the flow of time, exposing the present to the white light of an absolute demand for justice." For Caputo, justice demands we recognize that "the slightest imperfection in the present, the slightest injustice, is absolutely intolerable, and cannot be written off as a tolerable progress." In fact, "the intensity of the demand for justice is set by the tension between the moment and the to-come, by the absolute pressure exerted upon the present by the relentless demand for justice, the demand to make justice come, which we can never meet. For we will never have done enough."[83] Again, Caputo rightly points out that the "slightest imperfection . . . is absolutely intolerable" and warns us, like Derrida, to never rest on a notion of "tolerable progress" but to be constantly challenged by the impossibility of justice. Caputo thus maintains that the impossibility of justice should not come at the expense of smaller acts of justice in the present, but, in fact, should only intensify the demand for better and better acts of justice here-and-now.

Caputo goes even further in his response to Kuipers and Cudney, admitting that a "serious failure" of *Prayers and Tears* is his inability to "maintain the tension" between the poison and remedy that inhabits every institution and decision. This is a failure, Caputo admits, "to maintain them in their pharmacological undecidability," and he acknowledges that "[*Prayers and Tears*] appears to have broken the tension."[84] In fact, Caputo maintains: "deconstruction does not resolve contradictions. . . . Rather, deconstruction defines and stresses the tension in a phenomenon; it might even be thought of as a kind of phenomenology of torques."[85] This is precisely the reading of deconstruction that I am hoping to recover in the following chapter, one that does not re-solve but in fact *stresses* a pharmacological tension with regard to undecidability. It is clear from this selection of essays that although Caputo does not intend for any such relaxation of the aporetic double-bind, there is a way of reading his emphasis on openness and resistance to closure that suggests such. In fact, Caputo goes on in the same response to prefer openness to closure, stating: "if deconstruction were something, somewhere, if it did or did not do things . . . we would say that what 'deconstruction' does is keep the future *open*, and, by exposing the concrete messianisms to danger, protects them against themselves."[86] Here, Caputo appears to revert back to a notion of deconstruction that suggests remaining open is the ultimate goal, *telos*, or result, rather than appreciating that openness always, simultaneously accompanies the inescapability of closure. Put in terms more relatable to our present discussion, Caputo seems to suggest that not deciding would be preferable to any decision, because of the way that the latter cuts, divides, excludes. Again, Caputo's real critique is against the absolute certainty and surety of any decision, as well as the exclusivity of closure entailed, which is (part of) what deconstruction highlights. But what might get lost in such a strident critique of any actual decision is the inescapability, necessity, and exigency of being decisive, which is where my argument enters into the conversation and attempts to offer a corrective. In the reading of deconstruction that I offer below, I will argue that no such preference can be suggested by deconstruction; that deconstruction is in fact a phenomenology of torques, always defining and stressing the tension and thus can never show us the way out of the tension, but only reveals its tensity, or just how taut it is.

NOTES

1. Jacques Derrida, "*Sauf le nom* (Post-Scriptum)," in *On the Name*, ed. Thomas Dutoit, trans. David Wood, John P. Leavey, Jr., Ian McLeod (Stanford, CA: Stanford University, 1995), 35.
2. Walter Lowe, *Theology and Difference: The Wound of Reason* (Bloomington: Indiana University Press, 1993), 17.
3. John D. Caputo, *Radical Hermeneutics: Repetition, Deconstruction, and the Hermeneutic Project*, Studies in Phenomenology and Existential Philosophy (Bloomington: Indiana University Press, 1987), 3.
4. Catherine Keller, *On the Mystery: Discerning Divinity in Process* (Minneapolis: Fortress Press, 2008), ix.
5. Caputo, *Radical Hermeneutics: Repetition, Deconstruction, and the Hermeneutic Project*, 2. I have redacted Caputo's quotation where he says "resist the temptation to cut it down when it starts to look blue" because of the haunting imagery it elicits about lynching in the United States. See: James Cone, *The Cross and the Lynching Tree* (Maryknoll, NY: Orbis, 2011).
6. For a pertinent, exemplary approach of a reading of deconstruction that reflects Caputo's sustained influence, while continuing to break new ground in discussion with other discourses, see: Clayton Crockett, *Derrida after the End of Writing: Political Theology and New Materialism* (New York: Fordham University Press, 2017).
7. To clarify, the subsequent discussion of theological reception of Derrida is intentionally focused on Anglo-American engagement and contribution. While this certainly risks neglecting the significant, influential, and continued Continental engagement with a French philosopher on the topic of religion and theology (e.g., Jean-Luc Nancy, Jean-Luc Marion, Gianni Vattimo, etc.), it is for the purpose of honing in on a particular reading of Derrida and religion epitomized in Caputo, whose influence has gained the most traction in an Anglo-American context. And because this context is central to the argument put forward in this book—including the particular way(s) that the discourses discussed engage the topic of decisions that cut and divide—I have chosen to focus on, and remain within, this context. No doubt this is an illustration of the inherent, and problematic, exclusivity of decision that will hopefully become clearer further along.
8. See: Thomas Altizer, *Deconstruction and Theology* (New York: Crossroad Pub Co, 1982).
9. Mark C. Taylor, *Erring: A Postmodern A/Theology*, New edition (Chicago: University Of Chicago Press, 1987), 6.
10. See: John Milbank, Graham Ward, and Catherine Pickstock, *Radical Orthodoxy: A New Theology* (London: Routledge, 1999); John Milbank, *Theology and Social Theory: Beyond Secular Reason*, 2nd edition (Oxford, UK; Malden, MA: Wiley-Blackwell, 2006).
11. These include such pioneering works as: Kevin Hart, *Trespass of the Sign: Deconstruction, Theology and Philosophy* (New York: Fordham University Press, 1989); Walter Lowe, *Theology and Difference: The Wound of Reason* (Bloomington: Indiana University Press, 1993); Graham Ward, *Barth, Derrida and the Language of Theology* (Cambridge: Cambridge University Press, 1995); Ellen T. Armour, *Deconstruction, Feminist Theology, and the Problem of Difference: Subverting the Race/Gender Divide* (Chicago: The University of Chicago Press, 1999).
12. John D. Caputo, *The Prayers and Tears of Jacques Derrida: Religion without Religion* (Bloomington: Indiana University Press, 1997), xviii.
13. Ibid., xxix.
14. See: Geoffrey Bennington and Jacques Derrida, *Jacques Derrida* (Chicago: University Of Chicago Press, 1999).
15. This is a phrase that Derrida employs explicitly in *The Gift of Death and Literature in Secret*, trans. by David Wills (Chicago: University of Chicago Press, 2007), 50.
16. Bennington, *Jacques Derrida*, 154.
17. Caputo, *The Prayers and Tears of Jacques Derrida*, xix.
18. Ibid., xx.

19. Plenty has been written about Derrida's so-called "ethical" and "religious" turns, with various positions on Derrida's later engagement with religious and ethical/political themes and the extent to which this amounted to a genuine "turn." See: Simon Critchley, *The Ethics of Deconstruction: Derrida and Levinas* (Oxford: Blackwell Publishers, 1992); Clayton Crockett, *Derrida after the End of Writing: Political Theology and New Materialism* (New York: Fordham University Press, 2018); Michael Naas, *Miracle and Machine: Jacques Derrida and the Two Sources of Religion, Science, and Media* (New York: Fordham University Press, 2012); Herman Rappaport, *Later Derrida: Reading the Recent Work* (New York: Routledge, 2003); Carl A. Raschke, *Force of God: Political Theology and the Crisis of Liberal Democracy* (New York: Columbia University Press, 2015); James K. A. Smith, *Jacques Derrida: Live Theory*, annotated edition (New York ; London: Bloomsbury Academic, 2005).

20. I am in agreement with this more recent consensus about the lack of any significant departure in Derrida's later work, that, in the words of Carl Raschke, it "amounts less to a 'turn' away from pure deconstruction to matters ethico-political and religious than a kind of epochal elucidation of what has been tacit but not apparent in his philosophical enterprise all along" (*Force of God*, 16–17).

21. See: Jacques Derrida, "Of An Apocalyptic Tone Recently Adopted in Philosophy," trans. John P. Leavey, Jr., *The Oxford Literary Review*, vol. 6, no. 2 (1984).

22. See: Derrida, "How to Avoid Speaking: Denials," 73–142.

23. See: Jacques Derrida, *Specters of Marx: The State of the Debt, The Work of Mourning and the New International* (New York: Routledge, 2006).

24. See: Jacques Derrida, "Faith and Knowledge: The Two Sources of 'Religion' at the Limits of Reason Alone," in *Acts of Religion*, ed. Gil Anidjar (New York: Routledge, 2002), 40–101.

25. See: Derrida, *The Gift of Death, Second Edition and Literature in Secret*.

26. Ibid., 50.

27. Caputo, *The Prayers and Tears of Jacques Derrida*, xxi.

28. Ibid., xix–xx.

29. Ibid., 69.

30. Ibid., xxiv.

31. Ibid.

32. Ibid., 123.

33. Ibid., xxiii.

34. Ibid., xxiv.

35. Ibid., 101.

36. Ibid., xix–xx.

37. Ibid., 11.

38. Ibid., 6.

39. Ibid., 231.

40. Ibid., 246.

41. Ibid., 12.

42. On the opening page of *The Weakness of God*, Caputo confesses "a weakness for theology," despite his attempts to avoid it, especially in *Prayers and Tears* where he is more comfortable talking in terms of "religion." Now, however, he admits that he can no longer "deny that what I am doing here is theological." In the footnote to this statement, he argues that his desire to avoid "theology" was because it "suggests the onto-theological project, which takes God as an object of conceptual analysis" (p. 301).

43. John D. Caputo, *The Weakness of God: A Theology of the Event* (Bloomington: Indiana University Press, 2006), 2.

44. Ibid.

45. Ibid., 3.

46. Ibid., 4.

47. Caputo, *Prayers and Tears*, 246.

48. Ibid., 337.

49. Caputo, *The Insistence of God*, 9.

50. Ibid., 9.

51. Ibid., 10.
52. Ibid., 3.
53. Ibid., 4.
54. Ibid., 6.
55. Ibid., 7.
56. Ibid., 5.
57. Ibid., 8.
58. Ibid., 6–7.
59. Ibid., 4–5.
60. Ibid., 5.
61. Ibid., 7.
62. Ibid., 30.
63. Ibid., 31.
64. Ibid., 36.
65. Ibid., 37.
66. Ibid., 39.
67. Ibid., 36.
68. Ibid., 45.
69. Ibid., 144.
70. Ibid.
71. Ibid., 162–163.
72. Ibid., 34.
73. Caputo, *Prayers and Tears*, 14.
74. Derrida, "Force of Law," 24.
75. Caputo, *Prayers and Tears*, 25.
76. Ibid., 26.
77. Ibid., 63.
78. Ibid., 212.
79. Ibid., 225.
80. James H. Olthuis, ed., *Religion With/Out Religion: The Prayers and Tears of John D. Caputo* (London; New York: Routledge, 2001).
81. Jeffrey M. Dudiak, "Bienvenue—Just a Moment," in *Religion With/Out Religion: The Prayers and Tears of John D. Caputo*, ed. James H. Olthuis (New York: Routledge, 2002), 13.
82. Shane Cudney, "'Religion without Religion: Caputo, Derrida, and the Violence of Particularity,'" in *Religion With/Out Religion: The Prayers and Tears of John D. Caputo*, ed. James H. Olthuis (New York: Routledge, 2002), 46.
83. John D. Caputo, "Hoping in Hope, Hoping against Hope," in *Religion With/Out Religion: The Prayers and Tears of John D. Caputo*, ed. James H. Olthuis (New York: Routledge, 2002), 123–24.
84. Ibid., 128.
85. Ibid., 126.
86. Ibid., 127.

Chapter Two

Rereading Undecidability

An Appreciation for the Aporetic Double-Bind

> *No justice is exercised, no justice is rendered, no justice becomes effective . . . without a decision that cuts and divides. . . . But in the moment of suspense of the undecidable, it is not just either, for only a decision is just.*
>
> —Jacques Derrida, "Force of Law: The 'Mystical Foundation of Authority'"

> *We are always negotiating violence and our ideals of justice cannot be immune from contestation and struggle. Every ideal of justice is inscribed in what Derrida calls an "'economy of violence.' . . . There is no call for justice that does not call for the exclusion of others, which means that every call for justice can be challenged or criticized."*
>
> —Martin Hägglund, "The Radical Evil of Deconstruction"

Caputo's reading of Derrida and deconstruction emphasizes the movement toward avoiding, limiting, or remedying the problem of exclusion, and by extension reveals the problematic nature of decision. And we have already seen the significant influence this has had on understandings of undecidability and the problem of decision more generally. The goal now is to present an alternative reading that complicates any such attempt to remedy this problem by pushing undecidability even further. In my reading of deconstruction, undecidability is not meant to suggest that any position of indecision exists, but to reveal that in the midst of the impossible decision, we must still decide. In so doing, I will highlight how the deconstructive aporia or double-bind offers a different understanding of the deconstructive "impossibility," revealing the "necessity" and "inescapability" of (some form of) the problem, such that any attempt to eliminate, remove, or remedy it is impossible. Deconstruction certainly highlights an impossibility at the heart of language, justice, and religion, and this chapter will show that the Derridean aporia constitutes a double-bind wherein the situation is not only impossible (in a way similar, yet more radical than Caputo reads this impossibility) but also necessary and inescapable. An appreciation for the live tension of the Derridean aporia thus reveals a further complication of the problem of in/decision that we have been tracking and any attempts to navigate it.

My contention is that Caputo's reading of deconstruction separates out and overemphasizes one aspect of the deconstructive aporia, which results in a certain understanding of impossibility. Doing so distorts the movement of deconstruction, which can only be understood *as* or *in* this double-bind. Perhaps more accurately, it is my contention that Caputo leaves himself open to being read this way, even if and when there are moments—as I have shown above—where we seem to agree on this point. Deconstruction certainly entails an impossibility, yet my focus is more on the remedy to the situation that Caputo seems to propose where openness is preferred over closure, especially when said (ethical) remedy is understood as deconstructive. Caputo's emphasis on the impossibility in deconstruction, therefore, lends itself to being read as identifying a problem with a solution that can and should be avoided. In this particular case, the problem is that of decisions that cut, divide, and exclude. On ethical grounds, I agree that such exclusion is thoroughly problematic and affirm a desire to avoid it; any decision that cuts, divides, or excludes should be critiqued. In fact, we should continue to struggle against exclusion in its various forms. However, I do not think deconstruction can offer any such ethical critique or justification for such a critique. Deconstruction does not let us off the hook so easily, because it consistently reveals a predicament wherein the problem cannot be avoided or remedied; the problem is (always already) inescapable and even necessary. Thus, here, I will highlight this predicament by focusing more explicitly on the deconstructive aporia: the "impossibility" as well as "necessity" and "inescapability." In so doing, I offer a reading of Derrida that attempts to feel, grasp, and appreciate the tension—and pinch—of the double-bind (or "double binding" as Caputo calls it) of deconstruction, and then note the implications for the problem of decision.[1] Put simply, my goal by the end of this chapter is to show how deconstruction reveals that we are always already in the midst of exclusive decisions that we have identified as problematic. To the extent that this is the case, it will problematize any attempt to avoid or remedy this problem, even in Caputo's religion without religion, weak theology of the event, or God of the "perhaps." And, in so doing, it will offer us a clearer picture not only of the deconstructive aporia of in/decision, but, more importantly, of the problem of exclusive decisions, such that our struggle can be more rigorous, responsible, and transparent.

THE DECONSTRUCTIVE APORETIC DOUBLE-BIND

Let us begin by unpacking this notion of a deconstructive aporia that is central to my argument. In Derrida's earlier engagement with language, communication, and Western metaphysics, as well as Derrida's later work with religion and justice, deconstruction reveals a double-bind wherein something exists or occurs (i.e., is "possible") only in its deconstruction (i.e., its "impossibility"). Put differently, its impossibility is its condition of possibility. Western metaphysics, according to Derrida, is an attempt to return to the origin of self-presence; yet, in his early work, Derrida shows that such presence is illusory, thus revealing the deconstruction of a "metaphysics of presence." In his early essay, "*Différance*," Derrida is attempting to hold linguistic philosopher Ferdinand de Saussure's feet to the fire and spell out the metaphysical implications of Saussure's structuralist claim that language is a system of differences with no positive terms. In this essay, Derrida introduces the term "*différance*" as that which not only accounts for the spatial and temporal differences (deferrals) in language, but actually produces them. In other words, there is no "transcendental signified"—no structure, center, origin, telos, or that which ultimately puts a stop to the play of difference. There is nothing behind, above, beneath, or beyond language to which the signs refer. All we have are signs referring to signs—an endless chain of signifiers. In fact, all we have are traces of such signification; moreover, all we have are traces of these traces. At one point in the essay Derrida asks: "Has anyone thought that we have been tracking something down, something other than the tracks themselves to be tracked down?"—as if anyone thought we were actually following the tracks in order to arrive at something, because all we have are the tracks themselves.[2] There is no originary, self-present element or signified that we can ever get back to. All we have are the traces (of traces). As a result, language is always already underway. We cannot get back to the beginning, but always enter into the midst of dialogue and reference. Derrida takes this central structural insight and pushes it all the way in order to highlight its implications, which for him entails the deconstruction of everything that depends on language, including the philosophical underpinnings of Western metaphysics.

Derrida continues to reveal the deconstruction of Western metaphysics by turning to the speech/writing binary and the way that "writing" has been denigrated to "speech." If the sign is denigrated in Western philosophy because it is considered representation, as opposed to presence in meaning, writing is even further denigrated because it is considered the sign of the sign, which results in a further distancing from the immediacy of presence and meaning. Derrida's next main target, then, is the privileged position that speech gets in relationship to writing. In "Plato's Pharmacy," Derrida performs a close reading of *Phaedrus* and the way that Plato subordinates writing to speech in order to show how the former becomes a "dangerous supplement." In *Phaedrus*, Socrates recounts the origin of writing, calling it the "*pharmakon*," which can mean either remedy or poison. Derrida runs with this to show how writing is both given to speech and philosophy as a gift or remedy, in order to help with memory and knowledge, but, as the myth about the origin of writing in *Phaedrus* explains, it also becomes a poison as it causes further forgetfulness. Thus, writing becomes to speech both a remedy and poison. This leads to one of Derrida's most well-known quips: "there is no such thing as a harmless remedy. The *pharmakon* can never be simply beneficial."[3] Derrida points out how writing, the *pharmakon*, "is that dangerous supplement that breaks into the very thing that would have liked to do without it yet lets itself *at once* be breached, roughed up, fulfilled, and replaced, completed by the very trace through which the present increases itself in the act of disappearing."[4] Supplement is a key term for Derrida in this text as he uses it not only to mean addition, but also substitution. The implications of the *pharmakon* indicate that philosophy becomes trapped in an attempt to both police itself from the harmful effects of writing, while also relying upon it. This understanding of the *pharmakon* will be important to us moving forward. Derrida therefore illustrates the aporia of writing in relationship to philosophy: this policing is both necessary and impossible. It is necessary because it is inescapable; it is impossible because it can never purely purge its harmful effects. As a result, philosophy's best attempts to subordinate writing to speech are upset by the deconstruction of the speech/writing binary.

However—and this is the key to the double-bind—metaphysics *only exists* in this state of deconstruction. It can only ever be metaphysics if it attempts to do that (i.e., return to self-presence) which it cannot do. Derridean interpreter Geoffrey Bennington, writing what has come to be known as "Derridabase," tries to grasp this slippery notion: "This deconstruction is not something that someone does *to* metaphysics, nor something that metaphysics does to *itself* . . . *metaphysics only subsisted from its very beginnings through this deconstruction.*"[5] Later on, showing how this impacts all of Western philosophy, Bennington writes about the implications of the deconstruction of a metaphysics of presence: "This is also the constitutive double bind of philosophy itself, which cannot be comprehended by anything other than itself, but cannot comprehend itself either, although it just is the effort to do this."[6] In other words, the double-bind of philosophy is an attempt to explain itself by going beyond itself to an outside referent, which is, according to deconstruction, impossible, and therefore makes the entire enterprise incomprehensible. But we only know it is incomprehensible by way of, because of, philosophy. This is the deconstructive aporia: the notion that something "is" or "exists" *only* in its deconstruction. Deconstruction thus reveals that the condition of possibility is the very thing that is impossible; seen the other way around, its impossibility is its condition of possibility. Throughout his oeuvre, Derrida points out such an aporetic tension in several significant examples, including the "gift,"[7] "signature,"[8] "proper name,"[9] etc. For instance, the gift is annulled the moment it is acknowledged, because "your gratitude toward a gift I give you functions as a payment in return or in exchange, and then the gift is no longer strictly speaking a gift," since a gift by definition is freely given without repayment.[10] Thus the gift only exists in its deconstruction or impossibility, for how could it ever *be* without being acknowledged, which would no longer make it a gift—yet gifts are given every day. Similarly, although language is an endless chain of signifiers, it does "exist" (in this aporetic tension) in that we speak and write and listen and read.

In his later work, Derrida uses these deconstructive insights about language and communication (and their metaphysical implications) to point out the aporia of "the ethical" (e.g., justice, responsibility, duty, etc.), by showing how they too only exist or occur by, in, through their impossibility and deconstruction. Since Caputo takes Derrida's work and applies it more explicitly to religion and justice in order to show the limitations of determinate dogmas, doctrines, institutionalized religion, etc., especially in the ways such limitations exclude, we will focus more explicitly on these later Derridean texts that engage themes such as "responsibility," "duty," "justice," and most importantly, "decision." For Caputo, as we have seen, the messianic is always to come, never arriving, keeps us awaiting the future, which he understands as a very strident (ethical) critique of, for instance, Christian proclamations of the arrival of Jesus Christ as the messiah, or, more pertinent to this discussion, any decision that interrupts prematurely and forestalls what is to come, *à venir*. But what is in danger of being misrepresented in Caputo's emphasis on and understanding of the impossible is a fuller appreciation for the deconstructive aporia that also highlights an inescapability or necessity. Not only will the following reading indicate that one cannot have impossibility without inescapability, but that what is revealed to be impossible is any attempt to avoid or remedy the problem, even by way of any reading of deconstruction. With regard to decision, then, it will highlight an alternative understanding of undecidability, what I have been referring to as in/decision, i.e., that every decision is subject to deconstruction by being too early, presuming presence and certainty, etc., while also highlighting the impossibility of avoiding such limited decisions. This is the double-bind of in/decision.

Gift of Death: An Irresponsible Responsibility

In *The Gift of Death*, Derrida argues that to be infinitely or absolutely responsible, one must be irresponsible. This is what Derrida refers to as the "paradox, scandal, and aporia" of "responsibility" or "duty."[11] The first half of

The Gift of Death is a reading of Jan Patočka's history of European responsibility and its connection with Christianity. Derrida troubles Patočka's opposition between responsibility—which, as Derrida will demonstrate, is tied to and comes from religion—and secrecy (or mystery) by showing how responsibility can never rid itself of secrecy. If we have learned anything about deconstruction, we should be able to guess where Derrida is heading: having highlighted Patočka's binary of responsibility/secrecy, Derrida will show how that which is defined as responsible is only such because it is opposed to secrecy; however, this binary cannot hold as Derrida will show how secrecy is the condition of possibility for responsibility.

To that end, Derrida shows how for Patočka it is the gaze of God that rouses one to responsibility, resulting in the *mysterium tremendum*. Derrida suggests that for Patočka, the condition of possibility for responsibility is when the "Good [is] no longer a transcendental objective, a relation between objective things, but the relation to the other, a response to the other" which entails that "goodness forgets itself . . . a movement of the gift that renounces itself, hence a movement of infinite love." This love must be infinite, according to Derrida, because "only infinite love can renounce itself . . . to *become finite*" in order to love the other as a finite being. Since this becoming finite entails becoming singular for Derrida, "responsibility demands irreplaceable singularity."[12] Thus, the key to infinite responsibility is singularity—a singularity that Derrida argues only comes through death, as death is the only thing that is completely *mine*, "that which nobody else can undergo or confront in my place." One's irreplaceability, or singularity, is therefore "conferred, delivered, 'given' . . . by death." It is from this "perspective of death as the place of my irreplaceability" that one feels the call to responsibility, and thus "only a mortal can be responsible."[13] If singularity is the only thing that can make one truly responsible, and singularity is only "given" by death, then death is that which gives one responsibility; hence the call to responsibility, which entails singularity, is a "gift of death." To the extent that this is the case, infinite responsibility reveals its own deconstruction because it necessitates death, which means mortality or finitude, and therefore infinite responsibility is impossible by its very definition: "there is thus a structural disproportion or dissymmetry between the finite and responsible mortal on the one hand and the goodness of the infinite gift on the other."[14] Ultimately, then, responsibility entails—i.e., can never escape—guilt: "I have never been and never will be up to the level of this infinite goodness." Moreover, Derrida points out, such guilt is inescapable or originary, "like original sin." Before I commit any fault or wrongdoing "I am guilty inasmuch as I am responsible," because my singularity is given by death and finitude, which is "precisely what makes me unequal to the infinite goodness of the gift." Infinite responsibility is therefore shown to be always already irresponsible; its "guilt is inherent in responsibility."[15] One can never be responsible *enough*, able to live up to the level of infinite goodness, because of human finitude.

In order to illustrate the irresponsibility of (infinite) responsibility, in the second half of *Gift of Death* Derrida turns to a close reading of Kierkegaard's pseudonymous *Fear and Trembling*, which is itself a reading and commentary on Abraham's (attempted) sacrifice of Isaac on Mount Moriah in Genesis 22. First, Derrida draws on the necessary singularity of Abraham, because if Abraham is to be infinitely responsible—to God, who has given him the command to sacrifice his only son—then the responsibility must be his alone, he cannot share it with anyone. Abraham must not, and does not, tell his son Isaac where the sacrifice will come from; and he does not tell anyone else about this secret either, which makes him singularly responsible. By not disclosing the secret between God and him, Abraham "assumes the responsibility that consists in always being alone, retrenched in one's own singularity at the moment of decision."[16] Speaking or sharing this secret would deliver Abraham from his singularity, and thus his responsibility, which is why, in order to be responsible, one must be bound to silence and secrecy.

At the *same time*, however—and such *simultaneity* is important—secrecy undermines the very notion of responsibility because it means that Abraham will have a secret, which also entails irresponsibility, because in order to be responsible one must be held accountable for their actions; in other words, we must have no secrets. Whether it is according to "common sense" or "philosophical reasoning," Derrida admits that "the most widely shared presumption" is that secrets appear contrary to responsibility. There is always a "necessity of accounting for one's words and actions in front of others, of justifying and owning up to them." Yet, the discussion up to this point about "absolute responsibility" seems to entail a singularity, such that whatever I do, "to the extent that it has to remain mine, singular so," means that it is "something no one else can perform in my place," which in turn implies secrecy. "But what is also implied," Derrida continues, "is that, by not speaking to others, I don't account for my actions, I answer for nothing, I make no response to others or before others. It is both a scandal and a paradox."[17] Again, Abraham's singularity reveals the impossibility of responsibility because the very condition of possibility—singularity (in, with, by secrecy)—is the very thing that undermines it by making it irresponsible. Thus, the impossibility of responsibility does not render it something toward which to strive, but *structurally impossible* by the very fact that its impossibility is directly tied to it being necessarily so. In other words, the "scandal and paradox" is that the condition of possibility for responsibility is that which makes it impossible; therefore, attempting to avoid that which makes responsibility irresponsible is *impossible*.

Derrida also highlights the singularity of God as the one to whom Abraham is ultimately faithful and responsible as both necessary for responsibility, while at the same time that which undermines it. For Abraham to be infinitely responsible he needs to be faithful to God alone, but this means at the cost—or sacrifice—of all others, to whom Abraham is also responsible, which means that Abraham must be *irresponsible* toward all others. Again, the aporia is in play: absolute responsibility binds me singularly to one, which means that I must be irresponsible in relation to all others. Derrida reflects on this predicament: "Duty or responsibility binds me to the other, to the other as other, and binds me in my absolute singularity to the other as other. . . . As soon as I enter into a relation with the absolute other, my singularity enters into relation with his on the level of obligation and duty. I am responsible before the other as other; I answer to him and I answer for what I do before him." Yet, at the same time—again, note the simultaneity—the absolute responsibility that binds me in my own singularity to the absolute singularity of the other is the very thing that undercuts responsibility. And it does not just undercut it, but "immediately propels me into the space or risk of absolute sacrifice" because this other is not the only other. There are also others, in fact "an infinite number of them, the innumerable generality of others to whom I should be bound by the same responsibility." One cannot, therefore, respond responsibly, answer the request, meet the obligation "without sacrificing the other other, the other others." Moreover, "*every other (one) is every (bit) other* [*tout autre est tout autre*]; everyone else is completely or wholly other."[18]

In the case of Abraham, he exemplifies absolute duty by being responsible to the singularity of One (in this case, God). This is the condition of possibility for responsibility—the binding of me to the singularity of the other as other; anything less would constitute irresponsibility toward this other. But this infinite or absolute responsibility also entails irresponsibility because of how it neglects all others, all the other others—thus leaving infinite responsibility in a state of aporetic tension, unable to escape irresponsibility. Again, Derrida reiterates how infinite or absolute responsibility demands that one behave irresponsibly: "the concepts of responsibility, of decision, or of duty, are condemned *a priori* to paradox, scandal, and aporia."[19] Derrida emphasizes the paradox of responsibility, i.e., the *impossibility* of being ultimately responsible and ethical, because in order to attain absolute duty one must sacrifice ethics. But again, this is an inescapable predicament, for the very attempt to be responsible, is what makes it impossible.

In the context of our current discussion, then, let us pause briefly to note the implications for the problem of decision. This book enters into a conversation where there is a recognition about the problematic nature of decision, of deciding for one thing and against another, of deciding in a way that cuts, divides, or excludes. Again, it is important to keep in mind that this conversation has thus far remained in the abstract because we began our excursion into the problem of decision by looking at it structurally, via Derrida and deconstruction. But in the subsequent chapters this predicament becomes more concrete, taking on (literal) flesh and blood, when we discuss how decisions become even more problematic when deciding for one form of justice over and against another, or deciding about whether or not God decides. And this is why it was important to begin with Caputo, because he not only appreciates, as fully as anyone writing about these issues, the problematic nature of exclusivity—i.e., decisions that cut and divide, a decisiveness that prematurely interrupts the *à venir* by claiming presence, certainty, or absolute surety—but Caputo also understands deconstruction as revealing the impossibility of such.

In order to critically advance both Caputo's ethical instincts and reading of deconstruction, we need to highlight an even more precarious predicament. And part of the precariousness is an alternative understanding of impossibility. What Derrida highlights would mean that any attempt to avoid the difficult decision would be as problematic as any limited, problematic decision. Any attempt to be ethically responsible by avoiding exclusion is also impossible, because irresponsibility is unavoidable, inevitable, inescapable, and structurally necessary to the very attempt to be responsible. In other words, there is no safe ground to stand upon with regard to the difficult decision. Caputo has deftly highlighted how any decision is problematic, which is why he suggests a little word like "perhaps" as the way forward. And to the extent that one recognizes the limits of any decision, this is sound advice. But it is important, at least according to Derrida, that we also be wary of understanding this as a way *out* of the predicament, i.e., the difficult decision. Yes, any decision is subject to deconstruction, but so is indecision. Not deciding is as problematic as any decision, as we will see more clearly. But what *Gift of Death* already highlights for us is Derrida's understanding of the aporia of responsibility, that any attempt to be responsible—whether by avoiding decision or not—will always entail an inescapable irresponsibility. Abraham could not avoid irresponsibility; he either neglects his absolute duty to the singularity of the other as other, or he neglects his responsibility to all the other others. There is no good, i.e., purely responsible, decision here—this is the impossible predicament. But there is no way out of this dilemma either, for its impossibility emerges in the quest to be responsible in the first place. Again, *Gift of Death* paints the "scandal and paradox" of responsibility in this way: the condition of possibility for responsibility is that which makes it impossible; therefore, attempting to avoid that which makes responsibility irresponsible, as a way to be (more) responsible, is *impossible*. The same applies to the dynamic of decision—it is trapped in a scandal and paradox. Caputo has demonstrated the limits, i.e., the problematic nature, of decisions that cut, divide, exclude. But the scandal of decision is even more *scandalous* in that there is no avoiding such divisive, exclusive decisions.

Specters of Marx: Critique and Affirmation

Derrida also explicitly discusses the double-bind of the aporia in *Specters of Marx*. Throughout this text, one of Derrida's main targets of critique are those who declare the "end" of history, man, etc. (e.g., Hegel, Fukuyama, Kojeve, etc.). Derrida is particularly keen to critique any notion that we have arrived, and therefore portrays justice as more open-ended, always to come, in short, impossible. In the chapter, "Wears and Tears," Derrida shows just how bleak the situation is by outlining "ten plagues of the new world order" as proof that things are a long way from any such notions of arrival and finality. Much of what Derrida says here is certainly in line with Caputo's critique, who employs Derridean texts like these, that any declaration or definitive decision will betray the impossibility deconstruction highlights.

But in the midst of this critique, Derrida surprisingly affirms the movements, gestures, and decisions that have been made toward progress. These "plagues of the new world order" and their proof that we have not achieved any notion of finality "do not suffice to disqualify international institutions." Quite to the contrary, "justice demands," Derrida writes, "that one pay tribute to certain of those who are working within them in the direction of the perfectability and emancipation of institutions that must never be denounced."[20] Here we see that the impossibility of a justice that is always on the horizon to come, and awaited, does not equate to absolute negation of said attempts along the way. On the contrary, "however insufficient, confused, or equivocal such signs may still be, we should salute" them.[21] Thus, Derrida presents a deconstructive thinking about justice that offers both critique *and* affirmation: "There is a spirit of Marxism which I will never be ready to renounce, it is not only the critical idea or questioning stance.... It is even more a certain emancipatory and *messianic* affirmation, a certain experience of the promise."[22] And this promise, Derrida argues, must not remain "spiritual" or "abstract," but "produce events, new effective forms of action, practice, organization, and so forth."[23] Derrida expresses a concern that the impossibility and critique that has so preoccupied readings of deconstruction should also be accompanied by an affirmation of the limited, "insufficient, confused," problematic attempts at attaining them.

In my reading of the deconstructive aporia we find both critique and a certain sense of affirmation: a definitive critique of all attempts at justice, because justice is impossible, always to come, etc., which means that any determinate form of justice (i.e., law, institutions, decisions, etc.) will always fall short. But at the same time, however, we find a kind of affirmation of said attempts, because they are inescapable and necessary. Now, we must be careful not to slip too easily into an overly affirmative stance toward these limited attempts. This is one of Caputo's main fears, which is not misplaced. It is the fear that we might settle for "tolerable progress," wherein he reads deconstruction as always pointing out as intolerable "the slightest imperfection in the present, the slightest injustice."[24] I am not suggesting anything like this at all; I am simply urging us to reconsider how stopping at a critical stance toward the injustice of present forms (of religion and justice) "cannot be written off as a tolerable progress" either. The double-bind of deconstruction reveals that justice is always already trapped in a state of im/possibility, where every attempt is destined to fail, yet such attempts are necessary. Determinate forms of justice are problematic, because justice is impossible, always to come, open-ended, etc.; but it is only through closed, definitive, productive decision and action that justice can ever even be a possibility. This is the double-bind: we cannot, but we must. We must continue to strive for justice, discern and analyze such attempts, because they will always be incomplete. This is what I read as the "radicalization" deconstruction presents—a responsibility to never rest, keep working.

But such striving does not, and must not, equate to mere open-endedness either—this is the danger, in my opinion, of Caputo's reading (or readings of Caputo): it tempts us by suggesting a relaxation of the tension of the double-bind. On the one hand, Caputo's emphasis on the open-endedness of justice pushes us to continue striving for better, more just forms of justice, by revealing the limits of closure. But deconstruction also pushes us to not rest in any such identification of the problem. There is a sense in which if we merely identify closure and definitive forms of justice as problematic because they forestall the messianic justice to-come, then we can rest—at least partially—in such an identification. And while this is an important step in the movement toward justice (i.e., a realization that definitive forms of justice are limited, incomplete, unjust), this is only one-half of the insight of the deconstructive aporia. I understand the double-bind to be precisely that: two-fold in nature. There is the bind of the impossible—we cannot achieve justice completely, purely, absolutely; but there is also, and simultaneously, the bind of the inescapability—we cannot avoid closing, choosing, deciding.

"Villanova Roundtable": Incalculability Demands Calculation

At the "Villanova Roundtable," published panel discussions at the inauguration of a PhD program in Continental Philosophy, Derrida responded to several questions about his work, including those from Caputo himself. Of course, the question of justice and its impossibility came up, particularly as he addressed it in *Specters of Marx* and *Gift of Death*. In somewhat plainer language, Derrida asserts that justice is never, and can never be, fully present, because "justice, if it has to do with the other, with the infinite distance of the other, is always unequal to the other, is always incalculable."[25] The incalculability of justice is a theme that is most explicitly engaged in "Force of Law," which I will engage below. But here Derrida discusses how justice is incalculable because when the other—the *tout autre*—arrives on the scene, he or she introduces a relationship that cannot be reduced to law, right, or calculations: "That is what gives deconstruction its movement, that is, constantly to suspect, to criticize the given determinations of culture, of institutions, of legal systems, not in order to destroy them or simply to cancel them, but to be just with justice, to respect this relation to the other as justice."[26] Therefore, any instantiation of justice is to be critiqued by recognizing its impossibility, since "a justice that could appear as such, that could be calculated, a calculation of what is just and what is not just, saying what has to be given in order to be just—that is not justice."[27] Again, this is the inevitable critique that deconstruction brings in terms of the impossibility it highlights.

On the other hand, however, Derrida quickly adds: "This does not mean we should not calculate. We have to calculate as rigorously as possible."[28] Once more, it appears that the incalculability of justice does not suggest that we cease calculating. In fact, as we have seen, perhaps there is no way to stop calculating, as we cannot escape doing so. What's more, the incalculability of justice demands that we be as rigorous as possible in our calculations. *This* is the complex predicament that deconstruction reveals, that we *cannot*, but we *must*. We cannot achieve justice by calculation(s)—this is its impossibility. But we must calculate, because (a) there is no escaping calculations and (b) justice cannot have a chance if we do not calculate—this is its necessity. Thus, calculating, determining, closing, or deciding is necessary, even as we recognize their impossibility. Perhaps, then, the "best" we can do—what we might be urged to do in light of what deconstruction highlights—is to calculate, determine, decide, act, etc., with continuous rigorous analysis, scrutiny, and critique.

"Afterword: Toward an Ethic of Discussion": How to be Least Violent

Derrida continues to make the same point in other con/texts, this time again in a response to critics and those who he believes have misread him. In "Afterword: Toward an Ethic of Discussion," Derrida responds to questions, criticisms, and controversies that emerged after the publication of his early and influential essay, "Signature, Event, Context." In an interview-styled chapter included in the English translation of *Limited Inc*, Derrida begins by noting the inescapability of violence—something deconstruction had already implied in its earliest forms through the impossibility it suggested. However, the most interesting part of his response includes his suggestion that we have a certain responsibility to analyze and reduce such violence as much as possible. He begins by acknowledging "the violence, political or otherwise, at work in academic discussions or in intellectual discussions generally." Part of what deconstruction highlights is the impossibility of every attempt to avoid violence, because all such attempts will ultimately fail. He goes on, however, to clarify that this is not meant to advocate "that such violence be unleashed or simply accepted." Rather, Derrida argues, "I am above all asking that we try to recognize and analyze it as best we can in its various forms . . . And if, as I believe, violence remains (almost) ineradicable, its analysis and the most refined ingenious account of its conditions will be the least violent gestures, perhaps even nonviolent."[29] Here Derrida is suggesting something like discernment, as in discerning difficult decisions, is necessary in order that we might try to reduce violence by analyzing it "as best we can." What is important to note in Derrida's response is that although deconstruction, by definition, *deconstructs* every attempt at justice, responsibility, etc., this kind of analysis is not rendered null and void or futile by deconstruction, even if and when any attempt will always be subject to deconstruction itself. In fact, as we have already seen, it is the attempt to reduce violence that deconstruction reveals to be a form of inescapable violence. As he goes on to write: "For that is what we want, isn't it, to reduce [violence and ambiguity], if possible. Is it certain that we can, on one side or the other ever eliminate them? Is it even certain that we should try, *at all costs?*"[30]

The deconstruction of absolute purity, Derrida assures us, does not leave us with an "all or nothing" situation where we are left choosing between "pure realization" and "complete freeplay or undecidability," wherein the latter insinuates indecisiveness. On the contrary, distinctions are necessary. In response to one of his major critics, philosopher John R. Searle, Derrida discusses the role deconstruction plays regarding distinctions: "It can lead us to complicate—distinctly—the logic of binary oppositions and to a *certain use* the value of distinction attached to it. The latter has indeed certain limits and a history, which I have precisely tried to question. But that leads neither to 'illogic' nor to 'indistinction' nor to 'indeterminancy' . . . It never renounces, as Searle in the haste of a polemic seems to do and to advocate, clear and rigorous distinction."[31] Derrida's point is that deconstruction, by its very nature, complicates distinctions based upon binary oppositions; however, this does not abrogate distinctions altogether. Quite the contrary, Derrida insists distinctions, which are necessarily exclusive, must be made.

To illustrate the necessity of (exclusive) distinctions, Derrida uses the example of "the police" in response to a question about his statement "there is always a police and tribunal ready to intervene each time a rule is invoked in a case involving signatures, events, or contexts."[32] Whereas his earliest work seemed like an attack on the policing of rules—and to a certain extent it was that—Derrida maintains that his intention was not to suggest that "the law, the tribunal, or the police as political powers are *repressive in themselves*. . . . Every police is not repressive, no more than the law in general, even in [its] negative, restrictive, or prohibitive restrictions."[33] Again, distinctions are often in the crosshairs of deconstruction, as the distinctions collapse, break down, *deconstruct*; however, in pointing this out, Derrida realizes that we must not lose sight of the fact that we cannot escape making such distinctions. Ironically, the difference between making distinctions and their deconstruction is often a difficult distinction to make, Derrida admits; but it is a necessary and indispensable distinction. The law and the police, as restrictive and prohibitive, are not unjust simply because of their restriction and prohibition. Of course, Derrida makes the point that we should certainly be wary and critical of the "unjust brutality" of such forces and powers (which gains particular traction in light of recent events in the United States). But this is to be sharply distinguished from all restriction in general, as if restriction—in and of itself—equated to injustice, precisely because the distinction between justice and injustice has been troubled by deconstruction. Making such distinctions actually allows us "to avoid hastily confounding law and prohibition, law and repression, prohibition and repression."[34] "This is why," Derrida writes, "there are police and police. There is a police that is brutally and *rather* 'physically' repressive and there are more sophisticated police that are more 'cultural' or 'spiritual,' more noble."[35] Every institution or entity that enforces the law is a police, including, Derrida suggests, the academy. But society cannot exist without such policing, which is the double-bind of the aporia: a necessary impossibility. And the double-bind actually makes distinctions all the more important and valuable, because there are police and there are *police*. This, in my reading, is Caputo's point about why the "perhaps" is best understood as increasing responsibility—when we lose the certainty of *absolute* distinctions, it makes the limited, necessary distinctions all that more important (and dangerous). There are restrictions, prohibitions, laws, and rules that are unjust, power-driven, exclusive, etc.; but this does not render all prohibitions, laws, rules, or even all exclusions unjust, which is why we must distinguish and discern between the different kinds—itself a kind of policing, prohibiting, and excluding.[36]

Going further in his response, Derrida maintains that such policing is never "politically neutral either, never apolitical." Derrida argues that such political and ethical evaluation is always formulated within a given context, and, over against another politics, which will ultimately result in a kind of exclusion. He writes: "Once it has been demonstrated, as I hope to have done, that the exclusion of the parasite cannot be justified by purely theoretical-methodological reasons, how can one ignore that this practice of exclusion, or this will to purify . . . translates necessarily into a politics?"[37] And this kind of politics is unavoidable, as it "touches all the social institutions . . . more generally, it touches everything, quite simply everything." Contrary to the way deconstruction has typically been received, Derrida argues it is not that the restrictive, prohibitive nature of police is politically suspect in and of itself—as if we can critique the act of policing (which is itself an act of policing)—but that any attempt to police (e.g., fix the contexts of utterances) is *always* political. But even more than that, it is also inevitable, because "one cannot do anything, least of all speak, without determining a context. Such an experience is always political because it implies, insofar as it involves determination, a certain type of non-'natural' relationship to others." Derrida goes further: "Once this generality and this a priori structure have been recognized, the question can be raised, not whether a politics is implied (it always is), but which politics is implied."[38]

Here is where we begin to feel the sharpest pinch of the double-bind—a situation wherein one cannot escape a problem. Let's recap the twists and turns of Derrida's point above: if we cannot escape determining contexts, and such an act is political, which is also exclusive, then it would appear that exclusion is inescapable. This is precisely what I am attempting to demonstrate in this chapter. Derrida highlights a precarious predicament wherein one cannot escape or retreat to a safe (i.e., apolitical) ground, for we are always already in the midst of determinations, distinctions, decisions, contexts, politics, policing, etc., which all explicitly entail *exclusion*. Once we recognize this, Derrida proposes "you can then go on to analyze, but you cannot suspect [*whether* a politics is implied], much less denounce it except on the basis of another contextual determination every bit as political. In short, I do not believe that any neutrality is possible in this area."[39] Derrida seems to be suggesting that the "best" we can do is to analyze the kinds of politics, exclusions, and *decisions* that are always already in play, in everything we do. There is no escaping the problem; there is no neutral ground, for everything we do is trafficking in some version of this. If we are always in the midst of contexts—*il n'y a pas de hors-texte*—then we cannot denounce the exclusionary act of determining contexts *except* on the basis of *other* contexts, and hence other *exclusions*. It is not the enforcement, policing, determining, or deciding that is necessarily repressive—though it certainly may be repressive—but such enforcement is always political. In the midst of this aporetic double-bind, Derrida is suggesting that the "best" we can do is to be as rigorous as possible in discerning (i.e., exclusively) how we want to be political in our enforcement. *Which* politics? For what reason? *Which* exclusions? *How* will we decide? This includes recognizing that (exclusive) choices, distinctions, and decisions are as inescapable, necessary, and inevitable as they are problematic.

In "Afterword" Derrida seems to make the point that "necessity" and "inescapability" are as much in play as "impossibility"—or at least that impossibility needs to be understood in light of its inescapability, which highlights the aporetic tension of the deconstructive double-bind. Seen the other way around, the impossibility deconstruction reveals does not leave us in a state of indistinction or indeterminancy. On the contrary, exclusive determinations and distinctions are necessary, precisely because their impossibility is the condition of possibility that deconstruction highlights. And to the extent that every decision, by its very nature, entails distinguishing, determining, and excluding, it would mean that for all the ways deconstruction highlights the problematic nature of decisions, it also simultaneously reveals its inescapability. Consequently, this renders the notion of undecidability more complex than it initially appears. Just as every decision is deconstructible, so is a state of indecision or not deciding. The task then becomes discerning which determinations, which politics, which exclusions, and which decisions we will make.

"Force of Law: The Mystical Foundation of Authority": Ghost of the Undecidable

Perhaps the most explicit discussion of the predicament of in/decision and undecidability is found in "Force of Law: The 'Mystical Foundation of Authority,'" where Derrida pursues a line of questioning with regard to the difference between law and justice. One of the main points Derrida begins to ponder in this essay is that law implies force, the possibility of being "enforced," as "there is no law without enforceability." But this leads Derrida to ask: "How are we to distinguish between this force of the law . . . and the violence that one always deems unjust?"[40] Derrida is attempting to show that law, by definition, requires a certain amount of force; but force can—and should—make us nervous, especially if we are sympathetic to the notion that exclusion through the use and abuse of power is unjust, a point that Caputo has thoroughly demonstrated. In other words, given our ethical presuppositions and dispositions, which make us extremely wary of force and its association with law, force would seem to be that which is contrary to justice. The problem of force gains even more traction given the recent events that have transpired in the United States, most especially the use and abuse of violent force by the police. Piled on top of the numerous instances of police violence against African-Americans and immigrants prior to and since, the notion that force is problematic is fresh in all our minds. Although, unfortunately, this is not a new phenomenon, it has been exacerbated by the way the "law" and "justice" have *justified* this kind of use and abuse of violent police force by the criminal justice system, where officers who commit these acts of violence go unpunished, or the wrongness of these violent acts go unenforced. All of this makes discussion of force, as connected with law and justice, very problematic.

At the same time, however, Derrida urges us to consider how force might be required, or *necessary*, for justice—even the kind of justice pursued by those who deem force as unjust. Quoting Pascal, Derrida cites the necessity of force in justice: "Justice without force is impotent. In other words, justice isn't justice, it is not achieved if it doesn't have the force to be 'enforced.'"[41]

Derrida's point is that force without justice is "tyrannical," but equally, "justice without force is contradictory, as there are always the wicked."[42] Derrida uses Pascal to indicate that justice bears the mark of force: in order for justice to be *just*, it must be enforced. The only way to combat an oppressive or wicked force is with a just force—a point that will gain more traction in our discussion of the problem of exclusive preference in Chapter 4, wherein we will explore the extent to which liberation *from* exclusion entails some form of it.

Continuing his discussion of the difference between law and justice, Derrida cites the "aporia" of a justice "outside or beyond law."[43] Here he defines an aporia as that which "does not allow passage . . . a non-road." In the case of justice, this would mean that "justice would be the experience that we are not able to experience." Part of the reason for this is that justice cannot be reduced to the application of a "good rule to a particular case." When this happens "we can be sure that law (*droit*) may find itself accounted for, but certainly not justice," because "law (*droit*) is not justice." The former is based upon calculation, "but justice is incalculable." This is the unpresentable, incalculable form of justice that Caputo refers to, a justice that is always to come and never present, which is why we will never be able to fully experience justice here-and-now. But overemphasizing this point risks distortion by focusing on only one aspect of the aporia, its impossibility understood as that which is always to-come, never achieved or assured. However, Derrida goes on to add: "I think there is no justice without this experience, however impossible it may be, of aporia. Justice is an experience of the impossible." So while "justice is incalculable," it nevertheless "requires us to calculate with the incalculable." And these "aporetic experiences"—which are "impossible"—are in fact "the experiences, as improbable as they are necessary, of justice, that is to say of moments in which the decision between just and unjust is never insured by a rule."[44] These moments of an improbable and impossible justice can only ever be possible if/when a decision is made; in fact, the decision point is *necessary* in the midst of this impossibility.

In other words, Derrida's discussion of the aporia of justice highlights that its *impossibility* cannot be understood apart from its *necessity*, citing the double-bind of justice. As we have seen in the case of force, it is both problematic yet necessary for justice; it is that which can on the one hand be the source of injustice, while on the other hand that which is inescapable and necessary for justice—thus rendering justice as caught in "an experience of the impossible." "Everything would be simple," Derrida writes, if there were a clear and discernable distinction between justice and law (*droit*). But as it turns out, "*droit* claims to exercise itself in the name of justice and justice is required to establish itself in the name of a law that must be 'enforced.'" So "deconstruction always finds itself between these two poles" of the aporia, "between justice (infinite, incalculable, rebellious to the rule and foreign to symmetry, heterogeneous and heterotropic)" on the one hand, and "the exercise of justice as law or right, legitimacy or legality, stabilizable and statutory, calculable, a system of regulated and coded prescriptions" on the other.[45] Thus the aporia is the double-bind, the impossible possibility, of justice that is both *beyond* an enforceable law and *necessitates* it, of justice that is both *beyond* any decision and *necessitates* it.

Derrida continues to discuss the aporetic double-bind by turning toward a more explicit emphasis on the matter of decision and justice. He begins by reiterating that any decision that "simply consists of applying a rule, of enacting a program or effecting a calculation" would not be just because justice always requires "fresh judgment," which Derrida defines as a free and responsible interpretation of previous laws, not merely the blind application of them. At the same time, however, a decision is not just if it is made without the law. "In short," Derrida writes, "for a decision to be just and responsible, it must . . . be both regulated and without regulation . . . conserve the law and also destroy or suspend it . . . reinvent it in each case, rejustify it." So the decision, in order to be just, must be *both* beholden to the law *but also* free from it. Any decision that is merely the application of a law or rule is not just; any decision that is made without reference to a law or rule is not just. This aporetic double-bind is why, Derrida says, "there is never a moment that we can say *in the present* that a decision *is* just" or that any person is just, and "even less, '*I am* just.'"[46] Consequently, we can see why decision gets such a bad rap. Derrida has clearly outlined the impossibility of attaining, securing, achieving justice in any decision.

Continuing to outline the precariousness of decision, Derrida moves to the second aporia, which he calls "the ghost of the undecidable." Derrida cuts to the quick immediately as he admits that justice "is never exercised without a decision that *cuts*, that divides"; in other words, justice is dependent upon the cut, division, or exclusion that is inherent in every decision. Clarifying just what undecidable means, then, Derrida writes:

> The undecidable, a theme often associated with deconstruction, is not merely the . . . oscillation or the tension between two decisions; it is the experience of that which, though heterogeneous, foreign to the order of the calculable and the rule, is still obligated . . . to give itself up to the impossible decision, while taking account of law and rules. . . . But in the moment of suspense of the undecidable, it is not just either, for *only a decision is just*.[47]

Contrary to much of what Derrida has already said—in "Force of Law" and elsewhere—about the incalculability and undecidability of justice, here Derrida makes the point that the aporia points necessarily in the other direction as well: justice requires a decision. We are obligated, it appears, in the midst of an impossible decision, *to decide*, "for only a decision is just." Again, for

Derrida any decision that is merely the application of a rule or can be reduced to any sort of calculation is not only unjust, but not a real decision. As Derrida remarks elsewhere, "a decision worthy of the name . . . could not possibly be rapid or easy." The reality is that "it must be difficult to judge and to decide."[48] So anyone facing a genuine decision finds themselves caught in a moment of suspense, face to face with the undecidable, confronting the impossibility of the decision. However, in that moment of suspense, we are forced to decide—for remaining in a state of indecision would be as unjust as any decision.

Of course, once the decision has been made "it is no longer *presently* just, fully just," which is why we must "give up to the impossible decision."[49] This is why justice is impossible: either the decision has yet to be made and nothing allows us to call it just, or it has already followed some rule, which means it could be reduced to calculation. Thus, the undecidable remains caught as a ghost that "deconstructs from within any assurance of presence, any certitude or any supposed criteriology that would assure us of the justice of a decision."[50] Its impossibility is constitutive of the decision—yet, we must decide. And if decisions necessarily cut and divide, then the impossibility of justice necessitates such problematic exclusion and closure. Put differently, the incalculability and undecidability of justice also, simultaneously, demands calculation and decision.

This is why Derrida says that in the encounter with an impossible decision "we can recognize" and "indeed accuse, identify a madness."[51] And this madness is only intensified with the third aporia, where Derrida discusses the urgency implied in every moment of decision. In addition to an unsettling recognition that in the face of the impossible decision, in the moment of suspense, we must decide, there is also an urgency at play. Not only do we have to decide, but we have to do it now, "*immediately*, 'right away.'" There is no time to wait, ponder, or consider all the options. The decision does not allow time to "furnish itself with infinite information and the unlimited knowledge of conditions, rules," or hypotheticals. We are held, trapped, arrested by this moment that demands and requires an urgent response. "Justice," Derrida writes, "however unpresentable it may be, doesn't wait." Invoking *Philosophical Fragments*, Derrida agrees that "the instant of decision is a madness, says Kierkegaard."[52] Anyone who can recognize and appreciate (i.e., discern) the impossibility, and necessity, of a genuine decision would also recognize the madness it engenders.

Pushing even further, Derrida also rejects an understanding of a "horizon of knowledge" that could begin to act like a "Kantian regulative idea." Part of the point that Derrida is making in "Force of Law," which might be understood as a corrective to some of the ways he has been interpreted, is that we should be wary of looking at deconstruction as sketching some kind of a horizon that sets "a limit that defines an infinite progress."[53] If deconstruction merely points out the impossibility and unattainability of (something like) justice because it can never measure up to a justice "to-come," then this latter notion of justice is acting like nothing more than a Kantian regulative idea, a transcendental signified that is always attempting to be reached, but is still clear in our minds. The end result is that although justice here-and-now is critiqued and dismantled, the notion of justice to-come is still very much stable, secure, and certain. And the whole point of deconstruction is to reveal the *deconstruction* of this very process—not just to critique concrete instantiations of justice (which are also deconstructed) but also notions, ideas, and concepts of justice and the way that has operated in the history of Western metaphysics. In this discussion of the lack of horizons we find the phrase that Caputo capitalizes on: "'Perhaps,' one must always say perhaps for justice."[54] Yes, *oui oui*, we must always say "perhaps" for justice. In the moment of suspense, in the face of the undecidable, we have no guarantee—justice, perhaps. And this applies to any decision *as much as* it applies to any horizon by which we could critique any decision.

Consequently, what we get in the aporia of just decisions is an impossibility that appears even more *impossible* because the situation is such that we are obligated to do that which betrays justice. This process, of encountering the undecidable and deciding, "never proceeds without a certain dissymmetry and some quality of violence."[55] In other words, there is no escaping injustice. On the one hand, force—with its implications of violence—seems contrary to justice; on the other hand, force is necessary because justice without force can never be achieved. On the one hand, justice cannot be present once it has been decided; on the other hand, a decision is necessary because justice is not even given a chance if no decision is made. On the one hand, justice is incalculable; on the other hand, calculation is necessary because "incalculable justice *requires* us to calculate."[56] On the one hand, a decision without reference to the rules is unjust; on the other hand, any decision made as mere application of the rule is unjust. On the one hand, a decision made too hastily, without all the requisite information would be unjust; on the other hand, a just decision is required immediately. With regard to our present focus, we should note why decisions are often avoided or seen as so problematic. Derrida has literally put us in an impossible situation. But this does not give us an alibi for staying out of things, remaining in indecision, waffling between, back and forth, to and fro. Derrida has clearly pointed out that any decision is unjust, but so is not deciding. He has revealed the deconstruction of both decision and indecision. This is the aporia of in/decision. So what are we to do?

"Passions: 'An Oblique Offering'": I Can't, but I Must

Before attempting to respond to the above question, it is important to keep in mind that deconstruction cannot offer us a valid prescription or provide answers to questions posed to it, at least in my reading. Any response to the problem of decision, any philosophical, ethical, or theological reply "certainly cannot be by permission of Derrida," and we should be wary of any gesture in that direction.[57] The method of engagement with deconstruction in this book is to allow deconstruction's insights to inform our intentions, but to recognize that deconstruction cannot affirm, critique, or suggest alternatives to the problem, as I hope has already become clear. It follows the line of thinking that admits, in the words of Walter Lowe, that we "must honor the difference between [our] own task and Derrida's. Having learned what [we] can, [we] must proceed on [our] own, trusting [our] own best lights."[58] This does not render such an engagement with deconstruction fruitless and futile—on the contrary, deconstruction might help to sharpen our sights on the issues and what is at stake. By the end of this chapter, I hope to highlight how deconstruction can offer such a theo-ethical service, so long as we keep these limitations in mind.

Keeping that in mind, then, Derrida's own response to the deconstructive aporetic tension that always forces us to ask "so what are we to do?" might be insightful for our own. In "Passions: 'An Oblique Offering'" we find just that. Originally published in *Derrida: A Reader*, this essay was included as a kind of response to the other eleven essays about Derrida's work. In it, the topic of responsibility emerges, particularly whether or not deconstruction is political/apolitical, moral/amoral, responsible/irresponsible, etc. In typical fashion, Derrida refuses to answer such a question directly, and, recognizing how that might fuel even more criticism of deconstruction, it leads him to turn to an example to illustrate the problem of responsibility (or response-ability). He asks: "If, for example, I respond to the invitation which is made to me to respond to the texts collected here, which do me the honour or the kindness of taking an interest in certain of my earlier publications, am I not going to be heaping up errors and therefore conduct myself in an irresponsible way—by taking on false responsibilities?"[59] Having been addressed by these essays about his own work, Derrida is invited to respond. But such an invitation invokes a problem for Derrida, as it puts him in an impossible predicament, namely the task of having to do "justice" to their work in response, which Derrida sees as ultimately irresponsible. These irresponsible errors include, first of all, "disregarding the very scholarly and very singular strategy of each of these eleven or twelve discourses" through a hasty response. Derrida wonders: "By speaking last, both in conclusion and introduction, in twelfth or thirteenth place, am I not taking the insane risk and adopting the odious attitude of treating all these thinkers as disciples?"[60] Wouldn't his response, Derrida presumes, be considered the authoritative first or last word on their work, summarizing their efforts in a few short words or comments? Responding would mean that he felt "capable of responding" as if he had an "answer for everything" and saw himself as able to be up to the task of "answering each of us, each question, each objection or criticism."[61] Would that not entail some form of irresponsibility by not properly respecting the specificity, singularity, and complexity of each of these works? "To claim to do all this, and to do it in a few pages, would smack of a *hybris* and a naïveté without limit—and from the outset a flagrant lack of respect for the discourse, the work, and the offering of the other. More reasons for not responding." Perhaps, then, he ponders, a non-response would be the "best" response, "the most polite, the most modest, the most vigilant, the most respectful."[62]

By now we should recognize that Derrida's appreciation of his current predicament resonates strongly with a certain reading of deconstruction and understanding of the impossibility it highlights, precisely because it is a response *without* a response, where the "*sans*" is intended to respect the impossibility—of dogma, doctrine, decision, determinate religion or justice, and in this case, response. It might very well appear that to hold off, resist closure, continually wait, or refuse is the "best" response because it would avoid errors. Not doing so would seemingly betray deconstruction's insight that any closure, naming, deciding will always be too soon (i.e., impossible). Any such analysis would be akin to Derrida's "non-response" in this predicament, a recognition of the problems that arise by attempting to do that which deconstruction has rendered impossible, and thus one should avoid, hold out, and refuse to do just that.

But not so fast—it appears the non-response does not solve the problem either. Not responding might not be able to avoid irresponsibility altogether; or, as Derrida will go on to point out: is the non-response even "possible"? Can one inhabit a space of non-response, as if such a pure, present space existed, such that the *sans* (i.e., "without") becomes the appropriate (e.g., most ethical, just, responsible) response? Does it avoid the errors one commits by closing, naming, excluding, deciding, responding, etc.? Or has deconstruction revealed that such avoidance, such a space of non-response is (also) impossible?

Derrida continues his reflection. He admits that at first glance it would appear that one would be more responsible by not responding, that one "would avoid errors by not responding" because "it is more respectful to the other, more responsible in the face of the imperative of critical, hypercritical, and above all 'deconstructive' thought which insists on yielding as little as possible to dogmas and presuppositions."[63] Thus, a non-response seems to be the more ethical, appropriate, responsible response, even, Derrida admits, according to (supposedly) "deconstructive thought." On the other hand, Derrida suggests that not responding would equally entail a certain kind of irresponsibility; in fact, a non-response might even be worse. Not responding would indicate that he did not take seriously the persons, texts, ideas being offered here, or that they did not warrant his time, as if he were ungrateful or indifferent. The non-response can also be irresponsible to the other by its strategic nature. Under the pretext of giving them the "due respect" they deserve by taking the time to read through, ponder, and labor over every word, such a stance provides a kind of shelter from objection and criticism, which betrays the very notion of responsibility as having to answer for oneself. Just as presuming to respond adequately would "smack of a *hybris* . . . without limit," a non-response would also reflect a powerful, prideful, and privileged position to (choose) not to have to dirty one's hands with a limited, inappropriate response—a point that will gain more traction in Parts II and III.

Derrida then asks: "So, what are we to do?"[64] This is precisely the question deconstruction leaves *us* asking, after having seen the aporetic double-bind clearly (and one in which deconstruction—or Derrida—cannot answer for us).[65] On the one hand, Derrida recognizes that he cannot respond adequately, responsibly, to those who have addressed him and his work; on the other hand, he acknowledges that he must, in order to be responsible. On the one hand, responding (responsibly) is impossible; on the other hand, it is necessary for responsibility—precisely because what deconstruction reveals is that we are in the grip of structural forces prior and not subject to our agential, intentional, conscious (or ethical) decisions or desires. On the one hand, responding smacks of hubris; on the other hand, not responding entails just as much (if not more) hubris. Derrida reflects upon this predicament: "This aporia without end paralyzes us because it binds us doubly. (I must and I need not, I must not, it is necessary and impossible, etc.)"[66] Thus we are caught between the two poles of the deconstructive aporia: the impossibility and the inescapability. What are we to do? One of the main goals of this book is to ask ourselves this question regarding difficult decisions, having seen the problem in all its complexity. The more specific goal of this chapter is to recognize the complexity deconstruction reveals about this problem: that decisions that cut and divide are both impossible *and* inescapable. But the "so what do we do now" question is one that deconstruction might not lend us any help with, and it might only serve to reveal the structural predicament we are always already within, and the limits of our best efforts and attempts, because of this double-bind. Yet we must be wary of any reading of deconstruction that seems to offer a panacea to the problem(s) of religion and justice (that do not exclude), even when Derrida repeatedly assures us that deconstruction should always unsettle, disrupt, *deconstruct*.

Derrida actually addresses the moralism (or immoralism) of deconstruction in "Passions," noting that "some souls believe themselves to have found in Deconstruction . . . a modern form of immorality, of amorality, or of irresponsibility," which would be understandable given the impossibility deconstruction highlights. In other words, the initial reception of deconstruction as nihilistic, amoral, apolitical, and indeterminate is not entirely inaccurate. However, there are others, who, "more serious, in less of a hurry, better disposed toward so-called Deconstruction, today claim the opposite; they discern encouraging signs and in increasing numbers (at times, I must admit, in some of my texts) which would testify to . . . those things which one could identify under the fine names of 'ethics,' 'morality,' 'responsibility,' 'subject,' etc." In other words, while there are some who find deconstruction to bend toward nihilism and amorality, there are those who find resources for ethics, morality, and responsibility in deconstruction, and who interpret "encouraging signs" in it. Yet, Derrida warns:

> [I]t would be necessary to declare in the most direct way that if one had the *sense* of duty and of responsibility, it would compel breaking with both these moralisms . . . including, therefore, the remoralization of deconstruction, which naturally seems more attractive than that to which it is rightly opposed, but which at each moment risks reassuring itself in order to reassure the other and to promote the consensus of a new dogmatic slumber.[67]

Derrida appears equally as nervous at the extent to which deconstruction has been understood to provide ethical or political resources because of how it leads to a sense of assurance, something deconstruction always disrupts. And this leads us to ask to what extent prevailing readings of deconstruction—which would include readings of Derrida, Caputo, and others—allowed us to slip into such a "dogmatic slumber" by finding in deconstruction a reassuring moralism that, as attractive as it is, deconstruction can never support.

Derrida, continuing his questioning of responsibility, the "morality of morality," and "the ethicity of ethics," reminds us that neither he nor deconstruction can provide an answer to these questions. Deconstruction cannot side with either moralism or amoralism, the political or apolitical. Even though they are urgent questions, according to deconstruction, "they must remain urgent and unanswered."[68] And though this gives ammunition to those opposed to deconstruction by posing an amoralistic, apolitical, nihilistic stance, "isn't that preferable to the constitution of a consensual euphoria or, worse, a community of complacent deconstructionists, reassured and reconciled with the world in ethical certainty, good conscience, satisfaction of service rendered, and the consciousness of duty accomplished."[69]

And this is precisely the point of this chapter (and the overall argument of this book), to ask poignantly, to all readers of Derrida and those concerned about these issues—of which I include myself—who can appear ethically certain, satisfied, and with a good conscious reassured: has identifying exclusive decisions as the problem given us a sense of "consensual euphoria"? Is there a way in which Caputo's work—or any theo-ethical work that identifies and attempts to remedy this problem—leads us to a sense of security and reassurance? Have we become "a community of complacent deconstructionists"? Does avoiding difficult decisions leave us feeling "reassured and reconciled with the world in ethical certainty, good conscience, satisfaction of service rendered, and the consciousness of duty accomplished?" What I am proposing here is quite the opposite: to upset the euphoria, to question our assurance, to complicate our conscience, and render the task/duty of engaging the problem of decision as un-accomplished.

DECONSTRUCTING UNDECIDABILITY

As I have tried to show in the above reading, deconstruction only "is" (i.e., "exists"—to the extent that it "is" or "exists" at all) in an aporetic tension that does not inevitably collapse into an "impossibility" that privileges openness to closure, but presents a situation wherein closure—and by extension, decisions that cut and divide—are structurally inevitable and necessary. To the extent that this is the case, it would mean that any supposed remedy to the problem of decision relaxes the aporetic tension of the double-bind that deconstruction presents. Beyond any reading of deconstruction—including Derrida's, Caputo's, or anyone's reading of them—my targets are set more broadly on the general consensus about the problem of decision and anyone who might be culpable of the same move, wherein there is a relaxation of the tension, a sigh of relief, a justification or concession that we have achieved some progress (if not a solution) regarding this problem. This is the real target audience: those (of us) who agree that exclusion is ethically problematic and have attempted to remedy it without realizing the extent to which we cannot escape or avoid it and, in fact, need some form of it in our very attempt to combat the worse instances of it. Caputo represents a reading of deconstruction that attempts to do so. However, a reading of deconstruction that appreciates the aporetic tension problematizes, complicates, and renders increasingly problematic the problem of exclusive decisions, precisely because one can never escape it.

One of Caputo's fiercest critics and sparring partners, Martin Hägglund, also challenges Caputo's reading of deconstruction, from a non-religious—in fact, atheistic—perspective. I am not in full agreement with Hägglund on a number of matters, which include his theological views, understanding of "radical evil," and wholesale rejection of Caputo's approach. Nevertheless, there is some insight in his approach that supports the reading I have just presented. Hägglund's survey of the current academic debates about religion suggest that from both sides, "whether by those who seek to abolish or renew religious faith," the focus has been on religion's predisposition to violence and intolerance, with the critics pointing to this inherent flaw as the reason to discard religion, while the supporters of religion attempt to diagnose and remedy it.[70] In Hägglund's opinion, Caputo epitomizes the latter through his deployment of deconstruction, and as an astute reader of Derrida, Hägglund challenges Caputo's conclusions. In one of his debates with Caputo about Derrida and religion, Hägglund writes:

> According to Caputo, "deconstruction is a blessing for religion, its positive salvation" since it "discourages religion from its own worst instincts" and "helps religion examine its conscience, counseling and chastening religion about its tendency to confuse its faith with knowledge, which results in the dangerous and absolutizing triumphalism of religion, which is what spills blood."[71] All of Caputo's work on a supposedly deconstructive religion is structured around this opposition between a "good" religion that welcomes others and a "bad" religion that excludes others. The religion *without* religion that Caputo ascribes to Derrida would be a religion without violence, which repeats "the apocalyptic call for the impossible, but without calling for the apocalypse that would consume its enemies in fire" and "repeats the passion for the messianic promise and messianic expectation, *sans* the concrete messianisms of the positive religions that wage endless war and spill the blood of the other."[72] For Caputo, then, Derrida's work helps us move away from "the bloody messianisms" in favor of "the messianic" promise of a kingdom that is open to everyone.[73]

Hägglund's analysis resonates with the survey of the contemporary landscape that was presented earlier, about an assumed and assured conclusion that exclusion is the problem that should be remedied in religion, theology, philosophy, ethics, justice, etc. Additionally, his analysis of Caputo's work is accurate to the extent that Caputo seems to offer a remedy for religion that is "better" based on the premise that "good" religion welcomes and "bad" religion excludes, where the *sans* can mitigate the problem of exclusivity. Furthermore, Hägglund believes that to credit such a theo-ethical move to deconstruction is a gross misinterpretation of Derrida. Hägglund critiques Caputo's reading of deconstruction on two fronts: first, Hägglund reads "a logic of radical atheism" throughout Derrida's work that suggests an *antireligious* sentiment in deconstruction, rather than a religious one (as Caputo argues); second, that this "irreducible atheism at the 'root' of every commitment, faith, and desire . . . accounts for a constitutive violence that is at work even in the most peaceful approaches to the world, whether 'secular' or 'religious,' 'atheist' or 'theist.'"[74]

One of Hägglund's main disagreements with Caputo is the optimism Caputo finds in the impossibility deconstruction reveals. Caputo insists that the impossibility in deconstruction, which is emphasized in the *à venir* or "to come" of the messianic, is something hopeful and good—that what is to come is always desirable. For Hägglund, "it would be hard to imagine a more straightforward misreading of Derrida's notion of the *à venir*," which Hägglund reads as more precarious than that.[75] According to Hägglund, Derrida continually emphasizes that the "to come" may not always be desirable or good, or even subject to judgment or criteria, as if it were some-thing by which we could critique or judge (i.e., a transcendental signified). This leads Hägglund to suggest that "we must not exclude the possibility that the one who is coming is coming to kill us, is a figure of evil," or "that even the other who is identified as good may always *become* evil."[76] Thus one of Hägglund's main critiques of Caputo is that "religion without religion" presumes to escape an economy of violence by emphasizing openness over closure. Much like the concerns that we have been raising above, Hägglund argues that "Derrida is *not opposing* closure . . . in favor of openness," but rather that deconstruction reveals a situation in which openness and closure are always already co-implicated. Hägglund writes: "the openness of the future is not something that one can promote *against* the closure of determination; the unconditional openness of the future is rather what makes the closure of determination necessary and unavoidable while compromising its integrity from within."[77] This seems like a more accurate reading of the deconstructive aporia: a situation in which openness and closure, impossibility and inescapability, are always already structurally present. This would mean that any preference for the former betrays the insights of deconstruction by suggesting a way out, an escape from the tension of the double-bind in the aporia by preferring or prescribing openness to closure, the incalculable to calculations, the indeterminate to determinate, inclusion to exclusion, and indecision to decision. But what deconstruction actually reveals is the impossibility of avoiding the latter for the sake of the former, that the latter is always structurally inescapable, and in fact the condition of im/possibility for the former.

Hägglund's point, therefore, is that nothing escapes the deconstructive movement, including "religion without religion." Deconstruction, then, cannot offer a preference for openness or closure—precisely because deconstruction cannot offer a preference of any kind. The impossibility in deconstruction is more *impossible* than that: "the openness to the future is unconditional in the sense that one is necessarily open to the future, but it is not unconditional in the sense of an axiom which establishes that more openness is always better than less."[78] In other words, Caputo's "religion without religion" seems to suggest that openness is that which allows one to escape the deconstructive movement, or is what deconstruction prescribes, and Hägglund is arguing that a preference for openness is neither found in deconstruction nor a panacea to the problem itself, for deconstruction reveals an inescapable problem, an aporia, a poison that has no remedy that is not itself also poisonous.

However, Hägglund argues that the realization of the inescapability of violence need not collapse into an apolitical or nihilistic stance toward violence; on the contrary, it raises the stakes for analysis and discernment through a more rigorous appreciation of the problem, which is the very aim of this book. Hägglund writes:

> This notion of radical evil does not seek to justify violence or to reduce all forms of violence to the same. On the contrary, it seeks to recognize that we are always negotiating violence and that our ideals of justice cannot be immune from contestation and struggle. Every ideal of justice is rather inscribed in what Derrida calls an "economy of violence." . . . There is no call for justice that does not call for the exclusion of others, which means that every call for justice can be challenged and criticized. The point of this argument is not to discredit calls for justice, but to recognize that these calls are always already inscribed in an economy of violence.[79]

Although I am not prepared to "go all the way" with Hägglund here and suggest that "radical evil" is the underlying logic of all reality, I do agree with his reading of deconstruction that reveals a situation in which we cannot escape violence and exclusion. I also agree, on ethical grounds, that recognizing such does not abrogate responsibility or seek to justify exclusion, in whatever form it should take, but, quite the contrary, makes the pursuit of justice more rigorous by discerning between *which* exclusions. And that in so doing we must remember that "every call for justice can be challenged or criticized." That includes any definitive, exclusive decision, as well as indecision. My argument has focused on the latter, precisely because Caputo has so deftly demonstrated the problem of the former. My main point in this chapter is to problematize any attempted remedies for the problem of exclusive decisions and to suggest we think of responsibility, ethics, justice in relation to it differently, i.e., in terms of a renewed understanding of undecidability that urges us to discern difficult decisions.

Hägglund is not alone in understanding undecidability along these lines. Mary-Jane Rubenstein gestures toward a critical revisiting of undecidability as a corrective to any collapse into indecision that might seem to offer a way out of the deconstructive double-bind. In her chapter on decision in *Strange Wonder: The Closure of Metaphysics and the Opening of Awe*, Rubenstein tracks some of the same Derridean texts as above to reach a similar conclusion: "undecidability is *not* indecision; far more simply and far more inscrutably, undecidability refers to the situation that gives rise to any decision that can be called a decision." This kind of genuine decision, as we discussed above, is when "I find myself thrown into a position in which I *do not know* how to decide." This is the impossibility one confronts in the face of the undecidable—"and yet it is from this undecidability that I must decide."[80] Furthermore, she also argues: "This is not to say distinctions must never be made; to the contrary, responsibility demands nothing if not the distinctions that are made in decision."[81]

Rubenstein's main focus in this chapter is seeking to find a way to think *through* the madness of decision that Derrida highlights, namely "exactly *how* does undecidability give way to decision?"[82] While slightly different than our particular focus here, Rubenstein's reflections on undecidability resonate significantly, especially in her musing on Derrida's image of the hedgehog in a short piece entitled "Che cos'è la poesia?" where Derrida likens the poem to a hedgehog being thrown into the middle of a highway. "Frozen and blinded like a hedgehog in the headlights," Derrida suggests, "all alone in the middle of the road, facing oncoming cars and trucks, the poem *is* as sheer response to whatever comes its way."[83] Drawing on David Goicoechea's article about undecidability in Derrida and Kierkegaard, Rubenstein makes the point that the image of the hedgehog in the highway is akin to the moment of decision in the face of the undecidable: "For Goicoechea, the decision takes place the moment the hedgehog freezes and the truck either hits it or does not hit it."[84] But what Rubenstein finds most interesting about this endangered hedgehog, and what resonates most explicitly with our own reflection, "is that it is not simply receptive, rather, it is active in its very passivity, wounding in its very vulnerability, for it only exposes itself by means of the act of violence by which it seeks to defend itself."[85] There are several points to tease out here that are especially relevant. First, this is the very predicament that I have tried to sketch. In the face of the undecidable, we find ourselves as endangered as the thrown hedgehog. Frightened, "frozen and blinded" by the impossible situation we now find ourselves in with regard to the decision that cuts and divides. But, second, I have tried to disabuse the notion of pure passivity. We are facing the headlights that are fast approaching and, like the hedgehog, indecision offers no escape. Moreover, we become exposed by means of the act of trying to reduce, mitigate, or avoid the violence by which we seek to defend ourselves. In other words, like the hedgehog whose next move might risk further violence in the very act of defending against it, we too are exposed to violence by the very act of trying to avoid it. We have, thankfully, come to a keen recognition of the violence and danger of the oncoming headlights (of the difficult decision). But, like simply acknowledging the oncoming truck does not rescue the hedgehog, stopping at that recognition offers no safety. Whatever we do next will not offer any assurance of safety or security—but we must act. This is the predicament we find ourselves in with regard to the undecidable: an impossible, and exigent, situation wherein we must decide without assurance of safe destination. Whatever we do (or decide) next will likely, almost inevitably, end in violence; in fact, the very act of trying to defend ourselves from the violence will be that which exposes us to it—a point that will become clearer in the following chapters.

In Part I, the focus has been on revisiting undecidability and the problem of in/decision through the lens of deconstruction, where my real concern is that there seems to be an accepted remedy to the problem. My point, then, has been to offer a reading of deconstruction, critically analyzing Caputo's own, that complicates any remedy to the problem. Put simply, I think that one of deconstruction's most important insights includes the recognition that we are always already in the midst of structural, inescapable violence. More specifically, I agree with Hägglund that "there is no call for justice that does not call for the exclusion of others," which suggests that exclusion is a structurally inescapable problem—which is thoroughly *problematic*. And thus we are trapped in an economy of violence that cannot be remedied even if/when we recognize it as violent and problematic. In fact, it is the ethical desire to rid ourselves of exclusion, by attempting to avoid or remedy—*exclude*—it that deconstruction reveals to be structurally *impossible*.

Reflecting, as he often does, on the way deconstruction has been read and received, Derrida claims—this time in response to Paul de Man about the "impossibility" of deconstruction—that "deconstruction loses nothing from admitting that it is impossible." In fact, Derrida argues, "*possibility* is rather the danger, the danger of becoming an available set of rule-governed procedures, methods, accessible approaches."[86] In this chapter I have tried to stick with this "certain experience of the impossible" that Derrida speaks of and its implications for undecidability. To the extent that any reading of this impossibility renders undecidability as mere indecision, then it has become far too accessible and available—in a word, far too easy. In the two specific contexts wherein I will explore the illusion and lure of indecision—pursuits of justice and divine decision—the temptation for indecision is great, and is, I will argue, always related to power. In other words, undecidability as indecision can be, and is often experienced as, a relief. As I will go on to demonstrate in the subsequent chapters, however, indecision is a reflection of power and privilege, an ability to draw on the power supply to not get one's hands dirty with messy, risky, difficult decisions. And while it may "work"—people don't decide all the time—it is certainly no remedy to the problem. The impossible decision is one that cannot be reduced to a set of "rule-governed procedures, methods, accessible approaches"; it is impossible to decide. But this impossibility is more precisely an impossible possibility, because in the midst of this impossible decision, we must decide; indecision is no way out. Deconstruction lives in this im/possible moment, revealing the tension of the double-bind wherein we have to admit: "I cannot; but I must."

Derrida affirms that "the most radical programs of deconstruction" seek "not to remain enclosed in purely speculative, theoretical, academic discourses but rather to aspire to something more consequential, to *change* things and to intervene in an efficient and responsible, though always, of course, very mediated way."[87] This chapter has attempted to do just that—to intervene on the topic of decision, in a very mediated way. But this mediation does not take the form of some kind of middle ground or in-between; rather, the intervention deconstructs any resolution to the problem of difficult decisions, revealing that indecision is as problematic as (any) decision. Caputo has thoroughly highlighted the latter, the limits and problems of decisiveness and decisions, because no decision is just. My task has been to ensure that we do not lose sight of the simultaneous problem of any attempt to avoid decision(s) as a way out of the dilemma.

Caputo writes that theology should be measured "by the extent to which it avoids the pitfalls of a too-comforting piety."[88] I agree; but we must also be wary lest the "perhaps" lulls us into that very trap, either. Surely Caputo is intentionally unsettling those who rightly recognize the risk of the "perhaps" and try to avoid it because of their fear "of one small word." But I have tried in this chapter to point out an additional riskiness, one that does not merely retreat from "perhaps" into knowledge, presence, certainty, and surety, but that builds upon the risk that the "perhaps" elicits by revealing that indecision is as deconstructed as decision. That just as the "perhaps" continues to reveal the limits of every decision, it must not ever become an alternative to decision, leading us to any false sense of stability, safety, or security, even one as seemingly unstable and risky as "perhaps." Part I has intended to highlight both sides of the aporetic tension at work in the deconstructive double-bind. Chapter 1 highlighted how Caputo's work deftly illustrates the limits of decisions that cut, divide, and exclude. This chapter has attempted to maintain the tension by highlighting the other side of the double-bind, deconstructing undecidability as any sort of remedy to the problem. The task before us in Part II and Part III is to explore how the problem of in/decision relates to particular contexts.

NOTES

1. Caputo, *The Insistence of God*, 20.
2. Jacques Derrida, *"Différance,"* in *Margins of Philosophy*, trans. Alan Bass, Reprint edition (Chicago: University Of Chicago Press, 1984), 25.
3. Jacques Derrida, "Plato's Pharmacy," in *Dissemination*, trans. Barbara Johnson (University of Chicago Press, 1983), 99.
4. Ibid., 110.
5. Bennington and Derrida, *Jacques Derrida*, 37–38.
6. Ibid., 127.
7. See: Jacques Derrida, *Psyche: Inventions of the Other*, vol. 1, ed. Peggy Kamuf and Elizabeth G. Rottenberg (Stanford: Stanford University Press, 2007).
8. See: Jacques Derrida, *Limited Inc*, ed. Gerald Graff, trans. Jeffrey Mehlman and Samuel Weber, 1st edition (Evanston, IL: Northwestern University Press, 1988).
9. See: Jacques Derrida, *Glas* (Paris: Galilée, 1974).
10. Bennington and Derrida, *Jacques Derrida*, 188.
11. Derrida, *The Gift of Death*, 69.
12. Ibid., 51.

13. Ibid., 42.
14. Ibid., 52.
15. Ibid.
16. Ibid., 60.
17. Ibid., 61.
18. Ibid., 68–69.
19. Ibid., 69.
20. Derrida, *Specters of Marx*, 104.
21. Ibid., 104–5.
22. Ibid., 111.
23. Ibid., 112.
24. Caputo, "Hoping in Hope, Hoping against Hope," 123–24.
25. John D. Caputo, ed., *Deconstruction in a Nutshell: A Conversation with Jacques Derrida* (New York: Fordham University Press, 1996), 17.
26. Ibid., 18.
27. Ibid., 19.
28. Ibid.
29. Derrida, "Afterword: Toward an Ethic of Discussion," 112.
30. Ibid., 113.
31. Ibid., 127.
32. Derrida, *Limited Inc*, 105.
33. Derrida, "Afterword: Toward an Ethic of Discussion," 132.
34. Ibid., 133.
35. Ibid., 135.
36. This kind of an argument, about the necessity of police, and the difference between brutal, physical repressive police forces and "sophisticated . . . noble" police forces (Derrida's words) can easily be misinterpreted in this context. And context is important in this case—my reading, use, and deployment of Derrida in Part I is abstracted from particular contexts, given that the focus is on the structural dynamics in play with in/decision. This is why in Parts II and III it is important to take the conversation out of the abstract and focus on particular contexts and conversations. Nevertheless, a comment is warranted: for the record, this is not intended to be a kind of apologetic for police forces. Police brutality, excessive use of force (including deadly force), without repercussion by the US legal system needs to be rectified, its injustice eradicated. In fact, as the argument in Part II of this book will emphasize, the point that I am making here is that *in order* for this kind of justice to be realized, we will need to make distinctions. There is a distinction and difference that needs to be made with regard to police forces. I do not believe that anyone who is extremely critical of police brutality without repercussion would suggest that we should eliminate police forces altogether. And for those of us who stand firm in our conviction of rectifying the unjust use of police force in the United States, *my* point is that it will require navigating difficult decisions. It will require taking difficult stances and stands, making difficult distinctions. It will require—as I will demonstrate in Part II—discerning decisions that cut, divide, and exclude.
37. Derrida, "Afterword: Toward an Ethic of Discussion," 135.
38. Ibid., 136.
39. Ibid.
40. Derrida, "Force of Law: The 'Mystical Foundation of Authority,'" 6.
41. Ibid., 10–11.
42. Ibid., 11.
43. Ibid., 14.
44. Ibid., 16.
45. Ibid., 22.
46. Ibid., 23.
47. Ibid., 24 (emphasis mine).
48. Jacques Derrida and George Collins, *Politics of Friendship* (London: Verso, 2005), 15.
49. Derrida, "Force of Law: The 'Mystical Foundation of Authority,'" 24.
50. Ibid., 24–25.

51. Ibid., 25.
52. Ibid., 26. For an insightful exploration of Derrida's recurrent use of this Kierkegaardian phrase, see: Geoffrey Bennington, "A Moment of Madness: Derrida's Kierkegaard," *Oxford Literary Review* 33:1 (July 1, 2011): 103–27.
53. Ibid., 26.
54. Ibid., 27.
55. Ibid., 27.
56. Ibid., 28.
57. Boesel, *Risking Proclamation, Respecting Difference*, 270.
58. Lowe, *Theology and Difference: The Wound of Reason*, 16.
59. Jacques Derrida, "Passions: 'An Oblique Offering,'" in *On the Name*, ed. Thomas Dutoit, trans. David Wood (Stanford, CA: Stanford University Press, 1995), 18.
60. Ibid.
61. Ibid., 19.
62. Ibid., 20.
63. Ibid., 21.
64. Ibid., 22.
65. We might note a slippage here between Derrida and deconstruction, perhaps one that has been present all along, muddying the waters even further. I do not think we can assume that just because Derrida is asking, "So what are we to do?" that deconstruction can/does ask that question. Derrida here, might be put in the same position as the rest of us, now recognizing where he stands in relation to this deconstructive insight, and thus his question about what we ought/should do next implies intentionality, direction, telos, ethics, etc.—all of which deconstruction perpetually *deconstructs*.
66. Derrida, "Passions: 'An Oblique Offering,'" 22.
67. Ibid., 15
68. Ibid., 16.
69. Ibid., 17.
70. Hägglund, "The Radical Evil of Deconstruction," 126.
71. Caputo, ed., *Deconstruction in a Nutshell: A Conversation with Jacques Derrida*, 159.
72. Caputo, *The Prayers and Tears of Jacques Derrida*, xxi.
73. Hägglund, "The Radical Evil of Deconstruction," 127.
74. Ibid., 128.
75. Ibid., 139.
76. Ibid., 131.
77. Ibid., 140.
78. Ibid., 144.
79. Ibid., 146.
80. Mary-Jane Rubenstein, *Strange Wonder: The Closure of Metaphysics and the Opening of Awe* (New York: Columbia University Press, 2008), 145.
81. Ibid., 177.
82. Ibid., 151.
83. Ibid., 155.
84. Ibid., 156.
85. Ibid., 155–56.
86. Derrida, "Psyche: Invention of the Other," 15.
87. Derrida, "Force of Law," 8–9.
88. Caputo, *The Insistence of God*, 24.

Part II

Justifying Decisions

Chapter Three

The Injustice of Exclusivity

The option for the poor means an option for the God of the Reign as proclaimed by Jesus. The whole Bible, from the story of Cain and Abel onward, is marked by God's love and predilection for the weak and abused of human history.

—Gustavo Gutiérrez, "The Option for the Poor"

The people of color are [God's] elected poor in America.

—James Cone, *God of the Oppressed*

The task before us now is to explore how the structural nature of the aporia of in/decision presented in Part I plays out in a particular context. In Part II we begin that task by looking at how this problem relates to issues of social justice and liberation. We have already hinted at the problematic relationship between exclusion and justice and the implications that has for decisions that cut and divide. The implied ethical thrust of Caputo's work is driven by a desire to resist exclusion, which he calls "the height of injustice."[1] But our goal now is to explore this relationship more explicitly, diving further into the complicated entanglement of decision and its inherent exclusivity, with an eye toward how that has been navigated. The overall goal of Part II builds on the work of Part I by attempting to contextualize it. If the insights gained in Part I have led us to discern, i.e., reckon with, decisions that cut and divide, how does this structural insight relate to discourses that are engaged in the struggle for concrete liberation from material oppression and injustice? Again, the entry point and backdrop for our investigation here (as it is for the entire argument of the book) is the awareness of the limits of decision, choice, and preference for particular oppressed peoples and particular forms of injustice. Since this appears to be the growing contemporary consensus, we begin our task in this chapter by exploring such an awareness and identification of the problem of decisions that cut and divide. In the end, Part II intends to explore this problem more thoroughly, affirming and building upon the structural insight of Part I about both the problematic nature of decision and the inescapability of it.

Liberationist work emerged in response to the structural and material oppression, marginalization, and exclusion of certain groups, peoples, and identities. In the struggle against such systemic exclusion, liberationists recognized the need for a kind of "exclusive" preference for those oppressed and excluded, because anything less than such preference would not constitute a radical enough break with the unjust status quo. In liberation theologies this was framed in terms of a divine preferential option. Subsequent liberationist work, however, has been critical of the way exclusive preference for one oppressed group has resulted in the further exclusion of other oppressed groups, and thus identified these early liberationist moves as problematic. These critiques focused on how such preference or choice was based on "limited understandings of oppression, and especially of the multilayered nature of oppression," which, in turn, have "created new exclusions . . . through a narrow understanding of contexts."[2] More recent work in the fields of women's and gender studies, queer theory, postcolonial theory, critical race theories, and other liberation discourses has identified intersectionality, instability of identities, hybridity, and multiple sites of oppression and privilege that complicate the articulation of experience or identity in monolithic, homogenous categories, upon which such choice or preference could be made. In contemporary justice discourses, preference, choice, and decision *for* particular oppressed groups or forms of justice are considered problematic because such thick and totalizing categories obscure a much more complex and multilayered reality of persons, groups, and experiences. Here, in Chapter 3, we will explore these critiques and how they are related to the issue of decision, choice, and preference. We will do so by tracking the way that early liberationists recognized the need for preference in order to attain liberation, as well as the way more recent work has problematized such preference. In so doing, this chapter will highlight the first aspect of the aporetic double-bind by focusing on the problem of exclusivity in liberationist work and how that is navigated with regard to decision, choice, and preference.

Looking ahead, in Chapter 4 I will go on to make a similar argument as I made above (with regard to Caputo). While affirming the insights of more recent work that identifies how exclusive decision, choice, and preference for particular groups and forms of injustice perpetuates injustice, I merely highlight the ways in which indecision also perpetuates injustice. Whereas this chapter will underline the ways that deciding *for* is limited and problematic, Chapter 4 will argue that avoiding such decisions is equally problematic. To the extent that this is the case it would mean acknowledging an even more precarious situation wherein the struggle against the problem of exclusion (and oppression) necessarily, structurally, entails reckoning with difficult decisions that cannot avoid navigating a kind of strategic exclusivity.[3] Although part of the overall argument of Part II is suggesting how exclusive decisions are inescapable or necessary for liberation, keeping with the theme of this book I will also not neglect identifying the way(s) in which exclusion is also a problem—if not one of *the* major problems—that liberationists have and continue to engage. The overall goal is to continue to explore the problem of exclusive decision precisely as a problem, but one in which the remedies or alternatives present problems of their own, thus increasing our vigilance in the struggle against it. By the end of Part II, I will have shown how these difficult decisions are an inescapable problem for pursuit of liberation, something that liberationists must continue to grapple with, and will dissuade the notion that merely critiquing or avoiding them offers any kind of satisfactory remedy. If Part I revealed the impossibility of avoiding decisions that cut or divide, Part II seeks to explore which kinds of exclusive (and difficult) decisions might be necessary for those of us seeking to join the struggle for liberation against injustice and oppression. The key ingredient to this investigation, as we will see, is privilege. A central aspect of my argument in Chapter 4 will be that a more thorough analysis of privilege deconstructs undecidability as indecision with regard to these difficult decisions about justice.

In order to accomplish this goal, we will begin in this chapter by looking at the initial identification and response to the problem of exclusivity in "first wave" liberation theologies of the mid-to-late twentieth century, exploring the preferential option for a particular people or group through several strands within the liberation theological tradition: Latin American, black, gay and lesbian, and dalit liberation theologies.[4] In each of these discourses, we will highlight how liberation theologians understood such preference for the oppressed to be based upon "God's love and predilection for the weak and abused of human history."[5] Taking up the theme of the divine preferential option, liberation theologies present a contemporary understanding of divine election wherein God chooses to side with those who are excluded and oppressed in terms of poverty, race, sexuality, social location, identity, experience, etc. Exploring this divine choice for a particular group will also accomplish the task of highlighting the exclusive nature of the preferential option as a way of demonstrating the inevitable exclusivity of decision. As we will see, however, its exclusivity emerged in direct response to the fact that these groups were excluded. These early liberation theologians recognized that exclusion was inherently problematic, and therefore wrestled with how to understand the tension between a preferential option for the oppressed and the problematic exclusivity of that preference, since exclusion was one of the main problems the preferential option was attempting to remedy.

We will then explore some more recent liberationist work that has honed in on and further critiqued the limits of such an identification and preference. In the ensuing decades, harsher critiques of liberation theology's exclusive preference emerged, especially in terms of how preference for one oppressed group excluded other oppressed groups. These critiques include the way in which God's identification with one group results in further exclusion, not just of the oppressor but also of other oppressed groups, pitting one oppressed community's claims for liberation against another's, which in turn becomes a tool of hegemony—a divide-and-conquer strategy that continues to keep liberation out of the hands of the oppressed. Additionally, more recent work in this field has revealed the intersectionality of identity and experiences, complicating such preference for one stable identity or group, as well as the multi-layered nature of oppression and the way that complicates emphasis on particular forms of injustice. In the end, this chapter will provide us with a thorough sense of the way that exclusive preference has been identified as problematic for justice, something that liberationists have continued to wrestle with. In so doing, it will highlight how decisions that cut, divide, and exclude are problematic, setting the stage for the argument in Chapter 4.

PREFERENTIAL OPTION:
A (DIVINE) DECISION FOR THE EXCLUDED

Before diving into liberation theology's understanding about the divine preferential option for the oppressed and excluded as necessary for liberation, a word of clarification needs to be made regarding the way in which the divine preferential option is understood as a kind of exclusive divine choice, especially in relation to the eternality of such a choice. Traditionally understood within Christianity as "predestination," divine choice or election meant God's eternal, once-for-all decision; and, in terms of exclusivity, this meant that divine choice for one (person, group, etc.) was an absolute decree about eternal destinies. In other words, the history of the Christian doctrine of divine election typically suggested a divine choice for one/some as the elected (or included) and others as the rejected (or excluded), i.e., the former to heaven/glory and the latter to hell/damnation. Consequently, any discussion of divine election and exclusion warrants clarification about the eternality of such a divine decision, especially as we now turn to a more thorough investigation into a particular type of divine election in liberation theology's preferential option (we will explore divine decision more explicitly in Part III and its relationship to the theme of this book). When discussing the exclusive nature of the divine preferential option in this chapter, I want to clarify that this does not mean to imply an eternal, once-for-all decision, because this is not how liberation discourses have understood the preferential option. As we will see, the divine preferential option has always, necessarily, been tied to particular historical realities, communities, and experiences. In fact, the purpose of God's choice for the poor, oppressed, marginalized, excluded is with the intended goal of liberation from these material realities. Thus, this divine decision seems to be conditional on one's status in society, which means that if one (person, group, community, etc.) were to no longer be poor, oppressed, or marginalized, the implication seems to be that the preference is no longer needed. Again, the entire purpose of the preferential option is to liberate *from* this condition or situation. Therefore, in our subsequent discussion about the exclusivity of the divine preferential option we need to keep in mind that it is very much distinct from a divine choice about one's eternal destiny, since such historical realities can—and hopefully will—change.

But I also want to clarify that although the lack of eternality associated with the kind of exclusivity we will be discussing in this chapter might seem to mitigate against the offensiveness of the preferential option's exclusive nature, I want to keep our eyes focused on the ways in which it is still *exclusive*—even if not eternally so. And that is the real point of emphasis in this chapter: to highlight how the preferential option is (still) exclusive (on some level), and thus problematic. Consequently, perhaps "strategic exclusion" is a more fitting term to frame what we will be exploring. It is strategic in the sense that the purpose of the divine choice is to liberate and transform oppressive structures, which means it is different than an absolute decree with eternal destinies. But it is still exclusive, as I intend to show, in ways that are both problematic (in this chapter), yet inescapable and necessary (in Chapter 4). Liberation theology's insistence that God deals with the problem of exclusion by choosing those who have been excluded ensures they will always be God's chosen, while those who are oppressing others are not. The earliest iterations of liberation theology recognized that moving away from or reducing exclusive preference for the oppressed does not adequately deal with oppression and thus can become a tacit preference for the oppressor—or the oppressive situation—by keeping the status quo in place. Consequently, there appears to be a commitment to the notion that the only way to attain liberation is through exclusive preference for those on the underside of history, precisely because they have been excluded.

One more point of clarification is needed. As we explore these select strands of liberation theology, we cannot neglect to point out the choice involved in such a selection process—namely my own as author. Not only in the strands of this discourse, but also in the voices presented within each of these strands. While such an inevitable, and difficult, decision on my part reflects the very argument presented in this book, it is still worth pointing out (if not more so). The decisions made here are not intended to reflect a comprehensive overview of a discourse or discourses that are diverse, complex, and multivalent. Part of the goal of the next two chapters is, in fact, to highlight this complexity, in an attempt to bring the differing perspectives on this perpetual problem into conversation with each other in order to advance it. But there is still a need to clarify that doing so—especially in this chapter under these various headings—is not intended to collapse these strands into representative voices or thick categories in a reductive sort of way. Rather, the choice to categorize our investigation into the problem of preference is intended to highlight how these contextualized discourses approached this problem.

Latin American Liberation Theology: God's Choice for the Poor

The emergence of "liberation theology" was precipitated by several significant events and publications, one of which included Gustavo Gutiérrez's landmark work, *Teología de la Liberación* in 1971, with its English translation two years later. Through his pioneering work, Gutiérrez, a Peruvian priest, not only developed what became known as Latin American liberation theology, but can also be considered foundational for subsequent strands of liberation theology that would emerge in the ensuing decades, as he was one of the first to explicitly emphasize liberation as a central category for Christian theological reflection and analysis.[6] In the opening words of the English translation, *A Theology of Liberation: History, Politics, and Salvation*, Gutiérrez sets forth the significance of social location and liberation: "This book is an attempt at reflection, based on the gospel and the experiences of men and women committed to the process of liberation in the oppressed and exploited land of Latin America. It is a theological reflection born of the experience of shared efforts to abolish the current unjust situation and to build a different society, freer and more human."[7] The goal, Gutiérrez argues, is to reconsider the classical themes of Christian theology in the light of the particular experiences of those oppressed persons who work for liberation in Latin America.

Part of this work, according to Gutiérrez, is drawing attention to the "profound and rapid socio-cultural" changes taking place at that time that resulted in an extreme, economic discrepancy among nations. What's more, the growth of media had made many aware of such discrepancies, particularly acute in "poor countries where the vast majority of humans live" in "unacceptable living conditions."[8] According to Gutiérrez, this situation—the depth of poverty combined with an awareness of such inequalities—had called forth a "new historical era to be characterized by a radical aspiration for integral liberation" that demanded a Christian response.[9] In other words, for Gutiérrez, liberation theology begins with this situation and location, in the lives, experiences, and struggles against the injustice of poverty in Latin America. Its goal is the liberation of such people: "In the last instance we will have an authentic theology of liberation only when the oppressed themselves can freely raise their voice and express themselves directly and creatively in society . . . when they are the protagonists of their own liberation."[10]

Gutiérrez's desire for liberation of the oppressed continually emphasizes how it must include the poor being able to "freely raise their voice and express themselves" and be "protagonists of their own liberation," precisely because of how the poor have been excluded from this process. Gutiérrez contrasts this emphasis on liberation with the "'development' model . . . advanced by international agencies backed by the groups that control the world economy" in an attempt to provide "aid to the poor countries."[11] Although seemingly optimistic, Gutiérrez argues that in the development model "the alleged changes were only new and concealed ways to increase the power of the mighty economic groups," and thus keep the poor, oppressed in that state. As opposed to "development," which is an imposed strategy from the perspective of the oppressor, Gutiérrez suggests "liberation" is a more effective approach because of how "man begins to see himself as a creative subject; he seizes more and more the reins of his own destiny, directing it toward a society where he will be free of every kind of slavery." Simply put, liberation "expresses better the aspiration of the poor peoples," as opposed to an imposed strategy from the perspective of the oppressor.[12] What Gutiérrez is suggesting, therefore, is the inherent exclusivity of oppression, wherein the oppressed are not only materially oppressed structurally and systematically, but such oppression also includes being excluded from realizing one's own subjectivity and agency. This kind of inherent exclusivity lends insight into why Gutiérrez develops a notion of the preferential option.

Through Gutiérrez's pioneering work for the liberation of oppression in Latin America, a "preferential option" became one of the fundamental tenets in liberation theology's struggle against societal oppression based on class, race, ethnicity, gender, and sexual orientation. In order to address these injustices, liberation theologians argue that preference and priority should be shown to the oppressed in order to disrupt the status quo. As Gutiérrez notes in his landmark work, the discrepancy between the rich and the poor is so drastic that any attempt to bring about change within the existing order is futile, and thus "only a radical break from the status quo, that is, a profound transformation . . . and a social revolution . . . would allow for the change to a new society . . . In this light to speak about the process of *liberation* begins to appear more appropriate and richer in human content."[13] And, for Gutiérrez, such a commitment to liberation means a preferential commitment to the poor. Thus the preferential option—combined with liberation theology's emphasis on *praxis*—meant that Christians, as committed followers of Jesus

Christ, "cannot claim to be Christians without a commitment to liberation."[14] Consequently, a theology of liberation, Gutiérrez argues, is an attempt to "reflect on the experience and meaning of faith based on the commitment to abolish injustice and to build a new society; this theology must be verified by the practice of that commitment, by active, effective participation in the struggle in which the exploited classes have undertaken against their oppressors." He continues: "if—more concretely—in Latin America [theological reflection] does not lead the Church to be on the side of the oppressed classes and dominated peoples, clearly and without qualifications, then this theological reflection will have been of little value," which will only serve "to rationalize a departure from the Gospel."[15] For Gutiérrez, Christian theology is only *Christian* to the extent that it focuses on liberation, and we can only achieve liberation if there is a radical break with the status quo, which means commitment to a preferential option for the poor and oppressed, "clearly and without qualifications."

At first glance, it might appear that the preferential option mostly involves a human choice; as Gutiérrez has argued, liberation entails the "commitment to abolish injustice . . . by active, effective participation in the struggle." In other words, the preferential option emphasizes the Christian's (human) work and action to change the material realities of the poor. In fact, one of liberation theology's critiques of "classical" Christian theology is its over-emphasis on the spiritual, eschatological promises of Christianity at the expense of the material, here-and-now realities. Gutiérrez writes: "A poorly understood spirituality has often led us to forget the human message, the power to change unjust social structures, that the eschatological promises contain."[16] Thus, liberation theology is not a "wait-and-see what God will do" approach, but rather emphasizes the human praxis necessary to make concrete, political changes. Specifically addressing the preferential option and its significance for liberation theology, Gutiérrez maintains: "When all is said and done, the option for the poor means an option for the God of the Reign as proclaimed by Jesus. The whole Bible, from the story of Cain and Abel onward, is marked by God's love and predilection for the weak and abused of human history."[17] Again, it is a human option or decision "for the God of the Reign as proclaimed by Jesus." However, it is important to note how the human preferential option or decision is grounded in God's prior option or decision. For Gutiérrez, God is on the side of, or privileges, those who are on the underside of history: the abused, oppressed, poverty-stricken. And thus Gutiérrez, taking up this biblical theme of God's option for the oppressed, presents a contemporary understanding of divine decision wherein the object of God's choice is the poor in society.

In fact, Gutiérrez goes on to state that the human commitment to the liberation of the poor and oppressed is not a product of social analysis, human compassion, or experience of poverty—as valid as these are—but ultimately grounded in God's commitment: "as Christians, we base that commitment fundamentally on the God of our faith."[18] In other words, the preferential option of human work for liberation derives from the prior preferential option of God. Divine decision for, and election of, the poor is the basis for liberation theology's emphasis on human liberative praxis; thus humans should show preferential treatment to the poor because God has first chosen the poor as God's elect: "In the final analysis, an option for the poor is an option for the God of the kingdom whom Jesus proclaims to us. . . . This preference brings out the gratuitous or unmerited character of God's love . . . for [biblical voices] tell us with the utmost simplicity that God's predilection for the poor, the hungry, and the suffering is based on God's unmerited goodness to us."[19] Gutiérrez explains why it is significant to ground liberationist human praxis on God's prior commitment to liberation:

> The ultimate reason for commitment to the poor and oppressed is not to be found in the social analysis we use, or in human compassion, or in any direct experience we ourselves may have of poverty. These are all doubtless valid motives that play an important part in our commitment. As Christians, however, our commitment is grounded, in the final analysis, in the God of faith. It is a theocentric, prophetic option that has its roots in the unmerited love of God and is demanded by this love.[20]

No doubt this is a loaded passage for Gutiérrez, who was already getting accused of intermingling too much "social analysis" (i.e., Marxism) in his theology. Nevertheless, his point is still significant. Continuing to employ classical Christian theological themes and doctrines—like grace, divine love, kingdom of God, and divine election—Gutiérrez reframes them with liberation as the primary focus. Ultimately, for Gutiérrez, it is a notion of *divine* decision, understood as a preferential option for the poor, that demands that *humans* (i.e., Christians who hear and heed this call) decide to work for liberation from oppression. Additionally, as we have seen, the preferential option for the poor emerges in response to their exclusion, which is part and parcel of their oppression.

Leonardo Boff, who was one of the early voices in this conversation, continues along the same lines in his influential book, *Jesus Christ Liberator: A Critical Christology for Our Time*, which seeks to understand contemporary Christology—i.e., the significance and meaning of the person and work of Jesus Christ—in the context of the Latin American struggle for liberation. In the epilogue, Boff affirms that "to worship and proclaim Jesus Christ as Liberator is to ponder and live out our Christological faith within a socio-historical context marked by domination and oppression." Against this backdrop, such "faith seeks to grasp the relevance of themes that will entail structural changes in a given socio-historical situation" and "explore this relevance analytically," resulting in a Christology that "entails a specific sociopolitical commitment to break with the situation of oppression."[21] Boff reminds the reader of a central liberation theological insight: "Theologians do not live in the clouds. They are social actors with a particular place in society." Consequently, theologians emphasize different aspects of theology based on "what seems relevant to the theologian on the basis of his or her social standpoint." Continuing to expound upon the importance of social context, Boff argues:

> In that sense we must maintain that no Christology is or can be neutral. Every Christology is partisan and committed. Willingly or unwillingly Christological discourse is voiced in a given social setting with all the conflicting interests that pervade it. That holds true as well for theological discourse that claims to be "purely" theological, historical, traditional, ecclesial, and apolitical. Normally such discourse adopts the position of those who hold power in the existing system. If a different kind of Christology with its own commitments appears on the scene and confronts the older "apolitical" Christology, the latter will soon discover its social locale, forget its "apolitical" nature, and reveal itself as a religious reinforcement of the existing status quo.[22]

Boff's point about social context and location offers a liberation theological critique of any theology that presumes to operate objectively, "purely" theologically, or apolitically. If and when such a presumption is at work, Boff argues that we can be sure it is operating from, and adopting the position of, "those who hold power in the existing system." In other words, any such position of neutrality on these matters is deconstructed, which is why Latin American liberation theologians recognized the need for (divine) preference—anything less reveals "itself as a religious reinforcement of the existing status quo."

Jon Sobrino, another influential voice in this conversation, makes a similar point about the necessity for such (exclusive, divine) preference. In a more recent work, *Jesus the Liberator: A Historical-Theological Reading of Jesus of Nazareth*, Sobrino states the matter plainly: "Jesus is *for* some, the oppressed, and *against* others, the oppressors."[23] The scandal and offense of such partiality and preference is not lost on Sobrino; in fact, he highlights it as central to the liberative message of Christianity:

> The offense taken by the non-poor is an indirect but effective proof of the fact that the Kingdom of God belongs to the poor simply because they are poor, and that God is revealed as essentially on the side of the poor simply because they are poor. God's taking sides in this way seems to me to be a constant element of revelation. It is clearly shown by the choice God makes in support of some as opposed to and against others. The partiality that runs through the scriptures is therefore also a dialectical partiality. However obvious, we need to consider seriously how often scripture states what God and Jesus are against in order to show what they are for.[24]

Again, Sobrino makes the point that because of the systemic injustice of poverty, neutrality simply supports the unjust status quo. Thus, exclusive preference is needed to rectify this injustice. Theologically speaking, if God is *for* justice, then for Sobrino God is *against* injustice.

What already begins to emerge in this discourse is the way that it navigates the problem of exclusivity and preference. On the one hand, it is in response to the exclusion of the poor, even from participation in their own liberation; on the other hand, it already begins to recognize the need for clear and explicit—if not exclusive—preference for the poor, in order to sufficiently obtain the radical break from the status quo that is necessary for liberation. Additionally, Gutiérrez's discussion of the limits of the development model is important to note. As Gutiérrez points out (and Boff implicitly affirms), part of the problem with the development model is that it, like all perspectives, is always *from* somewhere. This is a significant liberation theological move, continually identifying how theologies, economic models, perspectives, etc., always come from somewhere, in defiant response to the notion that there is an objective, universal perspective. In this case, the development model is imposed upon the poor from outside, from above, from the perspective of the "first world" (wealthy) countries telling the "third world" (poor) countries how to fix the problem of poverty, i.e., by developing. Gutiérrez rejects this model because only a radical break with the status quo will suffice, not development *within* it. But he also emphasizes, like other liberationists, that the struggle must always emerge from the poor themselves, not from those removed from the situation and in a position of power. We will revisit this liberation theological move more fully in Chapter 4, and the insight it sheds on the way power distorts, as it pertains to the problem of justifying decisions, choice, and preference.

Black Liberation Theology: "Jesus is Black"

In liberation theologies the (divine) preferential option has not only been understood in terms of poverty, but also in terms of race, as in the work of another pioneer in liberation theology, James Cone, whose ground-breaking work emerged about the same time as Gutiérrez's. His two earliest works, *Black Theology and Black Power* and *A Black Theology of Liberation* were the first book-length treatments of what would come to be known as "black liberation theology"—the latter text being the first systematic, liberation theology ever published in English. In these texts Cone does not mince words and makes bold theological claims. Like Gutiérrez, Cone maintains that "Christianity is essentially a religion of liberation." Any aspect of it, or message put forward that is not directly related to the "liberation of the poor in a society is not Christ's message." Moreover, any supposed Christian theology that "is indifferent to the theme of liberation is not Christian theology." For Cone, and many other Christian liberationists, Christianity is fundamentally liberative; the entire contents of Christian theology (i.e., the Gospel, biblical witness, God's work and identity, etc.) are all intimately related to the movement of liberation—in fact they must be. This is why in a society or culture "where persons are oppressed because they are *black*, Christian theology must become *black theology*, a theology that is unreservedly identified with the goals of the oppressed and seeks to interpret the divine character of their struggle for liberation." For Cone, God's identification with the oppressed—in this case African-Americans—means not only that theology must become "black," but also that God becomes "black." Cone therefore warns his reader that it will become evident, if it hasn't already, that this text is "written primarily for the black community, not for whites," because an authentic understanding of it "is dependent on the blackness of their existence in the world."[25]

Part of the reason for Cone's insistence on "blackness" (i.e., the blackness of God, theology, reader), is because black theology emerges in response to "American white theology," which has been a theology of the white oppressor, and from the need for African-Americans to liberate themselves from white oppression. White theology is that which is written without any reference to the oppressed. In other words (as Latin American liberation theologians similarly argued in socioeconomic terms above), white theology, which is really just called "theology," entails the exclusion of everything other than the dominant, i.e., white, perspective. Thus white theology is exclusive in a twofold sense: it is exclusive in that it is "only" from this privileged racial perspective, written by and from the experience of whites; and it is also exclusive because in so doing it excludes and marginalizes the voices of others with different (racial) experiences. Black theology arises, however, "from an identification with the oppressed blacks of America," which means "it is a theology of and for the black community."[26] In fact, Cone claims that it "ceases to be a theology of the gospel," i.e., Christian theology, if and when it fails to arise out of the community of the oppressed.[27] For Cone, black theology is, therefore, a theology that is *of*, *for*, and *from* the black community. It is *of* in the sense that it is written by persons of a particular identity (dependent on "blackness"); it is *for* in that it is intended to liberate African-Americans from white oppression; and it is *from* in that it emerges from a particular location and/or community (black community). To put it another way, black theology must be preferential to African-Americans in order to be liberative. And since, for Cone, "Christianity is essentially a religion of liberation," Christian theology must become black liberation theology in a context where "theology" has typically been a theology of, from, and for the white oppressor to the exclusion of all "others."

Articulating the same sentiment as Gutiérrez, Cone argues that theology must be preferential because God is preferential. In other words, this preference does not originate in the theologian, but in God's (prior) preference. A few years later in *God of the Oppressed*, Cone writes:

> If theological speech is based on the traditions of the Old Testament, then it must heed their unanimous testimony to Yahweh's commitment to justice for the poor and weak. Accordingly it cannot avoid taking sides in politics, and the side that theology must take is disclosed in the side that Yahweh has already taken. Any other side, whether it be with the oppressors or the side of neutrality (which is nothing but a camouflaged identification with the rulers), is unbiblical. If theology does not side with the poor, then it cannot speak for Yahweh who is the God of the poor.[28]

For Cone, since God has chosen to side with the poor and oppressed and excluded—because of their exclusion—theologians must do likewise. And anything less than choosing in this way (i.e., exclusively) is merely a choice for oppression.

Emphasizing the social context of Jesus as evidence of God's commitment to and preference for the oppressed, Cone argues that Jesus's "historical appearance in first-century Palestine . . . is the clue to his present activity in the sense that his past is the medium through which he is made accessible to us today."[29] For Cone, analyzing this historical context leads us to acknowledge the importance of Jesus's racial identity as a Jew. And since this history (who Jesus *was*) is important for understanding him today (who Jesus *is*) Cone affirms the blackness of Jesus Christ. The historical significance of Jesus's appearance reveals God's identification with the oppressed and the divine work of liberation on their behalf because of God's incarnation in this particular context. Emphasizing the concrete particularity of this history, Cone correlates this with the context and circumstances of African-Americans in the United States. He writes: "The least in America are literally and symbolically present in black people. To say that Christ is black means that black people are God's poor people whom Christ has come to liberate."[30] Cone thus makes a profound declaration about the identity of Jesus: "He *is* black because he *was* a Jew."[31]

Moreover, because of Jesus's identification with blackness, which is an affirmation of God's identification with the oppressed, Cone also makes a statement about what this means for African-Americans: "the people of color are [God's] elected poor in America."[32] Thus we can see that Cone addresses the fact that God is partial by highlighting the sociohistorical context of divine decision in the incarnation, pointing to the blackness of Jesus Christ and its concomitant affirmation of divine election of African-Americans. Cone maintains that the God of biblical revelation is never impartial: "God is never color-blind . . . Yahweh takes sides . . . Jesus is not for *all*, but for the oppressed."[33] According to Cone, if God was impartial and "color-blind," it would mean that God was blind to injustice and oppression, which betrays the fundamental tenets of Christianity as a theology of liberation. Additionally, Cone is forthright that God's preferential option *for* blacknesss is inherently exclusive in the sense that it is also a choice *against* whiteness. Because the blackness of Jesus Christ affirms God's choice for such, "whiteness is the symbol of the Antichrist."[34]

Cone's understanding of this kind of divine decision as both for/against is important to note, given the way I have tried to sketch the inherent exclusivity of decision. As we have seen, sometimes the exclusivity is hidden, while other times it is more explicitly identified. Cone is not shy about discussing God's decision *for* blackness (those oppressed and excluded) and *against* whiteness (oppression and exclusion). But more than a mere boldness and polemical approach, the argument of this book is that perhaps Cone is just being more honest and transparent. What seems more offensive at first glance in his embrace of the exclusive edge of decisions that cut and divide, might actually be a more genuine approach to an issue that none of us can escape. And in the context of injustice, Cone is unambiguous that any decision that is not explicitly against injustice, is a tacit decision for it.

Gay and Lesbian Liberation Theology: The Queer Christ

Following James Cone's radical declaration of the blackness of Jesus Christ as a liberation theological move that highlights divine preference for African-Americans, several strands of liberation theology began to emerge that made a similar move with respect to other oppressed and excluded groups, namely that in the incarnation where Jesus *becomes* one of the oppressed, we see God's preference. One such strand included gay and lesbian liberation theologies, which emphasized the identity and experience of God's solidarity, and identification with, and justice and activism for, gays and lesbians.

Of course, we should pause to note that with any of these strands of liberation theology there are contours, debates, and trajectories that complicate any particular designation, categorization, or definition of these discourses, such that any attempt to do so will always be at the expense of their fluidity, difference, and complexity. This fact is magnified with gay and lesbian liberation theologies, where there tends to be an emphasis precisely on the fluidity, instability, and complexity of identities. Much of the development and trajectory of gay and lesbian liberation theology entails engagement—to various extents—with queer theory, which "destabilizes essentialist notions of sexuality, identity, and gender" that "renders fluid these cultural concepts and practices once considered stable."[35] Given the fact that gay and lesbian liberation theology, following the major tenets of its precursors in other iterations of liberation theology, presents a theology of/for those who identify as lesbian, gay, bisexual, transgender, or queer (LGBTQ), it has been critiqued by further engagements with queer theory. Consequently, "queer theology" began to emerge as a discourse that complicates the stable notions of sexuality and identity that gay and lesbian liberation theologies were necessarily based upon.[36] Although the "evolution" of gay and lesbian liberation theology is an interesting and complex trajectory, our current concern is with its earliest stages where God identifies, is in solidarity with, and displays preference for LGBTQ people because of its connection to the problem of exclusion, namely its development as a remedy to the problem of exclusion that entails its own exclusivity. The instability of identity, as queer theory argues, offers another layer to the problem, no doubt, because of how it reveals the problematic nature of identifying one group (over against another). As such, we will explore these issues further along in this chapter as we delve deeper into some more recent critiques of liberation theology's identification and (exclusive) preference for a particular group.

The designation of gay and lesbian theology as a "liberation" theology stems (at least partially) from the fact that its aim is not merely the full inclusion of gays and lesbians (because of their exclusion), but demonstrates how (gay and lesbian) *liberation* is at the heart of the Christian gospel and theology. As Laurel Schneider suggests, gay and lesbian liberation theologies "concern themselves with problems of exclusion and the need to obtain justice for gay, lesbian, bisexual, and transgendered people as full persons equal to their heterosexual neighbors in religious communities."[37] Again, the problem of exclusion is a central aspect of any liberationist approach, which will make our investigation into this problem all the more interesting and complex—i.e., the "exclusivity" of something like the preferential option is a response to how society, institutions, etc., *exclude* groups of people based on gender, sexuality, ethnicity, race, socioeconomic status, etc. Thus, gay and lesbian liberation theology's work for the LGBTQ community overlapped with Latin American and black liberation theologies at about the same time. Given what we have discovered, it should come as no surprise that gay and lesbian liberation theologies also argued "that God was not neutral and in fact had a preferential option for the poor and oppressed."[38] Patrick Cheng recounts several instances of this early move in precursors to gay and lesbian liberation theologies:

> For example, in 1968, the Anglican priest H.W. Montefiore published a controversial essay, "Jesus the Revelation of God," which suggested that Jesus' celibacy might have been due to his being a homosexual. If so, Montefiore argued, this would be "evidence of God's self-identification with those who are unacceptable to the upholders of 'The Establishment' and social conventions." That is, just as liberation theologians had argued in other contexts, Montefiore argued that God's nature was "befriending the friendless" and "identifying himself with the underprivileged."[39]

Cheng goes on to discuss other early works in gay and lesbian liberation theology, including the compilation of essays entitled *Towards a Theology of Gay Liberation*, where Giles Hibbert argues that a Christian understanding of liberation cannot be understood apart from gay liberation,[40] and minister Howard Wells's article, "Gay God, Gay Theology" that refers to a "gay God" who is "our liberator, our redeemer."[41]

In *Jesus Acted Up: A Gay and Lesbian Manifesto*, Robert Goss offers a thorough exploration of liberation theology in response to contemporary theology's lack of context and relevance for gays and lesbians. Goss defines this as a "queer liberation theology" that critically engages the oppressive context that forms the experience of gay and lesbian people, seeking to bring about political change. Given the importance of this experience, Goss is clear that no one "not involved in and committed to the struggle for gay/lesbian liberation can write a gay/lesbian liberation theology."[42] In this work Jesus's role as radical activist, social revolutionary, and one who embraces queer identity is highlighted to show God's solidarity with gay and lesbian people. For Goss, "the practice of God's reign actualizes Jesus' message that God is socially in the midst of queer struggle for sexual liberation"; thus "what Easter communicates is that God is passionately on the side of gay and lesbian people."[43]

In Goss's "Queer Christology," he emphasizes that it is through Jesus's "*basileia* practice of solidarity with the oppressed, his execution, God's identification with his crucifixion, and God's raising him from the dead that made Jesus the Christ," such that "Jesus asserted God as the saving reality of solidarity for the oppressed." Thus, God's identification with "the crucified Jesus" was "God's embodied action of solidarity and justice."[44] "Jesus embodied a preferential option for the oppressed," Goss argues, which includes most especially gays and lesbians.[45] He writes: "On Easter, God made Jesus queer in his solidarity with us. In other words, Jesus 'came out of the closet' and became the 'queer' Christ. Jesus the Christ becomes actively queer through his solidarity with our struggles for liberation."[46] Emphasizing the importance of Jesus's identification with, and hence God's preferential option for, gays and lesbians, Goss maintains:

> If Jesus the Christ is not queer, then his *basileia* message of solidarity and justice is irrelevant. If the Christ is not queer, then the gospel is no longer good news but oppressive news for queers. If the Christ is not queer, then the incarnation has no meaning for our sexuality. It is the particularity of Jesus the Christ, his particular identification with the sexually oppressed, that enables us to understand Christ as black, queer, female, Asian, African, a South American peasant, Jewish, transsexual and so forth. It is the scandal of particularity that is the message of Easter, the particular context of struggle where God's solidarity is practiced.[47]

Like other liberation theologians, Goss argues that anything less than God's identification with, and particular choice for, gays and lesbians turns the Gospel into "bad news" because it becomes a tacit affirmation of the status quo, which has perpetuated such oppression and exclusion of LGBTQ persons. Goss's point about the "scandal of particularity," which he understands as God's "identification with the sexually oppressed," is important to note, especially for the issues we will engage below. Such divine identification with one specific oppressed group has been critiqued because of its exclusionary nature—in other words, if Jesus is gay (or black, or dalit, etc.), then Jesus is not white, Latina, poor, etc. Again, this move is further complicated, and critiqued, because of more recent work in women's and gender studies and queer theory on identity that highlights the instability of particular identities and the intersectional nature of the way we inhabit these social constructions. Building upon these more recent discourses, Chapter 4 will return to the possible necessity of such particularity and exclusivity, precisely because of what Goss (and others) are suggesting here—that anything less than preference for the oppressed and excluded will only maintain their oppression and exclusion: "if the Christ is not queer, then the gospel is no longer good news but oppressive news for queers." Additionally, we will explore the even more problematic predicament wherein such exclusivity for one oppressed group or one form of justice can be in conflict with others.

Goss's book—like the others listed above—has most of the basic ingredients that constitute gay and lesbian liberation theology. His political goals, emphasis on how the oppressive context plays a significant role in gay and lesbian experience, privileging of that unique experience, and asserting God's solidarity and identification with gay and lesbian people are all key moves that are modeled after earlier forms of liberation theology. Although not framed explicitly in theological language of divine decision, gay and lesbian liberation theology's employment of earlier liberation theological notions can be understood as a divine decision *for* LGBT people. Just as Gutiérrez argued that liberation of the poor must be central to a Christian theology, so gay and lesbian liberation theologians argue that "queer liberation—that is, freedom from heterosexism and homophobia, as well as the freedom to be one's own authentic self—is at the very heart of the gospel message and Christian theology."[48] Similar to Cone's assertion of the blackness of Jesus as revelation of God's solidarity and preference for blacks in the United States, gay and lesbian liberation theology's notion of Jesus embracing queer identity reveals the identity of God as one who is fundamentally on the side of LGBTQ people who are oppressed.

Dalit Liberation Theology: Dalit Jesus

The final strand of liberation theology we intend to explore in terms of navigating the problem of exclusivity is dalit liberation theology. In the midst of the influx and spread of Christianity in India in the late nineteenth century that "sought to translate, adapt, and correlate the 'good news' of Christian proclamation by taking into consideration its Hindu philosophical and cultural framework," dalit liberation theology developed because certain Christians felt that this "Indian Christian Theology" did not adequately address the sociopolitical situation of dalits. Dalit liberation theologians argue that such a culturally-adaptive approach resulted in a Christianity that did not sufficiently challenge and critique "the culture and religion of a significant portion of its subaltern members who are not part of the Hindu community," namely the dalits, who "represent a large percentage of Indian society that did not come within the confines of the Hindu human community."[49] In order to better understand dalit liberation theology, we need to gain a bit more background on the situation of dalits, the caste system in India, and dalits' historical oppression.

The term "dalit" refers to a group of "untouchables" that are excluded from the fourfold Hindu caste system. They have been referred to by different names, including: *avarnas*, *Panchamas* (fifth caste), exterior castes, depressed castes, scheduled caste, and *Harijans*.[50] Dalit can mean: "(1) the broken, the torn, the rent, the burst, the split; (2) the opened, the expended; (3) the bisected; (4) the driven asunder, the dispelled, the scattered; (5) the downtrodden, the crushed, the destroyed; (6) the manifested, the displayed."[51] This historically oppressed people has not constituted a unified group, but have only been linked through the stigma of untouchability related to their polluting professions. Traditional dalit occupations included disposing of refuse (dead animals, rubbish, sewage), leather works, skinning, and carrying "night soil" (human excrement collected at night in buckets). Referring to dalits in his survey of Indian Christian history, John C.B. Webster writes: "Not only were [dalits] poor and powerless, if not actual slaves, but they also suffered from the stigma of untouchability and, in the extreme south, of unapproachability as well."[52] In rural sectors, dalits were segregated simply because of their impurity. As a result, dalits have been considered "the worst victims of the evil and divisive caste system in India."[53]

The situation began to change slowly, but significantly, for dalits in the nineteenth century with emerging opportunities due to a shift in the political and social landscape. Webster distinguishes three stages in this movement of change, with the first being mass conversion. He argues that converting to Christianity became the greatest leap forward for dalits in the latter half of the nineteenth and into the twentieth century. The gains made in this stage were not economic, however, and even the social and psychological advances were tenuous, as conversion "often raised the converts in the esteem of the landlords but it did not remove the problem of poverty."[54] The second stage of the dalit movement was characterized by Hindu and governmental efforts to improve dalit conditions. The 1920s to the present can be considered the third stage, and is marked by "the self-assertion and self-reliance on the part of the Depressed Classes themselves."[55]

It is within this last stage that we see the emergence of dalit liberation theology. One of its pioneers, Arvind Nirmal, observed that even as late as the 1970s Christian theology in India had still been bent toward the Brahminic, upper caste tradition and culture to the continued neglect and exclusion of the depressed classes. In so doing, Indian Christian theology revealed that "it had no time or inclination to reflect theologically on the dalit converts who formed the majority of the Indian Church."[56] Though things began to change with the rise of "Third world theology" and its connections to nascent liberation theologies, the unique situation of the dalits led Nirmal to contend, in 1986, that "dalit theology is still in the process of emergence."[57] In his estimation, theology still failed to see the dalit struggle for liberation as an appropriate subject matter for doing Christian theology in India. This, Nirmal claimed, was "all the more reason for our waking up to this reality today and for applying ourselves seriously to the task of doing Dalit theology."[58] Theologians heeded Nirmal's call and as a result dalit liberation theology has since established itself as "one of the most authentic expressions of the Indian liberation theology."[59]

The contours of dalit liberation theology during this time closely followed earlier strands of liberation theology and thus insisted that it become a theology *by* dalits, based on their own experience, sufferings, and goals. Unlike earlier expressions of Indian Christian theology *about* or *for* the depressed classes, Nirmal called for a theology *from* the dalits—a fundamental move of liberationists. Moreover, Nirmal insisted that dalit theology, as a counter-theology that developed in response to Indian Christian theology, necessitated a certain type of methodological exclusivism. Since it represented a "radical discontinuity with the classical Indian Christian Theology of the Brahminic Tradition" that excluded dalits, Nirmal maintained that dalit liberation theology must not allow any influence from the dominant (high-caste) theological tradition. Nirmal explains the importance of this kind of exclusivity in dalit liberation theology, as a response to the way dalits had been excluded from previous theologies: "What this exclusivism implies is the affirmation that the Triune god—the Father, the Son and the Holy Spirit—is on the side of the dalits and not of the non-dalits who are the oppressors."[60] This God, according to Nirmal, is a "Dalit God" witnessed to, by, and through the dalitness of Jesus, which is best symbolized by the Godforsaken-ness experienced by Jesus on the cross. Put simply, for Nirmal, God's preferential option for the dalits is indubitable and unambiguous, and, as we have seen, must be explicitly and exclusively so in order to be liberative.

Subsequent to Nirmal's proposal in the 1980s, several discussions and consultations began to emerge on the topic of dalit liberation theology resulting in the publication of a number of books and articles that addressed the unique oppression facing dalits because of the caste-based social order where their deprived status remained fixed for ages. It became clear that the particular experience of the dalits as the "lowliest of people" had been missing from Indian Christian theology.[61] As a result, one of the primary goals included focusing on the "concrete subjectivity" of the dalits, avoiding the "occluding, objectifying and abstract tendencies inherent in theological propositions."[62] In other words, some argued theology's attempt to speak about the poor or poverty, in general, actually concealed (i.e., excluded) the concrete situations of those living in these conditions and the reasons for their persistence. Thus, dalit liberation theology—as a distinct form of contextual, liberation theology—became a necessary corrective in order to speak from, about, and to the particular experience of this group of people. This kind of move, away from the universal and toward the particular, was intended to work for the inclusion of dalits in the struggle for their own liberation and humanity: "For a Christian Dalit theology . . . cannot be simply the gaining of the rights, the reservations and privileges. The goal is the realization of our full humanness or conversely, our full divinity, the ideal of the *Imago Dei*, the Image of god in us. To use another biblical metaphor, our goal is the 'glorious liberty of the children of God.'"[63] This meant establishing the subjectivity of dalits to be makers of their own history and of their own political liberation as well. In order for dalits to experience the fullness of this "glorious liberty," they would need to be freed from the oppressive structures that have excluded them, and this can only be accomplished through a particular emphasis on the concrete oppression of dalits in India, and God's preference and desire for their liberation.

Again, we see that the problem of exclusivity is dealt with by early liberationists with a recognition of having to navigate some form of exclusivity in order to rectify this problem. Dalit liberation theology recognized that speaking about the poor, in general, was part of the problem that did not allow the particular, concrete issues and experiences of dalits to be adequately addressed. It is also worth noting how dalit liberation theology developed in the midst of so-called "progress." Webster maintains that the situation of dalits began to improve in the late nineteenth century. However, it is here, in the midst of such "progress" that the radicality of dalit liberation theology emerged. There is something about this recognition of a need for a radical break in the midst of apparent progress that resonates with the goals and aims of this book. As I have already argued, this is the motivation for revisiting the

Navigating Exclusivity in Response to Exclusivity

problem of in/decision, such that we do not become complacent in dealing with it and the issues associated with it.

This brief foray into several strands of liberation theology is of course by no means intended to be exhaustive nor constitute an exclusive list. Not only have liberation theologies taken many different forms—including mujerista, LatinX, *minjung*, American Indian, etc.—but each contains a myriad of approaches and discursive complexities, as mentioned above. The goal was merely to explore some of this early work in order to highlight several of the significant methodological moves in liberation theologies, including the way that exclusivity and decision (divine or human) is already being navigated. These early liberationists sought to rectify oppression and exclusion through a preferential option in a way that appears to be inherently, or inescapably, "exclusive." These early liberationists wrestled with the notion that the remedy to the exclusion of oppressed groups entailed some version of "strategic exclusivity" in order to adequately attain liberation. At times we find a certain necessity for exclusive preference, while at others an inherent nervousness about such problematic exclusivity. An awareness of the problem of such exclusivity, therefore, has always been present in this discourse—especially since the early liberationists recognized that the preferential option was in response to the exclusion of those oppressed. While on the one hand, the earliest voices in liberation theology tended to be more radical in their claims for such preference, i.e., that God favors, chooses, or is "on the side of" the poor, oppressed, excluded, etc.; on the other hand, even those like Gutiérrez—who first championed God's preferential option for the oppressed—were nervous about exclusion. In a revised edition of his landmark work (almost twenty years later), *A Theology of Liberation*, Gutiérrez tries to clarify this negotiation of exclusivity:

> The very word "preference" denies all exclusiveness and seeks rather to call attention to those who are the first—though not the only ones—with whom we should be in solidarity. In the interests of truth and personal honesty I want to say that from the very beginning of liberation theology, as many of my writings show, I insisted that the great challenge was to maintain both the universality of God's love and God's predilection for those on the lowest rung of the ladder of history. To focus exclusively on the one or the other is to mutilate the Christian message. Therefore every attempt at such an exclusive emphasis must be rejected.[64]

Gutiérrez wrestles with the inherent, inescapable problem of exclusion and attempts to maintain the tension of both by asserting "both the universality of God's love" *and* "God's predilection for those on the lowest rung of the ladder of history." In so doing, Gutiérrez clarifies that his goal in liberation theology was never to advocate God's exclusive preference to the poor, but to show priority for those economically oppressed.

Even James Cone, whose poignant application of liberation theology and the preferential option led to bold claims about God's exclusive preference for African-Americans in the United States, admits significant "limitations" in his early work. In the "Preface to the 1986 Edition" of *A Black Theology of Liberation* Cone acknowledges "his failure to be receptive to the problem of sexism," both within the black community as well as in larger society, and that it was such a "glaring limitation" and "failure" that he "could not reissue this volume without making a note of it and without changing the exclusive language of the 1970 edition to inclusive language." He also admits a failure to incorporate "a global analysis of oppression" by limiting his focus to the North American context and the absence of a more focused analysis of economic and class oppression.[65] Ultimately, Cone recognizes that "an exclusive focus on racial injustice" without a more "comprehensive analysis of its links" with other forms of oppression, i.e., sexism, neocolonialism, capitalism, etc., was problematic because it illustrated both a limitation and failure on his part.[66]

A similar nervousness about exclusivity can be seen in the work for LGBTQ justice where the aim is to position the "universalist, fluid, 'Christian' and queer Jesus" against an exclusive, heteropatriarchal understanding of Christianity.[67] Robert Shore-Goss describes how "Jesus breaks many culturally religious laws and conventions. . . . He proclaimed the wild grace of God that stepped outside the ghettoized boundaries of his religious community that the exclusivist gatekeepers so violently protected."[68] For Goss, a liberationist understanding of Christianity offers a wholesale critique of exclusion, in whatever form it takes, especially the kind of exclusivity found in a Christianity that excludes LGBTQ people.

PREFERENCE FOR ONE AT THE EXPENSE OF OTHERS: COMPLEX IDENTITIES AND COMPETING INTERESTS

Even in some of liberation theology's earliest and foundational voices there is a concern about how an exclusive preference for one group, people, or justice can be problematic for the very liberation these theologies strive for. This concern was heightened even further in the ensuing decades as more voices and perspectives were considered. In one sense liberation theology succeeded in breaking the stranglehold of a single perspective, voice, and experience that had dominated the conversation, i.e., the dominant perspective in terms of socioeconomics, race, class, sexuality, etc. At the same time, as less voices were silenced, the complexities of identity and injustice became more apparent, complicating the early moves toward preference for one stable group of people or one particular form of justice. As a result, the instability and intersectionality of identity, and imbricated nature of oppression and domination, revealed the limits—and indeed pressing issues—associated with this early work. Combined with other factors that included the fall of socialism, the lack of dialogue and solidarity among liberation theologies, collapse into identity politics, and competing interests among those vying for liberation led many to declare that "Liberation theology is in crisis."[69] With some even going so far as to affirm that liberation theology is dead.

The primary focus now is how this pronouncement of the death of liberation theologies has been associated with the problem of preference and its connection to exclusivity. Angie Pears points out how such preference in early liberation theologies was based on "limited understandings of oppression, and especially of the multilayered nature of oppression," which, in turn, have "created new exclusions . . . through a narrow understanding of contexts." This "has had devastating implications for those that even these apparently radical and subversive theologies seem to have ignored." In so doing, Pears argues that early liberation theologies "repeated some of the same mistakes" that they were intended to rectify, namely exclusion.[70]

The inability to think across contexts and examine the multilayered nature of oppression has been one of the primary critiques of liberation theology over the last few decades, especially from those who are concerned about the issues liberation theologians began to critically engage. In a word, the problem is the recurrent issue of exclusivity. While an identification of the perennial problem of exclusion in liberation theologies has been present from the very beginning, more recent work has honed in on the exclusionary nature of the preferential option for one oppressed group at the expense of others and how it has mimicked the exclusivity of the status quo liberationists were trying to remedy. Here we will see that the problem is not necessarily the way the oppressors are excluded, though there appears to be some concern about a general universality or inclusivity. More specifically, the issue is how exclusive preference for one oppressed group, as found in these earlier liberation theologies, results in the exclusion of other oppressed groups, making the issue of exclusivity even more complex; which, in turn, makes the problem of decision that much more complex as well. Whether it's understood in terms of a preferential option or merely choosing to focus on one specific form of injustice, the issue of exclusivity remains a central concern.

Intersectionality and Complex Identities

One of the early and most influential critiques of the exclusivity of liberation theology can be found in the womanist work of Delores S. Williams. In

Sisters in the Wilderness: The Challenge of Womanist God-Talk, Williams reflects on her increasing awareness of the exclusion of black women in black liberation (as well as feminist) theologies,[71] noting that "what the sources presented as 'black experience' was really black male experience."[72] In other words, *black* liberation theology was not particular enough, because it still silenced, marginalized, and thus continued to oppress African-American *women's* perspective, experience, and voice by assuming that "black" was able to capture the entirety of African-American experience (male and female). What Williams identifies and is doing here is actually pushing one of liberation theology's major tenets further, and, in so doing, critiquing black liberation theology by "doubling down" on particularity. Cone—and other early liberationists in a similar way—argued that black liberation theology must emerge as a response to white theology that assumes and exclusively privileges a white perspective and experience, which, Cone adds, would include the inherent racism of this perspective. The real problem, however, is that white theology (i.e., theology from a white perspective) is masked because it is only presented as "theology," which reveals the dynamic in which the dominant perspective need not be named. Black liberation theology must emerge as a response not just to white theology, but to "theology" (in general), because the latter really is the former. Williams, therefore, is arguing similarly: *black* liberation theology only names and identifies the (male) racial experience and perspective, not the gendered experience and perspective, which, in a patriarchal society, means that women's perspective and voice gets silenced, marginalized, and hence excluded. Thus, Williams argues, *womanist* theology must emerge in response to black liberation theology as a "Christian theology from the point of view of African-American women."[73] Naturally—as feminist and liberation theologies have argued for decades—when what was once silenced is now given voice and included, there are significant theological implications, and Williams points out the difference this change in perspective makes theologically.

In *Sisters in the Wilderness*, Williams identifies biblical interpretation as one of the key challenges womanist theology presents to black liberation theology, specifically the way in which black liberation theologies have emphasized liberation in their reading of the Bible. Williams uses Hagar as the critical lens with which to challenge such an emphasis on liberation: "A womanist rereading of the biblical Hagar-Sarah texts in relation to African-American women's experience raises a serious question about its use as a source validating black liberation theology's normative claim of God's liberating activity in behalf of *all* the oppressed."[74] Through this womanist reading, Williams highlights how the oppressed do not always experience God's liberation, as seen in the case of Hagar. Black liberation theology's error, according to Williams, is that it has too readily identified with Sarah (Abraham's wife), and has failed to acknowledge the perspective of the "oppressed of the oppressed." Therefore, to read the bible, or make theological assertions, with a core assumption of liberation (as liberation theology does) only further marginalizes and excludes those who are already doubly oppressed—in this case, African-American women. Williams thus suggests an "additional hermeneutical posture—one that allows [black liberation theology] to become conscious of what has been made invisible in the text and to see that their work is in collusion with this 'invisibilization' of black women's experience,"—might enable black liberation theologians to read critically against their own (i.e., male) perspective.[75] Instead of a reading that understands the African-American community's relationship to Sarah (who is one of God's chosen people), Williams focuses on the Hagar texts in order to "demonstrate that the oppressed and abused do not always experience God's liberating power," and, in so doing, reveals a "non-liberative thread running through the Bible."[76] The importance of recognizing—and even identifying with—those who have been silenced in the biblical text is in order to see the "oppressed of the oppressed in scripture," those whose situation is most analogous to black women.[77] Consequently, black liberation theology would recognize that its core assumption of liberation at the center of Christianity actually functions to perpetuate oppression of African-American women. In terms of reducing the exclusivity of black liberation theology, Williams proposes that "wilderness experience" is more appropriate to describe African-American experience because it "expands the content" and is more "inclusive."[78]

Williams's point here is particularly relevant because of the way it highlights the latent problem of exclusion—through the silencing of African-American women's perspective—in liberation theology; and still more pertinent because of how such exclusivity is navigated and how it highlights the dynamics of power and privilege that are at work. According to Williams, black liberation theology's identification with Sarah has resulted in the further exclusion of black women as the oppressed of the oppressed. The implication here is that black liberation theologians—as predominantly male—have been unable to see things from anything but their own perspective, which they assumed to be universal. This reflection of power and privilege has functioned to silence and exclude anything *other* than that privileged position, in this case, Williams argues that includes the perspective of African-American women. Williams thus suggests identifying with the non-Hebrew (Hagar in this case), in order to avoid excluding black women. The move, then, on the one hand, is seemingly toward a more *inclusive* theology—one that does not exclude the lived realities and experiences of black women—but is only accomplished by being *more* particular.

Williams's womanist analysis is corroborated by others who consider the intersection of race and gender. Katie G. Cannon also identified the way black women have been excluded within feminist and black liberation theologies and thus insists on the need for a focus on "the distinctive consciousness of Black women." By "appropriating the human condition in their own contexts," Cannon argues, "Black women collectively engage in revealing the hidden power relations inherent in the present social structures." These include a recognition that "theo-ethical structures are not universal, color-blind, apolitical, or otherwise neutral" and thus a womanist voice is needed to rectify the "deafening discursive silence" that has been perpetuated by feminist and black liberation discourses.[79]

Kelly Brown Douglas argues similarly against the exclusionary tendencies of liberation theology that womanist theology has identified. Drawing on Alice Walker's definition of a womanist, Douglas recounts finding solace in the commitment "to survival and wholeness of an entire people, male *and* female."[80] There is still the particular emphasis on African-Americans, and even more particularly African-American women, yet Douglas asserts: "Womanist theology must make clear that authentic knowledge is not that which fosters any form of oppressive power. On the contrary, it is that which challenges dominating power, including the complex discourses that help maintain such power."[81] Douglas thus argues that womanist work has broadened its scope to include the dismantling of all oppressive structures and forces, in whatever form they may appear—including those of black liberation theology where the emphasis on race neglects the intersectional oppression African-American women face.

Douglas, Cannon, and Williams offer a strident womanist critique of liberation theology's emphasis on preference for one group and the way that has excluded other oppressed groups, namely the doubly oppressed, i.e., African American women. Turning liberation theology's best intentions back on itself, they identify that it is exclusive precisely to the extent that it is not particular enough: "black" actually works to silence those within the African-American community who are oppressed. In other words, "black"—as a category, label, identity—is not particular enough to account for the varied experiences and perspectives within that category, and thus womanist work attempts to give voice to African-American women and "construct Christian theology" from that point of view.[82]

Part of what womanist and black feminist insights introduced is the intersectional nature of oppression. Intersectionality is the notion that "inequality and privilege do not operate independently of each other and that our experiences of them are shaped by the interplay of our multiple social locations such as gender, social class, and race."[83] It was first introduced by Kimberlé Crenshaw in a pair of essays in law journals (in 1989 and 1991) that addressed the way black women were marginalized not only in antidiscrimination laws but also in feminist and antiracist, liberation discourses.[84] As "a method and a disposition, a heuristic and analytic tool," intersectionality functions to highlight how advocacy and preference within social movements can function to elide and marginalize people from other oppressed groups. Crenshaw's groundbreaking work exposed a complexity that further feminist and antiracist discourses would need to contend with, namely "how discourses of resistance (e.g., feminism and antiracism) could themselves function as sites that produced and legitimized marginalization."[85]

Of course, race and gender are not the only two markers—or even the two most important, one might argue—to account for any one experience, nor does any person securely inhabit any of these categories in any stable way. Consequently, more recent work in feminist, womanist, and other liberationist discourses has identified multiple sites of oppression and privilege that complicate earlier assumptions that categories like "poor," "black," "woman," "gay," etc., could be stable enough to cohere; and such instability of categories also adds to the complexity of identity. Feminist theories have for decades called into question any notion of essentialism, any "belief in the real, true essence of things, the invariable and fixed properties which define the 'whatness' of a given entity," which has led to a hotly-debated topic in the fields of race, gender, sexuality, and postcolonial studies.[86] Determining the true essence entails discovering these inherent and unchanging properties, because they constitute the most fundamental aspects of one's core identity. These essential characteristics must therefore be universally present in all instances of a given object, person, thing, etc.[87] In critical race and gender studies, such essential properties can be used to distinguish one race or gender from another, and within postcolonial theory essentialism has referred to the notion that individuals share an essential cultural identity. The critique of essentialism by feminist and postcolonial theorists has been influenced by the work on language and identity in post-structuralist theorists such as Jacques Derrida, Jacques Lacan, and Michel Foucault. These critiques gave rise to constructionism, which, in responsive opposition to essentialism, insists that "essence" is a cultural or historical construction and thus rejects the idea that any essential precedes the processes of social determination. In postcolonial studies, the political purpose of anti-essentialism includes exposing "the falsity of this mode of representing the colonial subject as an 'other' to the Self of the dominant colonial culture."[88] Similarly, some feminist theorists critique essentialism because it legitimizes women's historical subordination to men by making it seem like a natural fact, rather than a cultural product. Women, like the colonial "other," become defined in opposition to the dominant type—in this case men or "the masculine"—and thus have no identity of their own. More importantly, feminists point out that these essential properties are simply inaccurate because they fail to account for the complex reality of women's lives.[89] As a result, there is an increasing rejection of such modern definitions of essentialism and growing appreciation for ambivalence, border, and hybridity that more accurately describe the complexity of social and cultural relationships and identity.

More recent engagements with queer theory have also challenged earlier liberation discourses to reckon with the reality of unstable identities. As we have seen, early gay and lesbian liberation theologies seemed to rest on assumptions of a stable gay and lesbian identity, which was understood as necessary for grounding the desired political traction of this theological work. These assumptions are problematic however, because queer theory employs poststructuralist accounts of subjectivity that reject notions of an autonomous, unified, self-knowing, and static subject. As a result, queer theory is also "critical of the liberationist ideal of the liberation of the true self and of sexuality as a singular unified force that has been repressed."[90] One of queer theory's contributions to discourses about liberation, especially in its efforts "to struggle against the straightjacketing effects of institutionalization, to resist closure and remain in the process of ambiguous (un)becoming," is to point to the instability and contested nature of sexuality, such that even terms like lesbian and gay man are limited and limiting.[91] Additionally, this understanding of sexuality as split into two classifications is not only arbitrary but funds other dichotomies as well. Such an awareness offers the "sort of focus on the constructed, contingent, unstable and heterogeneous character of subjectivity, social relations, power, and knowledge, that has paved the way for Queer Theory."[92] Building on poststructuralist insight that knowledge, as well as the ways of being that they engender, naturalizes identity in culturally and historically specific ways, queer theory challenges ahistorical and universal notions of sexuality. These theorists expose the ways that sexualities—and their concomitant identities—are always contestable, unstable, and open to change. It could be said that the "essence" then, of queer theory, "is that there is no essential sexuality or gender. 'Queer' then is not actually another identity . . . but a radical destabilizing of identities and resistance to the naturalizing of any identity."[93]

One of the pioneering works of queer theology that took seriously such a perspective, Marcella Althaus-Reid's *Indecent Theology: Theological Perversions in Sex, Gender and Politics*, challenges liberation theological discourse by unmasking its heterosexual and patriarchal assumptions.[94] Drawing not only on queer theory but also postcolonial criticism, Marxist studies, and Continental philosophy, Althaus-Reid calls attention to the fact that poverty and sensuality (as well as their interface) have been excluded in theology, despite what she sees as theology's appreciation of discontinuity over stability—especially liberation theology's hermeneutics of suspicion and constant questioning. Thus Althaus-Reid questions the traditional context of doing liberationist theology and prompts it to continue its work of recontextualization and serious doubting by following its own best intentions, probing the reasons why it has been indifferent to the sexual realities of the poor in the first place. This context includes the accepted social codifications that bind theology to epistemologies and sexual constructions that limit its work—a context that queer theory has fundamentally critiqued. What emerges in this process is, for Althaus-Reid, an indecent theology—or sexual political theology that rewrites both theology and sexuality—because a theology from the poor needs to be sexual. Challenging earlier liberation theologies, Althaus-Reid utilizes a genealogical critique to both draw attention to and subvert sex and gender codes. Pointing to the constructed nature of these codes, Althaus-Reid "'outs' the heterosexuality of the dominant discourses of liberation theology."[95] But the real advance, perhaps, is not just the critique mounted against these assumptions but the constructive theological—indecent—work she attempts, especially in light of the instability and complexity of identities and experiences.

The burgeoning recognition of intersectional forms of oppression and privilege, combined with an appreciation for the complexity of identities, problematizes early liberationist work that seemed to emerge from concrete identities and for particular forms of oppression. All of this makes the problem of decision all the more complicated. In terms of a preferential option, it would reveal that any preference—divine or human—for a particular group will always be limited. Additionally, if oppressive structures do not form neat boundaries, then social movements that are focused on one aspect of injustice can be implicated in perpetuating other forms of injustice, making the problem of deciding and choosing all the more difficult.

Problem of Essentialist Notions of God's Preference

Theologically speaking, essentialist notions of divine preference have been recognized as a significant problem, leading to identity politics and competing claims for divine favor among oppressed groups, which has, consequently, undermined liberationist work. Sathianathan Clarke identifies this problem and challenges the parochial nature of contextual liberation theologies and their tendency toward exclusivity. Through an investigation of dalit and tribal theology in South India, Clarke reflects on the segregation between dalits themselves as well as the division between the dalit community and the Adivasi community, another oppressed and marginalized group in the village, with the latter "considered to be so low in rank and status that they were also looked down upon by the dalits."[96] Clarke found these kinds of divisions, and even inter/intra-group animosities, to be disheartening, but unfortunately not atypical. Though he admits that much has been achieved in contextual liberation theology since the 1980s, Clarke still concludes: "Dalit Christian communities may have concretized and contextualized the Christian gospel into their own particular historical context but this has not enabled them to broaden the scope of this good news to build community solidarity with similar oppressed communities."[97]

Pointing to the ways that oppressed communities exclude one another, Clarke calls for a reexamination of contextual and liberation theology that, among other things, allows for a "roomier conception of community" and "is less prone to becoming insular."[98] This leads Clarke to ask pressing questions about the connection between the particularizing of theology and its propensity toward such parochialism and exclusivity. Part of the way he addresses this is by critically analyzing preference for one oppressed group, especially through some kind of divine preference, at the expense of other oppressed communities with whom it might be beneficial to build solidarity. Clarke recognizes the need for such theological particularity, however, given how hegemony operates. Utilizing the work of Antonio Gramsci on the "subaltern," Clarke highlights how the dominating elite weaves convincing, all-embracing worldviews making oppression acceptable and even meaningful for the oppressed. This works to legitimize the conditions of domination by offering a rationale for the dominated to actually participate in their own domination. In response to this, liberation theology counters such tendencies by calling for a preferential option for the poor, oppressed, and excluded.

The problem with liberation theology's solution, for Clarke, is that "God's preferential option is actualized in essentialist terms," which leads to further exclusion of other oppressed groups.[99] By critiquing liberation theology's employment of a preferential option in "essentialist terms," Clarke is arguing against exclusive priority in terms of a stable, ethnic identity; in other words, that dalits receive divine preference because of some essential characteristic (i.e., experience, ethnicity, caste position, etc.). Rather, Clarke contends that these liberation theologies should interpret a preferential option for dalits more "in terms of process," not some essential characteristic. Clarke clarifies just what this means: "Thus, in advocating God as preferentially opting to covenant with subalterns we are stressing that God is aligned with the *activity* of people who participate in countering hegemony and embracing their own authentic freedom and dignity."[100]

Clarke maintains that interpreting divine favor in essentialist terms "negates the dynamic that was initiated and mediated by Jesus as the Christ."[101] In Clarke's analysis, part of what Jesus inaugurated was a new understanding of the covenant, ending "traditional" understandings of divine preference with a certain people in terms of ethnicity. God's presence is now experienced and expressed through the "dynamic movement of people struggling for life and liberty." In other words, we come to know that God is on our side by participating in the cooperative struggle, alongside God. Hence, there can be no claim to an "ontological privilege" (based on some essential characteristic or identity) in one's relationship with God, but "rather, claiming God is conceived of as participating in God's working." Even though God is the same for any who would participate in the struggle, Clarke makes the point that those who are oppressed—in this case, dalits—are typically the ones who want to subvert unjust structures; thus they will more likely join in the divine work for freedom and life. Clarke contends that this kind of "participatory knowing" assuages concerns about divine preference for a particular group, to the exclusion of others, yet remains contextual and liberative because the oppressed "will inevitably take the side of God" and therefore receive God's favor.[102]

Clarke's proposal attempts to negotiate the tension in liberation theology's preferential option by confronting the way it excludes other oppressed groups, while retaining its liberative and contextual character. Clarke shows how liberation theology's greatest strength—its preferential option for the poor, oppressed, marginalized, excluded—can present its own issues of exclusion and parochialism as oppressed communities vie for *the* essential characteristic that leads to divine favor. In contrast, Clarke argues that his proposal does not privilege any "ethnic reality" and as such "is a move away from the hierarchical mindset that leads to claims of exclusive priority of God's favor."[103] In other words, the problem is the inherent exclusion of the preferential option and the way that leads to competing claims from oppressed groups for divine (or human) preference. But rather than abandon it altogether, Clarke understands the divine preferential option in terms of participation rather than identity. God chooses, favors, or is on the side of those who join in the struggle for liberation, freedom, and life. And since those who are oppressed are more likely to—or even "inevitably will"—participate in God's working, Clarke maintains that preference is still more germane to dalits.

Solidarity and Expansive Notions of Justice

Many contemporary liberation theologians and ethicists echo Clarke's concern for competition over exclusive preference (divine or otherwise) and the damaging effects that has for the work of liberation. Ivan Petrella addresses the issue of how early liberationist work resulted in a lack of dialogue across various liberation theologies and suggests that there must be "a combination of particularity and global vision." Each of the different contexts from which these theologies of liberation emerge will—and should—converge, he argues, because "none exists in isolation." As a result, Petrella goes on to frame his project as one that will also "be contextual," keeping in line with liberation theology's emphasis on particular, concrete contexts. But, he continues, "it will be contextual of American liberation theology as a whole," thinking "across particular liberation theologies to reveal the overarching context within which a liberation theologian of any stripe must work." Focusing on convergence and solidarity is necessary, Petrella argues, because "each struggle for liberation is related to all other struggles" and different agendas inevitably obstruct the pursuit of justice.[104] Liberation ethicist Miguel De La Torre similarly argues that liberative work "should not be conducted from only one marginalized perspective," as is the case when an oppressed group claims exclusive divine preference, because "keeping the marginalized groups separated insures and protects the power and privilege of the dominant culture."[105] In fact, Darryl Trimiew argues that "the refusal of various liberation movements to concern themselves with the fates of others is the self-issued death warrant of these moral movements."[106]

Theologian and cultural critic Thandeka points out that keeping oppressed communities at odds with each other is a well-oiled "divide and conquer strategy" of the dominant position. Using the history of colonial North America to illustrate this point, Thandeka highlights how wealthy white Virginians prevented poor whites from building natural allegiances to black slaves (with whom they had a shared economic plight), by infusing racist laws and endowing whites with privileges over blacks.[107] Prior to this, the white ex-indentured servants were an oppressed and despised group, considered to be the "rabble of Virginia."[108] But white masters' fear of an uprising of the oppressed—by both poor whites and black slaves—"required a new strategy for social control, for the affinities between indentured servants and slaves presented a danger to the masters. . . . With a swelling slave population, the masters faced the prospect of white freeman with 'disappointed hopes' joining forces with slaves of 'desperate hope' to mount ever more virulent rebellions."[109] The "solution," argues Thandeka, was "the sinister design of racism," which fostered a division among groups who could have, and should have, been in solidarity with each other based on a similar experience of oppression. Perpetuating racism, and hence division among these groups, however, protected the power of elite whites by seducing poor whites into despising newly freed blacks, whom they should have been in solidarity with. Liberationists, like De La Torre, point out that such insight about the machinations of domination is something that we should take seriously: "Then, as now, the dominant culture's privilege is maintained because different marginalized groups fight with limited resources for black justice, Latino/a justice, Amerindian justice, gender justice, Asian-American justice, and so on."[110]

The problem becomes even more complicated when we also realize, as other recent work has pointed out, that these identities (e.g., black, African-American, Caribbean, Latino/a, Hispanic, etc.) are constructions that the dominant culture has used to separate, oppress, and marginalize that which is "Other." Sociologist Manuel Mejido Costoya notes that "the plurality of perspectives that attempt to grapple with the coming of age of U.S. Hispanic reality—Chicano, borderland, Latino/a, poco, diasporic, feminista, mujerista, etc.—lack a common root or ground."[111] This kind of "fragmentation," which "is the U.S. Hispanic mestiza/o reality" results in a lack of unity, "which fragments and turns mujerista vs. feminista, east vs. west, etc."[112] In other words, the attempt to be more particular and true to the realities of the experience of an oppressed group that denies any label (e.g., "Latino") the dominant culture imposes, has the unintended result of only maintaining the separation and fragmentation of those oppressed and marginalized, which perpetuates the oppression.

Moreover, such critiques raise questions over the value of being even more particular in liberation work, as was the case with the womanist response to black liberation theology. We should recall that part of Cone's analysis of (white) theology was that by not naming the dominant perspective (i.e., "white") it perpetuated the exclusion of "other" perspectives, thus black liberation theology emerged in response to the exclusion of a black perspective. Womanist voices pushed even further by asserting that "black" was not particular enough to account for the intersectional experience of black women and thus needed to become even more particular, in order to be less exclusive. But the above critiques seem to propose that a lack of unity among oppressed groups can also perpetuate oppression, which suggests that particularity can be both resource and poison, thus only further complicating the work for liberation.

What we see emerging in these critiques and developments is the dynamic that has been at the fore throughout this entire book: does choice—or even preference—necessarily, and problematically, exclude? The issue becomes even more complex when we begin to recognize the problem of decision, choice, and preference pertains not only to peoples and groups, but also to particular forms of injustice. Reflecting on this complexity, Kate Ott raises this question in terms of work for justice: "How do we better integrate our justice work so we are not advocating for one issue over and against another, but out of an awareness of and commitment to ending all oppression/injustice? Said more directly, when we choose one 'justice' to focus on (because of our identity affiliation), are we in turn doing injustice to others?"[113] These questions emerge as Ott discusses specific concerns for justice (i.e., feminist, sexual, reproductive, etc.). In order to illustrate the issue and present an alternative, Ott walks us through a reading of Jesus's encounter with the Syrophoenician/Canaanite woman in the Gospels, where we find Jesus's infamous denial of healing, seemingly insensitive response about being sent only to the lost sheep of Israel, and taking the children's food and throwing it to the dogs. Ott suggests a reading that relates Jesus's response to this woman's plea for justice in a similar way to ours: "There is only so much justice one person can do, and [Jesus] has a tall order just dealing with his own community. We do the same thing . . . we parcel out what resources we have (monetary, time, interest) based on proximity of those in need, entitlement toward those like us, and safety of our own self and community."[114] But through the encounter with the Syrophoenician/Canaanite woman, Jesus realizes the limits he placed on his ministry and the injustice that resulted. Jesus's experiential frame limited his understanding of justice; but once challenged by this woman he realized "he had to push beyond the limits of *who* he had thus far included."[115] Ott argues that this story teaches us about ourselves, our limits on who gets included in our understandings of justice, and the ways in which we can push beyond such limits through challenging encounters to our experiential frame. Thus Ott suggests that we "should be erasing modifiers of justice," because "when we base justice work on categories of oppression, we may easily fall prey to saving some people's daughters without working to change the world so all daughters have a chance at a fulfilled and healthy life."[116]

Ott's point is well taken, and offers another significant critique of the problem of exclusive preference for one group or form of justice. Those who work for justice need to continually identify our limitations, push beyond them, become increasingly aware of injustice, lessen and avoid exclusion and violence as much as possible. We need to continue to become aware of our ignorance, exclusions, "other-ings," stereotypes, limited worldviews, racism, sexism, heterosexism, etc. Moreover, the issue of power and privilege is always lurking and seeping into these analyses, such that even our best attempts at moving beyond our limited perspectives are always met by strict limits. As we have also seen, recognizing and attempting to remedy such exclusivity is not easily navigated, as some are calling for more and more particularity (in order to be more inclusive), while others are suggesting less particularity (in order to be more expansive). Already, then, we see that any attempt to remedy this issue, and focus on liberation and justice, is complicated and thorny.

EXCLUSIVE PREFERENCE UNDERMINES JUSTICE

The above-mentioned complexities highlight the issues associated with the preferential option in liberationist work and the ways in which that undercuts the work for justice that is their main goal. Consequently, what we see emerging more and more in response to these critiques is an ever-increasing move toward broadening, expansion, and openness, which further complicates any move toward priority, preference, and decision. We should recall from Part I that this is a familiar move: the movement away from closure and exclusion, epitomized in the theological engagement with deconstruction and Caputo. Not surprisingly, then, we also find that so-called "postmodern" engagement with liberation theologies follows a similar dynamic, highlighting a foregoing consensus and the potential influence that Caputo's work has had, by identifying the limitation, closure, and exclusivity found in liberation theologies—especially the preferential option—and a movement toward a more expansive field of vision. Put simply, in order to avoid closure, like that of exclusive preference or decision, postmodern engagement with liberation theology often concludes that we must broaden and expand the vision and scope of justice work.

In an introduction to a compilation of essays on postmodern engagement with liberation theology and the preferential option, Joerg Rieger describes the benefit of adding new visions and voices: "The collaboration of authors writing from the (mostly hybridized perspectives) of Latinos and Latinas, Latin Americans, African Americans, Asian Americans, Euro-Americans, Euro-Africans, and Europeans, both male and female, produces a much-needed broadening of the horizon and uncovers new sources of energy in the life-and-death struggles of people all over the world today."[117] Rieger opens by describing how "opting for the margins"—which is the title of the book—has become more and more passé in theological, ethical, and philosophical discourses because of its tendency to be exclusive (as we have seen). While taking these critiques seriously, this project revisits one of liberation theology's most significant concepts through a postmodern lens. Rieger writes: "In this volume we deal with such challenges from various points of view and develop new ways of interpreting the option for the poor in a postmodern world."[118] The result is a recognition that it is no longer possible to speak *for* or *from* the perspective of one, stable, pure identity; on the contrary, we need a "broadening of the horizon," which includes increasing the particularities of various oppressed groups, and hence a move beyond particularity and preference for one oppressed group.

The move toward openness, broadening, and expansion can also be seen in *Wading through Many Voices: Toward A Theology of Public Conversation*. This compilation of essays seeks to bring together the voices of Latino/a, African American, Asian American, Native American, and Euro-American scholars to produce a dialogue of public theology in order to find a common ground for justice. This self-described "multiethnic perspective" is intended to counter the divisive identity politics that are often the result of too much emphasis on one particular group or people. The goal, therefore, is to build a coalition of forces to work on issues of freedom and justice in order to "develop a shared public theology that addresses aspects of the current state of society, while offering a social and political vision broad enough to bring various and different groups together to collaborate for an improved understanding of the common good for our pluralistic, democratic society."[119] Although there are times in which the various essays in *Wading Through Many Voices* explicitly challenge or critique liberation theology's preferential option and its exclusivity, the movement toward openness and broadening as a move beyond such particularistic and exclusive notions is present throughout. In the introduction, the editors write: "These essays in shared public theology will in various and different ways provide categories and building blocks to correct the exclusionary interpretation of the common good and for understanding responsible citizenship in public life."[120] Moving beyond exclusive interpretations and understandings, identity politics, and achieving a political vision "broad enough," means expansion, which becomes a consistent theme throughout the essays in this work. Marcia Riggs explicitly identifies the problem with choice that leads to polarizing various oppressed groups and puts them at odds with other marginalized people: "This polarized thinking is constitutive of an ethical dilemma wherein choice is between loyalty to the race and collusion with or co-optation by white racist oppression because of disloyalty to the race." In other words, Riggs argues that African-Americans feel the need to choose race as the primary focus of justice and liberation in order to maintain solidarity and loyalty against racism and white supremacy, or else they are implicitly siding with it. But Riggs's goal is "to expose how making either choice promotes oppression" by construing too narrow a view and making one identity marker (e.g., race) the key determinant.[121]

In *Liberation Theologies, Postmodernity and the Americas*, we see another engagement between liberation theologies and postmodern discourse with a similar move toward broadening, expansion, and resisting closure that excludes. In the opening pages the goal is clearly stated: "Its many-side grounding and method of de-centering one dominating voice put liberation theology in natural dialogue with postmodern analyses."[122] According to the editors of this volume, both liberation theologies and postmodern analyses relativize the absolute claims of dominant ideologies and critique universality, which is always at the expense of particular vantage points. At the same time, however, the volume argues that postmodern discourses challenge the emphasis on particularity, dualism, and exclusivity in liberation theologies. In her essay, "Dancing with Chaos: Reflections on Power, Contingency, and Social Change," Sharon D. Welch maintains that even though she has supported the preferential option in liberation theologies, it is not without its faults: "While these theologies criticized the dualistic logic that excludes most of humanity, they often merely reverse the division of humanity into legitimate and illegitimate knowers and actors."[123] In other words, liberation theologies address the exclusion of those on the margins through an exclusive choice, option, or preference for those on the margins. Welch argues that this kind of dualistic reversal is subject to postmodern critique. In her analysis, "a postmodern analysis recognizes that epistemic inclusion does not require or presume closure, purity, definitive insights, or the final word," but rather "takes seriously the open-ended nature of social activism."[124] Again, given our exploration of deconstruction and its theological engagement, we should recognize this move away from closure and exclusion and toward openness, which Welch applies more particularly to liberation theologies.

From its earliest iterations to its more recent developments, liberationists have been concerned about the problem of exclusion. Gutiérrez and Cone, two of the earliest voices in this discourse, both identified the problematic ways that the preferential option could be understood as too exclusive, and, in revised editions of their landmark works, clarified or corrected previous claims in order to counter this trend. Subsequent work has also highlighted and critiqued such exclusivity, particularly the way oppressed groups continue to be excluded when preference for one is employed. As we have seen, this is directly related to the problem of decision—preference, choice, or priority of focus (divine or human) on one group or one form of injustice is problematic. It leads to identity politics, further exclusions, and pits oppressed communities against each other vitiating the solidarity needed to disrupt the unjust status quo. This is the backdrop, and consensus, where the constructive work of Part II intends to enter the conversation. Given this dynamic and these insights, where does that leave us with regard to making difficult decisions about justice?

NOTES

1. Caputo, *Prayers and Tears*, xx.
2. Pears, *Doing Contextual Theology*, 170.
3. As I will go on to show, this exclusivity is "strategic" in the sense that it is not absolute, but provisional and temporal, a distinction that becomes especially pertinent when such exclusivity is tied to a concept of divine election. "Strategic exclusion" calls to mind postcolonial theorist Gayatri Spivak's "strategic essentialism" as a way to forge a collective identity in political movements. There is actually a significant point of resonance between what I am attempting in this chapter and Spivak's work, especially in terms of identity, experience, and the work for liberation. Unfortunately, exploring some of this resonance is beyond the scope of this chapter or book. See: Gayatri Spivak, "Subaltern Studies: Deconstructing Historiography," in *The Spivak Reader: Selected Works of Gayatri Spivak*, eds. Donna Landry and Gerald Maclean (New York: Routledge, 1996): 203–36.
4. The appellation "first wave" is merely intended to connote the early liberation theologians who called themselves such in the 1960s and 1970s, as contrasted with more recent work that challenges and builds upon this earlier work. For an alternative, earlier understanding of "first wave" liberation theology, see: Gerd-Rainer Horn, *Western European Liberation Theology: The First Wave (1924–1959)* (Oxford: Oxford University Press, 2008).
5. Gustavo Gutiérrez, "Option for the Poor," in *Systematic Theology: Perspectives from Liberation Theology: Readings from Mysterium Liberationis*, eds. Jon Sobrino and Igna Ellacuria (Maryknoll, NY: Orbis Books, 1993), 27.
6. Like any discourse or movement, it is difficult to track the genealogy to a specific starting point or origin. In addition to the conferences and conversations that were beginning to emerge in the late 1960s in South America, James Cone's work in Black Liberation theology also began around this time, and it is contested as to how much each other knew of, or were influenced by, the other's work.
7. Gutiérrez, *A Theology of Liberation: History, Politics, and Salvation*, xiii.
8. Ibid., 13.
9. Ibid., xvii.
10. Ibid., 174.
11. Gustavo Gutiérrez, "Notes for a Theology of Liberation," *Theological Studies* 31, no. 2 (June 1970): 246.

12. Ibid., 247.
13. Gutiérrez, *A Theology of Liberation*, 17.
14. Ibid., 81.
15. Ibid., 174.
16. Gutiérrez, "Notes for a Theology of Liberation," 256.
17. Gutiérrez, "Option for the Poor," 27.
18. Gutiérrez, "Option for the Poor," 27.
19. Gutiérrez, *A Theology of Liberation*, xxvii.
20. Ibid.
21. Leonardo Boff, *Jesus Christ Liberator: A Critical Christology for Our Time* (Maryknoll, NY: Orbis Books, 1978), 264.
22. Ibid., 265–66.
23. Jon Sobrino, *Jesus the Liberator: A Historical-Theological Reading of Jesus of Nazareth* (Maryknoll, NY: Orbis Books, 1993), 13.
24. Ibid., 83–84.
25. James H. Cone, *A Black Theology of Liberation*, Fortieth Anniversary Edition (Maryknoll, NY: Orbis Books, 2010), ix.
26. Ibid., 5.
27. Ibid., 1.
28. Cone, *God of the Oppressed*, 65.
29. Ibid., 106.
30. Ibid., 125.
31. Ibid., 123.
32. Ibid., 126.
33. Cone, *A Black Theology of Liberation*, 6.
34. Ibid., 8.
35. Robert E. Shore-Goss, "Gay and Lesbian Liberation Theologies," in *Liberation Theologies in the United States: An Introduction*, ed. Stacey M. Floyd-Thomas and Anthony B. Pinn (New York; London: New York University Press, 2010), 189.
36. The situation is further complicated by the fact that the terms used do not also designate the difference between earlier LGBT *liberation* theologies and later queer theologies (which focus more on destabilizing identities), such that some will use the word "queer" to identify their work while others argue this is a misnomer. Part of the contestation is over the use of the word "queer," with some arguing that earlier liberationist theologies cannot employ that term because of how it is based on notions of a stable identity, which Queer Theory has complicated. For more on the trajectory and development of Queer Theology, see: Grace Jantzen, "Contours of Queer Theology," *Literature and Theology* 15, no.3 (September 2001): 276–85; Elizabeth Stuart, *Gay and Lesbian Theologies; Repetitions with Critical Difference* (Burlington, VT: Ashgate, 2003); Mary Elise Lowe, "Gay, Lesbian, and Queer Theologies: Origins, Contributions, and Challenges," *Dialog* 48.1 (March 2009): 49–61; Patrick Cheng, *Radical Love: An Introduction to Queer Theology* (New York: Seabury Books, 2011).
37. Laurel C. Schneider, "Homosexuality, Queer Theory, and Christian Theology," *Religious Studies Review* 26, no. 1 (January 2000): 3.
38. Patrick Cheng, *Radical Love: An Introduction to Queer Theology* (New York: Seabury Books, 2011), 30.
39. Ibid., 30–31.
40. Giles Hibbert, "Gay Liberation in Relation to Christian Liberation," in *Towards a Theology of Gay Liberation*, ed. Malcom Macourt (London: SCM Press, 1977).
41. Cheng, *Radical Love: Introduction to Queer Theology*, 31.
42. Robert Goss, *Jesus Acted Up: A Gay and Lesbian Manifesto* (San Francisco: Harper San Francisco, 1993), xvii.
43. Ibid., 171.
44. Ibid., 77–78.
45. Ibid., 82.
46. Ibid., 84.
47. Ibid., 85.

48. Cheng, *Radical Love*, 30.
49. Sathianathan Clarke, *Dalits and Christianity: Subaltern Religion and Liberation Theology in India* (Delhi: Oxford University Press, 2000), 18.
50. V. Devasahayam, "Pollution, Poverty and Powerlessness—A Dalit Perspective," in *A Reader in Dalit Theology* (Madras: Gurukul Lutheran Theological College, 1990), 1.
51. A. P. Nirmal, "Doing Theology from a Dalit Perspective," in *A Reader in Dalit Theology* (Madras: Gurukul Lutheran Theological College, 1990), 139.
52. John C. B. Webster, "From Indian Church to Indian Theology: An Attempt at Theological Construction," in *A Reader in Dalit Theology* (Madras: Gurukul Lutheran Theological College: 1990), 96.
53. Israel Selvanayagam, "Waters of Life and Indian Cups: Protestant Attempts at Theologizing in India," in *Christian Theology in Asia* (Cambridge: Cambridge University Press, 2008), 61.
54. Webster, "From Indian Church to Indian Theology," 98.
55. Ibid., 98–100.
56. Arvind P. Nirmal, "Towards a Christian Dalit Theology," in *A Reader in Dalit Theology* (Madras: Gurukul Lutheran Theological College: 1990), 56.
57. Ibid., 58.
58. Ibid., 57.
59. Selvanayagam, "Waters of Life and Indian Cups," 61.
60. Nirmal, "Towards a Christian Dalit Theology," 59.
61. James Massey, "A Review of Dalit Theology," in *Dalit and Minjung Theologies: A Dialogue* (Bangalore: South Asia Theological Research Institute, 2006), 4–5.
62. Saral K. Chatterji, "Why Dalit Theology?" in *A Reader in Dalit Theology* (Madras: Gurukul Lutheran Theological College: 1990), 23.
63. Nirmal, "Towards a Christian Dalit Theology," 62.
64. Gutiérrez, *A Theology of Liberation*, xxv–xxvi.
65. Cone, *A Black Theology of Liberation*, xx–xxi.
66. Ibid., xxii.
67. Linn Marie Tonstad, "The Limits of Inclusion: Queer Theology and Its Others," *Theology and Sexuality* 21, no. 1 (2015): 3.
68. Robert E. Shore-Goss, "The Holy Spirit as Mischief-Maker," in *Queering Christianity: Finding a Place at the Table for LGBTQI Christians*, ed. Robert E. Shore-Goss (Santa Barbara, CA: Praeger, 2013), 102.
69. Daniel M. Bell, Jr., *Liberation Theology after the End of History: The Refusal to Cease Suffering* (London: Routledge, 2001), 43.
70. Pears, *Doing Contextual Theology*, 170.
71. Although Williams challenges both black liberation *and* feminist theology's exclusion of African-American women's perspective(s) respectively, we will focus mainly on the former here because of the way these two discourses unfold and develop, especially as it pertains to the topic of this book. As we have seen, liberation theology's emphasis on the preferential option represents a pertinent example of problematic exclusivity in theology; feminist theology, on the other hand, did not typically emphasize such an exclusive divine choice for women. Of course, a case could be made for further exploration into the ways in which feminist theologies—especially in their earliest iterations—paralleled a similar move that could be read as exclusive in order to counter women's oppression. But for the sake of clarity of focus we will concentrate predominantly on the way in which these problems manifest themselves in liberation theologies. Ironically, such a *choice* performs and instantiates yet another example of the very thing I have set out to explore: the inevitability, necessity, and problematic nature of exclusive choice and decision.
72. Delores S. Williams, *Sisters in the Wilderness: The Challenge of Womanist God-Talk* (Orbis Boks, 1995), 1.
73. Ibid.
74. Ibid., 144.
75. Ibid., 149.
76. Ibid., 144.

77. Ibid., 149.
78. Ibid., 158–60.
79. Katie G. Cannon, "Hitting a Straight Lick with a Crooked Stick: The Womanist Dilemma in the Development of a Black Liberation Ethic," *The Annual of the Society of Christian Ethics* vol. 7 (1987): 171.
80. Kelly Brown Douglas, "Twenty Years a Womanist: An Affirming Challenge," in *Deeper Shades of Purple: Womanism in Religion and Society*, ed. Stacey M. Floyd-Thomas (New York: NYU Press, 2006), 145.
81. Ibid., 147–48.
82. Williams, *Sisters in the Wilderness Challenge of Womanist God-Talk*, 1.
83. Lorena Garcia, "Intersectionality" *Kalfou* 3.1 (Spring 2016), 102.
84. See: Kimberlé Crenshaw, "Demarginalizing the Intersection of Race and Sex: A Black Feminist Critique of Antidiscrimination Doctrine" *University of Chicago Legal Forum* (1989): 139–68; Kimberlé Crenshaw, "Mapping the Margins: Intersectionality, Identity, and Violence against Women of Color" *Stanford Law Review* 43.6 (1991): 1241–1300.
85. Devon W. Carbado, Kimberlé Williams Crenshaw, Vickie M. Mays, "Intersectionality," *Du Bois Review: Social Science Research on Race* vol. 10.2 (2013): 303–4.
86. Diana Fuss, *Essentially Speaking: Feminism, Nature and Difference* (New York: Routledge, 1989), xi.
87. Serene Jones, *Feminist Theory and Christian Theology* (Minneapolis: Fortress Press, 2000), 25.
88. Bill Ashcroft, Gareth Griffiths, and Helen Tiffin, *Post-Colonial Studies: The Key Concepts* (London: Routledge, 2001), 78.
89. Jones, *Feminist Theory and Christian Theology*, 29.
90. Nikki Sullivan, *A Critical Introduction to Queer Theory* (New York: NYU Press, 2003), 41.
91. Ibid., v.
92. Ibid., 42–43.
93. Stuart, *Gay and Lesbian Theologies; Repetitions with Critical Difference*, 10.
94. See: Marcella Althaus-Reid, *Indecent Theology: Theological Perversions in Sex, Gender and Politics* (London: Routledge, 2001).
95. Stuart, *Gay and Lesbian Theologies; Repetitions with Critical Difference*, 102.
96. Sathianathan Clarke, "Subalterns, Identity Politics and Christian Theology in India," in *Christian Theology in Asia*, ed. Sebastian C. H. Kim (Cambridge, UK; New York: Cambridge University Press, 2008), 272.
97. Ibid., 273.
98. Ibid., 274.
99. Ibid., 276.
100. Ibid., 276–77.
101. Ibid., 276.
102. Ibid., 277.
103. Ibid.
104. Ivan Petrella, *Beyond Liberation Theology: A Polemic* (London: SCM Press, 2008), 2.
105. Miguel A. De La Torre, *Doing Christian Ethics from the Margins* (Maryknoll, N.Y: Orbis Books, 2004), 18–19.
106. Darryl M. Trimiew, "Ethics," in *Handbook of U.S. Theologies of Liberation*, ed. Miguel A. De La Torre (St. Louis, MO: Chalice Press, 2004), 108.
107. Thandeka, *Learning to Be White: Money, Race and God in America* (Bloomsbury Academic, 2000), 46.
108. Ibid., 43.
109. Ibid., 45.
110. Torre, *Doing Christian Ethics from the Margins*, 20.
111. Manuel Mejido Costoya, "Rethinking Liberation," in *Rethinking Latino(a) Religion and Identity* (Cleveland: The Pilgrim Press, 2006).
112. Ibid.

113. Kate M. Ott, "Feminism and Justice: Who We Are, What We Do," in *Faith, Feminism, and Scholarship: The Next Generation*, ed. Melanie L. Harris and Kate M. Ott (New York: Palgrave Macmillan, 2011), 38.
114. Ibid., 40–41.
115. Ibid., 42.
116. Ibid., 42–43.
117. Joerg Rieger, ed., *Opting for the Margins: Postmodernity and Liberation in Christian Theology*, 1st edition (New York: Oxford University Press, 2003), 5.
118. Ibid.
119. Harold J. Recinos, ed., *Wading through Many Voices: Toward a Theology of Public Conversation* (Lanham, MD: Rowman & Littlefield Publishers, 2011), 6.
120. Ibid., 7.
121. Marcia Riggs, "Escaping the Polarity of Race versus Gender and Ethnicity," in *Wading through Many Voices: Toward a Theology of Public Conversation*, Harold J. Recinos, ed. (Lanham, MD: Rowman & Littlefield Publishers, 2011), 11.
122. David Batstone et al., eds., *Liberation Theologies, Postmodernity and the Americas* (London; New York: Routledge, 1997), 1.
123. Sharon D. Welch, "Dancing with Chaos: Reflections on Power, Contingency, and Social Change," in *Liberation Theologies, Postmodernity and the Americas*, ed. David Batstone et al. (London: Routledge, 1997), 126.
124. Ibid., 127.

Chapter Four

The Injustice of Indecision

We must make decisions about where God is at work so we can join in the fight against evil.

—James Cone, *A Black Theology of Liberation*

We can give the impression of neutrality, of not choosing at all, because to support the established order is to engage in routine, to move with the flow, to refrain from deliberation and perhaps even to disattend from the situation.

—Patricia McAuliffe, *Fundamental Ethics*

The previous chapter painted a bleak picture for liberation theologies. Intersectionality, the multilayered and imbricated nature of systemic oppression, and the insight that no identity or experience is stable and pure, have all contributed to the declaration of the death of liberation theologies. One of the reasons for the consensus that we should move beyond liberation theologies is because it oversimplifies that which is more complex. In its early stages, declaring that God is on the side of the poor, African-Americans, or LGBT persons initiated a radical and liberative break with the unjust status quo wherein these groups were subordinated, oppressed, excluded. But the bloom was not on the rose for very long, for as we have seen, injustice and identity are not so easily defined. And so one of liberation theology's central tenets, the preferential option, was exposed for its limits; in fact, it was shown to actually exacerbate the problem. Movements based on preference for a particular group, identity, or form of justice were discovered to have deleterious effects on the very struggles for justice that motivated them by obstructing solidarity, keeping power at the top and out of the hands of the oppressed, and further occluding and silencing identities and experiences. In light of these insights, it is no wonder that we would continue to be wary of decisions that cut, divide, exclude. In short, when justice and liberation is the goal and aim, such decisions appear thoroughly problematic.

Without rejecting these insights, this chapter is an attempt to probe deeper into this problem by asking what is lost if and when our pursuits for justice move further and further away from difficult decision points. Without wholeheartedly endorsing decisions that cut, divide, and exclude, it seeks to highlight how indecision is just as—if not more—problematic than such limited decisions for a particular group or form of justice. It is an attempt to continue the conversation, by embracing the importance and necessity of more recent work in liberation discourses, while also gleaning insights from its early work, through an appreciation of the inescapability of making limited, difficult decisions for particular forms of justice or targeted groups. My fear is, as always, that we might slip into thinking we have solved the problem, that we have moved beyond these limited views and stand in a privileged position over them. In fact—as a bit of foreshadowing here—privilege might be an important factor to keep in mind.

In an attempt to pull this off, this chapter follows a similar pattern to Chapter 2. Just as the goal there was to critically analyze foregoing understandings of undecidability so that we do not rest easy thinking we have safely avoided the dilemma, here too there is a parallel objective. While current conversations about the complexity of identity acknowledge blind spots in early liberationist work that perpetuated injustice, more recent discussions might also be subject to a mistaken belief that one could avoid difficult decision(s), and in so doing also perpetuate injustice. More than an apologetic about whether or not liberation theology is still considered a viable approach—in the pursuit of justice or as a method of theological engagement—the main focus of this chapter is to glean insights from early liberationist work, taking into consideration and building upon recent discourses, in order to more responsibly deal with the problem of in/decision. It is truly in the spirit of advancing and continuing the conversation that began decades ago and resurrecting some of the early insights. To that end, I will argue that the predicament is such that we must make difficult (i.e., inescapably divisive) decisions for justice, even while recognizing their limits. In so doing it will paint a more complicated picture of this predicament, such that there is no way to have the right perspective on things, no way to see it all or avoid the complexity and muddiness of the dilemma. Building upon and seeking to make concrete the insights of Part I, this chapter explores the relevance of Derrida's reflections on justice and the inescapability of decision where he writes: "No justice is exercised, no justice is rendered, no justice becomes effective . . . without a decision that cuts and divides."[1] Simply put, this chapter seeks to explore to what extent such choice, preference, and decision might be inescapable and necessary for the pursuit of liberation from material oppression, even if/when such decisions might inevitably be problematic.

Furthermore, I will focus primarily on the way that power and privilege distort our understanding of difficult decisions. I will argue that one only ever mistakenly inhabits the illusory position of indecision, i.e., standing outside the decision point, as a reflection of power and privilege. Drawing on insights in women's and gender studies and critical race theories about how privilege is defined as the ability to exist—or believe one exists—outside or beyond gendered, raced, sexualized identity markers, I argue that the belief that one could avoid the difficult decision reflects such privilege. Even more specifically, I am seeking to dispel the illusion of a safe ground, upon which one might retreat to, with regard to problematic, messy, complicated, and difficult decisions. Simply put, power and privilege can blind us into thinking that we are outside, above, beyond the decision point, such that we might be able to avoid the difficult decision.

THE ILLUSION OF INDECISION

We begin straight away by seeking to dispel the notion of indecision, at least as any sort of remedy to the problem. This was, indeed, one of the main goals of Part I—to highlight that there is no escaping or avoiding decisions that cut, divide, exclude. But given the import and emphasis on context in Part II, it is worth exploring how that general, structural, deconstructive insight applies to more concrete and specific circumstances concerning justice and liberation. We should also recall from Chapter 3 that the early liberationist voices recognized the need to navigate some form of exclusivity, as a remedy to the problem of exclusivity. Although not explicitly stated in the previous chapter, it is insightful to point out here the connection between that move and the insights of the deconstructive *pharmakon*. More importantly, it is important to also tease out the connection between the *pharmakon* and subsequent critical reactions to these early, limited liberationist moves and attempted remedies of them.

As you might remember from our discussion of the *pharmakon* in Chapter 1, Derrida describes it as that which is both remedy and poison. We find a sustained reflection on the *pharmakon* in "Plato's Pharmacy," where Derrida performs a close reading of *Phaedrus* as a way of demonstrating the frustrated attempts of philosophy to maintain an appropriate relationship with writing, which is the *pharmakon* to speech. Writing was given to speech as a gift or remedy, in order to help with memory and knowledge, but, as the myth about the origin of writing in *Phaedrus* explains, it also becomes a poison as it causes further forgetfulness. Hence, writing functions as both a remedy and poison for speech.

Early on in the essay, Derrida draws upon a conversation between Phaedrus and Socrates, where the former reminds Socrates that those citizens of high regard and stature, the ones with the greatest influence and dignity, feel ashamed at speechwriting because of its connection to sophistry. The reason for their shame, Phaedrus explains, is that these citizens do not want to be considered "sophists," those who do not intend to communicate the truth, but merely play with words and language in order to make spurious arguments. As Phaedrus confirms, writing—as opposed to speech—is associated with the "logographer," a ghost writer who composes speeches that he himself will not deliver; in fact, this ghost writer will not even be present at the time the speech is given. These writings will, therefore, "produce their effects in his absence." Such absence is key to Derrida's investigation into the de/valuation of writing in Western philosophy, as you might recall. In the speech/writing binary, the former attempts to distance itself from the latter because of the binary of presence/absence, where speech is associated with presence and writing with absence. Derrida elaborates on the danger and fear of writing that is assumed in this binary and its relation to speechwriting: "In writing what he does not speak, what he would never say and, in truth, would probably never even think, the author of the written speech is already entrenched in the posture of the sophist: the man of non-presence and of non-truth."[2] Writing is significantly denigrated to speech in Western thought because the former entails distance and absence, and, in so doing, it retreats further and further from the (pursuit of) truth. If Western philosophy is a series of attempts to return to the origin of self-presence (i.e., what Derrida calls a "metaphysics of presence") as a way of attaining what is true, then writing will always be suspect and secondary because it is constituted by absence—writing (always) produces in absence of the writer.

Derrida continues his reading of *Phaedrus* when Socrates tells a myth explaining the origin of writing. As the story goes, the god Theuth presents writing as a gift to the Egyptian king and "father" of the gods, Thamus, as a remedy for forgetfulness. Theuth had previously brought many gifts to Thamus, "numbers and calculation, geometry and astronomy, not to speak of draughts and dice"; and each time "Thamus questioned him about the usefulness of each one." Again and again Theuth thoroughly defended the value of the gift given to the god-king, but even more so in this case: "when it came to writing, Theuth said, 'This discipline, my King, will make the Egyptians wiser and will improve their memories: my invention is a recipe (*pharmakon*) for both memory and wisdom.'"[3]

Derrida pauses here to reflect on this interaction. Even though the value of writing as a gift has been spelled out to the king, it is the king, ultimately, who will determine its value: "The value of writing will not be itself, writing will have no value, unless and to the extent that god-the-king approves of it." In other words, writing has no value until the king decrees it as valuable. This gift "comes to him from outside but also from below," and as such it "awaits his condescending judgment in order to be consecrated in its being and value." Even though Thamus does not know how to read or write, i.e., doesn't need writing, this ignorance or inability "only testifies to his sovereign independence" over writing—he is not beholden to it in anyway because he stands outside or above it. The god-king only needs speech, not this gift-supplement to it: "He has no need to write. He speaks, he says, he dictates, and his word suffices. Whether a scribe from his secretarial staff then adds the supplement of a transcription or not, that consignment is always in essence secondary."[4] The god-king has the power to de/value writing, because it is always a supplement to the power, presence, and effectiveness of his speech. He has no need for writing himself, that is the work of those who are secondary, beneath and below him. He is independent, sovereign; he speaks and it happens. And if he does decide to accept this supplement of writing, it will always be depreciated. Moreover, the god-king will always be suspicious and watchful toward it.

Derrida of course makes the connection between the de/valuation of writing by the god-king and the way in which writing is viewed in Western philosophy, following Plato. We ought "to pay systematic attention," Derrida argues, "to the permanence of a Platonic schema that assigns the origin and power of speech, precisely as *logos*, to the paternal position." Moreover, this indebtedness to Plato, "which sets up the whole of Western metaphysics in its conceptuality," follows suit and illustrates "with incomparable subtlety and force" the de/valuation of writing.[5] In other words, in the indebtedness to Plato that follows in Western philosophy, speech has always been understood to have power and presence, while writing can only ever be associated with supplement and absence.[6]

However, the supplement is not *only* secondary, as Derrida goes on to illustrate. Writing is given to speech as a remedy in order to help with memory and knowledge; and the translation of *pharmakon* as remedy "is not, of course, inaccurate," Derrida maintains. But at the same time, as the myth of the origin of writing corroborates, "the effectiveness of the *pharmakon* can be reversed: it can worsen the ill instead of remedy it."[7] Thus *pharmakon* can mean both remedy and poison. It is "always caught in the mixture" between cure and ill, pleasure and pain. This leads Derrida to declare: "There is no such thing as a harmless remedy. The *pharmakon* can never be simply beneficial."[8] As we see in the story told by Socrates, writing both helps the forgetfulness that accompanies speech by being able to record what is communicated; but it also becomes a poison as it causes further forgetfulness, for there is now no need to remember as we can rely upon the written text. That which was added to speech and memory, as supplement, as secondary, has now infected them, revealing how "the outside is already *within*" and how "the evil slips in" unsuspectingly, unwillingly.[9] In fact, the infection of the outside within is only realized, i.e., happens, precisely when there is an attempt to remedy, purify, and protect. In other words, when one's intentions were quite the opposite. The poisonous effects of the *pharmakon* are only felt when it is administered as remedy—one only ever experiences the so-called "side effects" of a drug when it is ingested as remedy to an ailment. The unintended result of the gift of writing, therefore, is the revelation of an absence and secondariness that speech itself could never be immune from, that it was always already trafficking in.

Having revisited this notion of the *pharmakon*, let us draw some connections with our present focus. Early liberationists recognized the need for exclusive preference as a response to the problem of exclusivity and oppression. In this way, that move can be understood as a manifestation of the *pharmakon*—the remedy that entails poison. Every remedy will contain traces of that which it is intended to avoid, eliminate, and rectify. That which writing was meant to fix or cure becomes the unintended, deleterious, and dangerous result of the cure itself. Writing was meant to remedy memory, but ends up being detrimental to it in the process. Seen the other way around, writing as a cure for forgetfulness manages to perpetuate and exacerbate forgetfulness. Similarly, the remedy to exclusivity and injustice in early liberationist work manages to perpetuate and even exacerbate both, as we have seen in the previous chapter. In a sense, then, more recent work has called out the way that early liberationists could not escape the problem of exclusivity, were always navigating some form of it, and have thus critiqued the limits of these earlier approaches that never escaped the problem they intended to rectify. Exclusive preference for one group or form of justice perpetuated injustice, exacerbating it by pitting oppressed communities against each other and by occluding the complexity of identity and injustice, further silencing and marginalizing other Others. This was the conclusion reached in Chapter 3.

However, there is a further connection to be drawn with the discussion of the deconstructive aporia in Part I. The above analysis is, unfortunately, the accepted reading and understanding of deconstruction, full stop. It is that which allows us to recognize the limits of every attempt (at anything). Just as the deconstruction of the speech/writing binary reveals that the problem is never solved, so readings of Derrida are enlisted to muster a similar kind of critique of any such attempt (at anything). Prevailing readings of Derrida (and Caputo) are thus employed to critique institutions, religious doctrines and dogmas, and decisions, using the former to highlight the limits of the latter, the impossibility of doing what they set out and intend to do, showing how they could never resist, escape, or avoid the very thing intended to be remedied. In the most present case, this is the critique leveled against early liberationist work that could never escape the problem of exclusivity, injustice, and oppression. Its best attempts always came up short as recognition and appreciation for the complexity of identities and injustice increased.

But as I argued in Part I, while such a critique is indeed accurate, it represents only one aspect of what deconstruction reveals in the double-bind. Stopping there initiates a new binary, wherein previous attempts are denigrated to some new, higher, better approach. Because if we rest merely on the critique, if we just focus on the limits of every attempt, then we end up repositioning ourselves in a similar binary, which is the very thing the *pharmakon* deconstructs. If the *pharmakon* offers any insight, it is that *all* attempts to fix, solve, or rectify a problem will come up short—including critiques of every limited attempt. Stopping at the critique inevitably leads to privileging one approach to another. In this case, it would mean privileging indecision to any limited decision. However, the revelation of the *pharmakon* that every remedy will always contain the very thing it intends to cure includes those critiques of every limited attempt. In fact, the *pharmakon* reveals its poison precisely at the moment when it is used to remedy. The outside is always already within. It has slipped through the back door unsuspectingly. There is no way to escape or move beyond it, no pure remedy that would solve the problem once and for all. This includes, most especially, even those that identify the limits of every attempt and rest in that critique. What this means, then, is that even the best, most sophisticated attempts to avoid priority, preference, decision in the pursuit of justice—as we saw in Chapter 3—can never be pure remedies to these issues. Just as priority, preference, and decision for particular groups or forms of justice were revealed for their limits, attempting to avoid such will also have its limits. More than anything else, that is the insight that I am hoping to make clear in this chapter (and throughout the book as a whole).

In fact, it is the problem with any attempted "move beyond" that might offer the insight most pertinent to the pharmacological issue of decision with regard to injustice. Let us also consider, for a moment, the standpoint of the god-king. He stands outside, beyond, above. Writing, as a gift-supplement to him is below, beneath him. He has no need of it, for his spoken word has power and effect, it actualizes and is causal, which means he has no need of this supplement that is secondary. As a result, he can look down upon writing and see it "clearly" for its limits. The god-king sees that it does not accomplish what it should or even what it intends to; it is limited in its effectiveness. Worse still, it is something that we—or He—should keep a watchful eye on because even though it is secondary, it is still dangerous. Again, Derrida relates this position and stance of the god-king to the Western metaphysics of presence in the speech/writing binary. It is from this fatherly, transcendent location, "from the position of the holder of the scepter" that "writing is indicated, designated, and denounced."[10]

What I seek to draw our attention to in this chapter is a similar connection between a supposed space of indecision and this kind of detached, powerful, privileged position. This place that stands beyond or outside, wherein decisions can be "indicated, designated, and denounced." I seek to sharpen our critical analysis on the position where difficult decisions are seen as merely secondary, supplementary to something else, something better. This is the space of indecision that reflects the power and privilege to stand outside, above, beyond, where, like the god-king, there is no need to make limited decisions. In short, part of what this chapter intends to highlight is the way that power and privilege leads us to make such pronouncements and denouncements about decisions that are limited, that cut and divide. It is an attempt to reflect upon such an identification and the desire to avoid these decision points because we (at least some of us) have the power and privilege to do so.

By drawing our attention to the role that power and privilege plays in navigating the problem of in/decision, I want to be as clear as possible and reiterate the importance of context. In the subsequent argument I will suggest revisiting the necessity for making difficult decisions in the pursuit of justice and how power and privilege has an ability to distort one's perspective about this predicament, tempting us to retreat to a place of indecision. It is important to note—and clarify—however, that the argument is radically contextual and thus aimed at an analysis of the function of such power and privilege. Of course, the very topic of systemic injustice and oppression should draw our attention to the fact that some are not (always) afforded the opportunity and occasion of making decisions, which is surely a privilege in and of itself. Some are, unfortunately, stripped of that ability by circumstantial or societal situations. My argument for making difficult decisions, then, could be seen as exacerbating the issue by assuming a certain supply of power and privilege that affords one the ability to do so. This is certainly not my intention, as the argument is very much directed at those who do in fact have the opportunity and privilege of not deciding. In fact, it is intended to urge those of us with such privilege to continue to struggle to recognize it, and, as a result, make decisions that critically engage the circumstances and societal apparatuses that deprive certain individuals with the ability to make their own decisions. And the first step in that process is a more thorough analysis of the positions of power and privilege that we inhabit.

If and when we pause and reflect upon the impact of power and privilege, it will not lead us to a place wherein we wholeheartedly endorse decisions that cut, divide, and exclude or reject the insights explored in Chapter 3 about the problems that this engenders. What it will do is heighten our vigilance with regard to these issues, causing us to further reflect upon and analyze difficult decision points—at least that is my intention. In so doing it might urge us to reconsider stopping at the denouncement of limited decisions and recognize the inescapability and necessity of them as much as we critique them. Similar to the argument in Part I, this chapter is an attempt to resist the collapse into a simple either/or. Recent discourses have, fortunately, drawn attention to the complexities of identity and injustice, revealing the limits of earlier work and decisions that continue to cut, divide, exclude. I am merely urging us to reconsider how moving too far in that direction can be problematic as well, and thus what is needed is an equally strong argument for resisting indecision.

In a sense, then, the early liberationists—in their limited, imperfect attempts—were more transparent about what they were doing, recognizing, as they often did, the confines and issues of an inescapable, problematic dilemma. Such transparency is part of what we are after as we revisit some of these insights, seeking to expose and highlight the problem of indecision and critique it as harshly as any limited, problematic decision. In so doing, a more complex and complicated predicament will emerge wherein we might acknowledge that there is no remedy that is not also poison. Again, the goal and intention of the argument is not to collapse into a nihilistic or apathetic state with regard to these issues, but to heighten our vigilance, advance the conversation, and continue in the struggle against injustice in its various forms.

Indecision as Decision for the Status Quo

In order to fully understand the way power and privilege might lead us to a place of indecision and the concomitant problems that emerge as a result, it is worth revisiting one of the central tenets of liberationist work as a way of exposing the multiple layers of this issue. As we saw in the beginning of Chapter 3, the recognition of the necessity for exclusive preference emerged in response to the material conditions of oppression. Early liberationists recognized that only a radical break with the unjust status quo would suffice in order to attain liberation from these injustices, not development or progress *within* it. Anything less would remain trapped in the power dynamic of dominance and oppression. Patricia McAuliffe highlights these conditions of oppression, hegemony, and exclusion, which always form the backdrop and context of these issues that we need to keep in mind:

> Our experience of the world is not one of harmony, order, a God-given plan. Rather it is overwhelmingly one of disharmony, disorder, suffering, oppression. People are being destroyed due to their class, sex, sexual orientation, color, religion, language, because they are "too" old or because they are "handicapped" . . . ; other species and the environment are being destroyed because they are seen as mere means to some people's ends. We are an "already damaged *humanum*" in an already damaged cosmos.[11]

This obvious entry point for liberationist work cannot be overstated. The central premise is that we are already in the midst of disharmony, suffering, oppression; there is no clean slate here from which to work. As McAuliffe goes on to reassert, the reality of these structural injustices require or necessitate a paradigm shift in liberationist ethics: "Unless resistance to suffering and oppression is at the center and core of our ethics, unless it is its *raison d'être*, then ethics, our ethical lives, ourselves as ethical beings cannot be taken seriously."[12] McAuliffe's point echoes one of the most fundamental tenets of liberationist work: an awareness of systemic oppression and exclusion, the identification of a need for a paradigm shift to adequately address it, and the necessity of making liberation the center of this work. Consequently, she therefore agrees with the liberationist conviction that any movement away from exclusive preference or priority will always undercut the work for liberation.

McAuliffe also goes on to argue, however, that choice and preference are inevitable and inescapable. Furthermore, she maintains, the more we are convinced that we are not choosing sides, the more likely it is that we are supporting the status quo, i.e., the systemic injustice, oppression, and exclusion that is the current structural reality:

> In spite of the fact that our very historicity implies that we have to take sides, there are situations which create the illusion that: (1) we are being neutral, we are not choosing when, in fact, we do and must choose, or (2) we are being objective in the sense of supporting a value-free situation when the situation we support is but an option which is value-loaded, or (3) we are choosing a universal such as universal love, when we are being partial, choosing to side with some who are in conflict with others. In all these cases, it is when we choose the established order, the structures that are in place, the powers that be, the status quo, that our choice may give the appearance of being objective or universal or simply a neutral nonchoice. *We can give the impression of neutrality, of not choosing at all, because to support the established order is to engage in routine, to move with the flow, to refrain from deliberation and perhaps even to disattend from the situation.*[13]

McAuliffe touches on several important insights that this chapter seeks to flesh out. One of the most central is teasing out those "situations which create the illusion" of indecision, of retreating to a space where we come to believe that "we are not choosing, when, in fact, we do and must choose." Part I intended to dispel the general, structural illusion of indecision, and our task here is to relate that to the context of struggles against injustice. Additionally, I will argue that this illusion of indecision is a by-product of power and privilege such that when we think we are being "objective," "value-free," or "choosing a universal," we are inevitably "choosing to side with some who are in conflict with others." For McAuliffe the illusion of neutrality or nonchoice is often, and in fact likely, just a disguised decision for the status quo. She challenges us to consider that when we think we have avoided such problematic choice and preference we have merely decided "to engage in routine, to move with the flow" of the unjust established order. This is an important point to reflect upon, especially as it relates to decision and power.

Beverly Tatum, attempting to help white people understand the way that racism functions, uses two fitting analogies that describe the inescapabilty of being affected and infected by the ubiquity of racism in a society that normalizes, and thus hides, this reality. The first is her description of racism as smog: "Cultural racism—the cultural images and messages that affirm the assumed superiority of Whites and the assumed inferiority of people of color—is like smog in the air."[14] Tatum points out that in a racist society we are continually bombarded by images and "misinformation about people different from ourselves" that reinforce white superiority. From early on in our life, and throughout, we experience continued segregation, which means we do not often interact with, or learn about firsthand, "others," i.e., those who are "racially, religiously, or socioeconomically different from ourselves."[15] Consequently, this secondhand information—if and when we do receive it—is at best incomplete and often distorted. And Tatum argues that such "omitted information" about others who are different than us can be as problematic as distorted information because it leads us to believe, and trust, that the information we are learning about society is accurate. She describes repeated experiences with her college students who admit to never having learned about black authors or thinkers, leading one frustrated white male student to declare: "It's not my fault that Blacks don't write books." While certainly disheartening, Tatum reflects on what circumstances would have led an otherwise bright and educated person to conclude this: "Had one of his elementary, high school, or college teachers ever told him that there were no Black writers? Probably not. Yet because he had never been exposed to Black authors, he had drawn his own conclusion that there were none."[16] This student, like all of us who live in a society that reinforces the superiority of whites, had been inhaling the smog of racism his entire life.

Smog is such a fitting analogy because it is not immediately visible and apparent, despite the fact that it is always present. "Sometimes it is so thick and visible," Tatum admits—and recent events in the United States (and globally) continue to corroborate explicit, overt racism at work. Other times, in fact most often I would argue, this smog is less apparent. "But always, day in and day out, we are breathing it in."[17] Of course, none of us want to admit to being "smog-breathers." And this is even more the case when the result of breathing in such smog means that we have developed prejudices and been infected by a racist society.[18] Tatum asks us to consider, however:

> But if we live in a smoggy place, how can we avoid breathing in the air? If we live in an environment in which we are bombarded with stereotypical images in the media, are frequently exposed to the ethnic jokes of friends and family members, and are rarely informed of the accomplishments of oppressed groups, we will develop the negative categorizations of those groups that form the basis of prejudice.[19]

This is inevitable. To believe that one can avoid the infection of racism and white supremacy is as foolish as believing that one can somehow avoid being infected by smog, even if the pollution is not immediately apparent or the effects are not often felt.

Recent studies by the Kirwan Institute for the Study of Race and Ethnicity scientifically verify the way in which prejudice and bias infect us unsuspectingly. In one of its first iterations of the "State of the Science: Implicit Bias Review" in 2014, the report documents "30 years of findings from neurology and social and cognitive psychology showing that hidden biases operating largely under the scope of human consciousness influence the way that we see and treat others, even when we are determined to be fair and objective."[20] The studies by the Kirwan Institute reveal how our understanding, actions, and decisions are affected by implicit bias, unconsciously, involuntarily, and without awareness or intentional control. Moreover, everyone is susceptible to implicit biases and the studies refer to it as "an 'equal opportunity virus' that everyone possesses, regardless of his/her own group membership."[21] In fact, that is precisely how racism—like other forms of systemic domination and oppression—functions: those who benefit most from it cannot see it, because the system is working to their advantage. We will return to this important insight about privilege below.

But the image of racism as smog might lead us to believe that since it is not "our fault" we are somehow relieved of the responsibility for addressing it. This is why Tatum also employs the image of the conveyor belt, where racism is like a conveyor belt that every one of us find ourselves standing on. In this analogy, "active racist behavior is equivalent to walking fast on the conveyor belt," as when walks with the moving walkway at an airport. This is the case for those who actively identify with the ideology of white supremacy and are seeking to advance it. Again, this is certainly, and unfortunately, evident in contemporary society and worth addressing at every turn. But the analogy (literally) gains even more traction when we also come to recognize that "passive racist behavior is equivalent to standing still on the walkway." When no overt, explicit effort is made, Tatum explains, the conveyor belt still "moves the bystanders along to the same destination as those who are actively walking" with it. Even though the intention might be completely different, passivity will lead to the same destination, albeit in a much slower and less deliberate way. This strongly resonates with McAuliffe's point above, that we might give the impression of neutrality or not deciding, but in reality, we are just standing on the conveyor belt of the racist, unjust status quo and, therefore, still implicitly supporting (i.e., deciding for) it. Thus Tatum concludes that unless someone actively decides to walk "in the opposite direction at a speed faster than the conveyor belt—unless they are actively antiracist—they will find themselves carried along with the others."[22] Returning again to the smog analogy, Tatum reinforces the need for decisive action in order to resist racism:

> We may not have polluted the air, but we need to take responsibility, along with others, for cleaning it up. . . . Am I perpetuating and reinforcing the negative messages so pervasive in our culture, or am I seeking to challenge them? If I have not been exposed to positive images of marginalized groups, am I seeking them out, expanding my own knowledge base for myself and my children? Am I acknowledging and examining my own prejudices, my own rigid categorizations of others, thereby minimizing the adverse impact they might have on my interactions with those I have categorized? Unless we engage in these and other conscious acts of reflection and reeducation, we easily repeat the process. . . . It is not our fault, but it is our responsibility to interrupt this cycle.[23]

What Tatum is describing here is what McAuliffe mentioned above—that unless we are explicitly deciding *against* injustice (e.g., racism), we are inevitably deciding for it. Unless we consciously and decisively walk faster in the opposite direction, we inevitably will be carried along with it. As Tatum points out, it is not enough to merely stop moving with it, for inaction and indecision in the midst of injustice is ineluctably a tacit decision for supporting it. If the smog is ubiquitous, then there is no escaping it. There is no option to merely step off the conveyor belt. The best that we can do is to decide to walk even faster in the opposite direction of the conveyor belt if any ground is to be gained. Similarly, I am arguing that there is no way to "step off" or avoid the issues I have tried to highlight, to retreat to an illusory position of indecision, because one is either moving with the unjust status quo (and the multiple forms of injustice that entails) or actively moving against it.

Discussing a similar issue, Ada Maria Isasi-Díaz recounts the problem she faced in *Mujerista Theology: A Theology for the Twenty-First Century* by attempting to give voice to "grassroots Latinas" struggling against injustice and "using" or "speaking for" them. While such issues of "representation" are certainly concerning and pressing, Isasi-Díaz maintains that she cannot assume a "retreat position." Invoking the work of Linda Alcoff, Isasi-Díaz argues: "to retreat from all practices of speaking for others assumes that one *can* retreat into one's discrete location and make claims entirely and singularly within that location that do not range over others, that one can disentangle oneself from the implicating networks between one's discursive practices and others' locations, situations, and practices." She goes on to write: "But there is no neutral place to stand free and clear in which one's words do not prescriptively affect or mediate the experience of others . . . even a complete retreat from speech is of course not neutral, since it allows the continued dominance of current discourses and acts by omission to reinforce their dominance." This is precisely the argument I am making in this chapter about the illusion of retreating to a space of indecision with regard to difficult choices about justice. The reason for the illusion of an ability to retreat to this so-called safe place, Isasi-Diaz argues, is the assumption of "the autonomous conception of the self in Classical Liberal theory."[24] This autonomous conception of the self is synonymous with the concept of privilege that we will hone in on.

As McAuliffe points out, if "nonchoice," neutrality, or impartiality is an illusion—*and* such decisions and partiality are revealed to be problematic—then we should be even more careful and discerning about which choices we are making and what we are choosing to support. More poignantly, McAuliffe stresses the need for ethics to be concrete, and given the fact that the condition we live in is one of "disharmony, disorder, suffering, oppression," those concerned about liberative justice should recognize that "not choosing at all," or limiting the exclusivity, partiality, or preference of the choice for specific, particular oppressed groups or forms of justice, will only continue to perpetuate these oppressions. McAuliffe goes on to argue that in order to gain equality and liberation, in order to work against the injustice of inequality, oppression, marginalization, and exclusion that is the current reality, we might need to be impartial, preferential, and exclusive, because to do anything less is to merely engage in the "business as usual" approach of injustice:

> We argued that if there is to be justice, and the love which includes everyone in the benefits of society, we cannot merely treat everyone as though she or he were equal. We must engage in equalizing by favoring the worst off. This is the only means by which we can even approach universal justice and love. Besides, we cannot avoid taking sides. To attempt to be neutral, to do nothing, is to support the structures that are in place; if we do not explicitly side with the oppressed . . . we will at least implicitly side with oppression.[25]

McAuliffe's point certainly resonates with the consensus among early liberationists—that the movement away from exclusive preference can become a tacit preference for oppression. In a hierarchical, stratified society, not explicitly working against particular forms of injustice results in implicitly siding with them. Exclusive preference is necessary for justice, because "equalizing"—or even including—means favoring those currently deprived of justice. "If there is to be justice, and the love which includes everyone," then such preference is a necessary ingredient.

Despite the fact that such preference is complicated, as we have seen, by any stable, pure identification of oppressor/oppressed, throughout the navigation of this issue there has been a similar recognition. Particularly in womanist and intersectional responses to black liberation discourses, the way in which the problem of exclusion—i.e., the exclusion, silencing, marginalization of African-American women inherent in the category "black"—is navigated. It appears that the only way to account for the experience that is silenced in the broad category (i.e., black) is to name said experience (i.e., womanist) more particularly. To put it differently, to be more "inclusive" one might need to be more "particular," because broad, thick, "universal" categories simply cannot capture the more specific, particular experiences of complex identities. Thus, we see a counter-intuitive dynamic at work wherein broadening might mean being more specific, otherwise those who are silenced, marginalized, and oppressed will always remain so. This is the very nature of marginalization and oppression—the dominant perspective normalizes and hides itself, in order to remain in power. For example, "theology," without any prefix or indicator, assumes an objective, universal viewpoint; but as liberationists argue, all theology is contextual: "The idea of theologizing from a position of complete 'objectivity' is a myth constructed to protect the privileged space of those with the power to determine how the discipline is to be defined. In short, objectivity is the dominant culture's subjectivity."[26] Thus, anything "other than" the dominant perspective (e.g., white, male, Western, European, heteronormative, etc.) warrants an adjectival label: e.g., African American/black, Womanist, Latino/a, Native American, LGBTQ, etc. In other words, because "the center is secured," all other theologies (and disciplines) are understood as deviating from this male, Western, Eurocentric, heteronormative perspective, and consequently, understood as less authoritative, significant, and important, which only perpetuates marginalization and oppression. Some liberationist work, therefore, suggests a move toward greater particularity—including priority, preference, and decision—in order to limit or avoid the inherent exclusivity of the status quo.

The foregoing argument is not one that any of the voices in Chapter 3 would necessarily disagree with. The critiques about the limitations of preference are not suggesting that we simply do nothing, inhale the smog and stand still on the conveyor belt of racism, sexism, homophobia, etc. And it is certainly not my intention to suggest that this is the consensus. At the same time, however, I am arguing that we should be wary of how the complexities of identity and machinations of injustice might lead us to forget this central insight and be lured into the illusion of indecision—or at least an ability to escape the difficult decision point(s). These early insights, though limited in their approach to the issues, were indeed insightful. And my point is not to negate the more recent critiques and complexities in an attempt to return to a simple identification of the problem wherein exclusive preference, choice, and decision are unleashed in a way that perpetuates further injustice and oppression. It is simply to point out, as poignantly as more recent critiques, the dangers of indecision about particular forms of justice and how that also perpetuates injustice.

Where this argument gains the most traction is when we also come to recognize, in light of more recent insights, that there is not just one conveyor belt of injustice (e.g., racism). Identity and injustice are not so simply understood. To continue to play with this analogy, we have to acknowledge that while one person may indeed be walking *against* one conveyor belt, they might find that they are now walking *with* another. This is the real predicament that I am trying to highlight. And it is this insight that has led to the critiques and resistance of preference for one particular group or form of justice. While my argument is not intended to ignore these critiques, it is intended to challenge us to recognize that walking in the opposite direction of conveyor belts, i.e., making difficult decisions, is still necessary in light of this complexity.

COMMITMENT TO PARTICULAR FORMS OF JUSTICE: THE NECESSITY OF PRIORITIZING (AND EVEN OPPOSING)

In the essay, "Is a Womanist a Black Feminist? Marking the Distinctions and Defying Them: A Black Feminist Response," Traci C. West makes several important points regarding the relationship between womanist and black feminist scholarship. But there is one brief point toward the end of the essay that is especially pertinent to, and illuminating for, our present focus. In discussing her work on violence against black women, West states that such work entails prioritizing women's safety and well-being, even if and when that might conflict with womanist commitments to racial solidarity. West writes:

> My work on the experience of intimate violence against black women requires the privileging of support for their wholeness. It involves my adamant opposition to maintaining silence about black male violence against them, a silence that is too often demanded out of concern for what image of black people descriptions of this black male violence might invoke in the minds of white people. Because my allegiance to women's wholeness takes priority, the womanist commitment to the wholeness of the black community as an expression of its communalism would not necessarily be an essential goal for me. Also, my liberationist commitments to pointing out the problem of black male clergy who sexually harass women congregants . . . may generate divisiveness that violates womanist notions of black communal unity.[27]

Here West admits that womanist commitments to black communalism and unity—in order to fight the injustice of racism in the United States—ran up against her own commitments to the safety and wholeness of black women. Thus, West's "adamant opposition" to silence about black male violence against women may have violated womanist concerns about black unity and solidarity, especially because of how it might be co-opted to reinforce stereotypical images of violent black men and thus reinforce racist views. In other words, West acknowledges that her allegiance to women's wholeness must take "priority" over her allegiance to "black communal unity." Put differently, West recognizes that the commitment to black unity and the protection of black men's image because of racial injustice was in conflict with her commitment to women's wholeness because of the injustice of intimate violence. For West, at some point these commitments part ways, and then a difficult choice must be made: *which* commitment takes priority? As West presciently acknowledges, it appears that we cannot have it both ways, for a both/and approach—as is a common response to the problematic nature of complex identities, intersectionality, identity politics, etc.—will not work. In this case, West identifies that priority must be shown in order to adequately work against the injustice of intimate violence against black women because silence, inaction, or indecision will only continue to perpetuate these injustices. West's recognition and admission that these kinds of difficult decisions are necessary if particular forms of justice are to be realized is extremely insightful. It highlights not only the imbricated nature of oppression and injustice, whose boundaries are not easily identified, but an appreciation for the difficulty in navigating this reality.

In "Heteropatriarchy and the Three Pillars of White Supremacy: Rethinking Women of Color Organizing," Andrea Smith corroborates the complicated terrain of work for justice by highlighting the complex machinations of white supremacy and the limits of previous attempts to engage it. "The premise behind much 'women of color' organizing," Smith writes, "is that women from communities victimized by white supremacy should unite together around their shared oppression."[28] But this approach—like the attempted avoidance of difficult decisions—is limited, Smith argues, because "it tends to presume that our communities have been impacted by white supremacy in the same way" and "that all of our communities share similar strategies for liberation," when, in fact, "our strategies often run into conflict."[29] In other words, Smith points out that because of the complexity of oppression—in this case, white supremacy—oppressed groups often become complicit in the further oppression of other oppressed groups.

Outlining what she calls the logic of three pillars of white supremacy, Smith highlights how victims of one pillar of white supremacy actually become complicit in another form of it by being "seduced with the prospect of being able to participate in the other pillars." Smith's three pillars demonstrate how white supremacy is constituted by separate, but still interrelated, logics: slavery/capitalism, genocide/colonialism, and Orientalism/war. The mistake is when we substitute the workings of one of these pillars for another, and, in so doing, continue to perpetuate the logic of one pillar of white supremacy even while working against another. Worse still, is assuming that one pillar of white supremacy is the only one. Because white supremacy is a complex system of domination, it is structured in such a way that in each of these three logics there is the seduction of participating in another's oppression in order to elevate oneself: "For example, all non-Native peoples are promised the ability to join in the colonial project of settling indigenous lands. All non-Black peoples are promised that if they comply, they will not be at the bottom of the racial hierarchy. And Black, Native, Latino, and Asian peoples are promised that they will economically and politically advance if they join U.S. wars to spread 'democracy.'"[30] In each of these pillars of white supremacy a subjugated group is invited to participate in the subjugation of another. Smith thus argues that such complexity must further heighten the vigilance needed in order to address injustice and oppression—a point that I have been trying to make throughout this book. To draw a connection between Smith's three pillars and Tatum's analogy of the conveyor belt, the notion that we can step off of one conveyor belt means that we inevitably end up on another. Or, perhaps even worse, as we walk in the opposite direction of one conveyor belt we might find that we are now walking in the same direction as another.

Again, it is an awareness of the complicated nature of injustice and identity that has led to the resistance of decisions that cut, divide, and exclude. But West's distinction among priorities raises an important issue for liberationists to reckon with: might the necessary work for liberation demand such difficult decisions, choices, and priorities? Might (concrete) liberation entail a kind of specificity, particularity, and even exclusivity that runs up against *other* commitments—even "adamant opposition" to them (as West admits)? And might such an acknowledgment entail a kind of transparency, accompanied by an increased vigilance in dealing with the reality of such difficult decisions? In light of the logic of the three pillars of white supremacy, Smith suggests "making strategic alliances," which is indeed a necessary ingredient in the struggle for solidarity. But might we also need to recognize that at times these alliances will also run up against other alliances? And yet might we still be wary that such a recognition of the problem need not lead us to back away from such commitments to particular forms of justice, lest we end up merely riding on a conveyor belt?

Of course, the complexities continue to multiply, and I must address at least one more layer to this problem, of which the key ingredient is power and privilege. I raise the above questions bearing in mind the pertinent and sober warning West highlights in the opening of *Disruptive Christian Ethics:*

When Racism and Women's Lives Matter: "The inevitability of conflict over moral issues seems to grant permission to wound those one opposes by targeting and trampling the most vulnerable, manipulating those who are least informed and most fearful, and doing whatever else seems necessary to claim moral superiority and power over others."[31] West makes an important point that resonates with the consensus of critiques in Chapter 3 about conflict over moral issues. But she also adds a focus on the reminder of how power operates in these dynamics. All along I have been suggesting that there are limits to avoiding priority, preference, and decision with regard to justice, and more recently, how doing so might also inevitably lead to conflict among those who work for justice. In so doing, there is a real danger that I might be read as trying to highlight "the inevitability of conflict" in order "to grant permission to wound" as a way "to claim moral superiority and power over others." This is an extremely pertinent point, and I cannot stress enough that this is certainly not my intention. Raising a concern of inevitable conflict may indeed be subject to this critique—especially coming from a position of power, privilege, ability, and history of wounding those at the margins—but my intention is quite the opposite: I raise this issue *because* of my concern for and commitments to justice, liberation, and the dismantling of oppression and privilege.

More importantly and fundamentally, however, my argument is pointed in the opposite direction because it is an attempt (however limited in scope) to highlight how critiquing priority, preference, and decision might also be a way of claiming superiority and working from a place of power and privilege. It is an attempt to highlight how the critiques levied against decisions that cut and divide can also be read as, and with, a representation and enactment of such superiority, privilege, and power. It is aimed at those of us who are concerned about injustice as an attempt to resist the temptation and disrupt our thinking that in so doing we have solved the issue. It is an attempt to defy the very lure and deception of power and privilege through a more transparent recognition of the complexities, which is the target of West's critique in the preceding quotation. Moreover, it is attempting to build on West's admission of the necessity for priority, preference, and decision, even if and when they run up against other commitments for justice—especially when we too also want to engage in those struggles as well. As a result, this entire argument is intended to continue the conversation through a further analysis of power and privilege and therefore resist any temptation to grant permission to wound and trample.

With an appreciation for these concerns in mind, then, I urge us to consider: do our commitments for justice and the priorities they entail mean that at some point we will inevitably have to part ways, even with others who are working for justice? If so, what does that mean for our attempts at "building a shared ethics"?[32] Might each of us, depending on our justice commitments, have certain non-negotiables or priorities that preclude us from such a shared ethic, or at least a recognition that we might have to part ways, we might have to choose or prioritize, we might have to adamantly oppose other commitments? In other words, might we have to make difficult decisions that cut, divide, and exclude?

The kind of "exclusivity" I am suggesting here is not meant to insinuate permanent, absolute, once-for-all exclusive decisions; it is, as I have been arguing, "strategic" in that it is temporal, conditional, contingent. I am merely trying to highlight the edges of difficult decisions and choices entailed in the work for liberation. Thus it is still *exclusive*, even if not permanently or absolutely so. If systemic injustice and oppression means a stratified, hierarchical society where those targeted will remain there because the dominant position is perpetuated through power, then justice might entail a kind of strategic, exclusive priority *for* particular oppressed, marginalized, excluded groups (and *against* particular forms of injustice), because anything less than such will not be radical enough to disrupt the status quo. In other words, if liberation—concrete, particular liberation—is not made an explicit priority, then it will never occur. To the extent that this is the case, it would mean that liberationist work for "justice" or "the oppressed" as abstract categories might never be particular or concrete enough to do the work it intends to do. This, in turn, would cause those of us striving for justice to discern *whose* liberation to pursue, *which* injustice to work against, and therefore a recognition of the necessity of limited, problematic, exclusive decisions required in such work. We are now beginning to reach the pinnacle of what this chapter intends to highlight: a "truth in advertising" moment—the work of liberation, as a way to remedy exclusion, entails some version of strategic (i.e., temporary) exclusivity. And it is up to us who desire to join the struggle for liberation to acknowledge this, partly to "be honest," but more so to maintain vigilance in recognizing that there is no remedy to the problem that is not itself also poisonous. I affirm the nervousness about such preference, choice, and decision, and why it is so problematic, which is why vigilance is so necessary in the navigation of such. My suggestion that resisting the notion that we have escaped some version of the issue dovetails with the Derridean insights of Part I, and might help aid liberationist work by revealing the structural impossibility to remedy the problem of exclusion without navigating some form of it, because the problem is inescapable. As always, I must remind the reader that my goal in highlighting such a dynamic is never intended to be nihilistic or, worse, an apologetic *for* exclusion, but a keener evaluation of the predicament in order to increase our vigilance in engaging it.

LIBERATION DEMANDS PARTICULARITY

How might such insight affect the strident critiques about the problem of exclusivity that were raised in Chapter 3? In particular, Kate Ott suggested that integrating our work for justice should be concerned about working for one justice over and against another, because "when we choose one 'justice' to focus on (because of our identity affiliation), are we in turn doing injustice to others?"[33] As I stated above, this is a pressing concern that should be taken seriously. At the same time, however, Ott's response to this insight now bears more critical reflection, as she suggests that we "should be erasing modifiers of justice" in order to be more broad, expansive, and inclusive enough of all forms of injustice.[34] But should we not also be concerned about the erasure of such modifiers? This movement toward expansion, broadening, inclusion is important, but perhaps we should also be concerned about letting it become the pervasive movement in our work for justice because, as Ott maintains: "Justice-seeking requires that we start somewhere. It is a concrete action."[35] Justice demands concrete action, which, it appears, is a movement toward particularity and closure, lest the erasing of modifiers of justice become erasures of particular identities and the way they are the targets of particular forms of injustice. Liberationist work seems to suggest that in order for there to be concrete justice at all, we must take stands, choose, prioritize, show preference—even if/when such choices are problematic (i.e., exclusive). Perhaps returning to an acknowledgment of the veracity of one of liberation theology's fundamental insights is important to keep in mind, namely that in order to rectify and redress injustice, priority must be shown, otherwise it will perpetuate.

What I am suggesting, however, is not an unbridled move to preference and priority without concern for exclusion. Much to the contrary, I am not suggesting—or could suggest—a remedy that might both avoid exclusion (because of priority, preference, and decision—i.e., limiting justice—as Ott suggests) *and* result in justice for those in desperate need of it (because justice can only ever be achieved, even for some, through priority, preference). I think the best that we might be able to do, at this point, is raise the issue: can we ever achieve a justice without modifiers; or does "erasing modifiers of justice" also result in injustice? Might liberation demand particularity and specificity with regard to the justice it seeks to achieve, recognizing the limited nature of such and the necessity of making tough, limited (exclusive) decisions? The work for justice might entail a specificity, particularity—even exclusivity—in order to adequately attain the justice pursued, as "justice for all" might not be specific or concrete enough. Precisely because of the complex nature of stratification, oppression, and domination, those of us concerned about concrete justice—defined as naming and working against the injustice of those particular oppressed groups—should be aware of the predicament liberationist work must engage.

In a somewhat recent compilation of essays entitled *No Salvation Outside the Poor: Prophetic-Utopian Essays*, Jon Sobrino highlights this very dynamic by exploring "voices of hope" in the Latin American liberation theological tradition to address the contemporary reality of "cruel inhumanity." Sobrino begins by writing:

> The underlying reflection is about our present world, a world of poverty and opulence, victims and victimizers; about the salvation and humanization that are so urgently needed; and about where that salvation and humanization might come from. They are all based on the words of Ignacio Ellacuría in his last speech, given in Barcelona on November 6, 1989, ten days before his assassination: "The civilization is gravely ill—sick unto death, as Jean Ziegler says; to avoid an ominous, fatal outcome, the civilization must be changed." With absolute and radical clarity Ellacuría added, "We have to turn history around, subvert it, and send it in a new direction." Today's world, the official and politically correct world, refuses to listen, and in any case to take the radical action required by the utter gravity of the problem.[36]

Here, Sobrino, through Ellacuría's speech, is highlighting the urgency and exigency of the current globalized, neoliberal socioeconomic society in which we live, and the desperate need for prophetic voices to awaken us "from the sleep of cruel inhumanity," and force us to confront the accusations: "Are these not human beings? . . . Do you not see this? Do you not feel it? How can you stay in such lethargic sleep?" Sobrino is invoking the liberationist sentiment that we need something radical to disrupt "the drawn shades of indifference"[37] that plague our contemporary situation.[38]

In Sobrino's chapter on liberation theology's option for the poor, however, we find the tension of attempting to urge the radical shift necessary to disrupt such indifference, while also navigating the inherent exclusivity in the preferential option. On the one hand, Sobrino—heeding the concerns expressed in Chapter 3—highlights the issue: "the option becomes a way to move toward a truly human and *inclusive* globalization that does not paradoxically become antihuman and *exclusive*."[39] Throughout his chapter on the preferential option, Sobrino affirms the critiques of its exclusivity, maintaining that it is, was, and remains "'preferential' but 'not exclusive.'"[40] On the other hand, although Sobrino explicitly names exclusion as problematic, he also suggests that it—or something close to it—might be necessary.

Sobrino insists on four elements in order to properly understand the preferential option for the poor in today's world. First, he suggests a "dialectic element" that requires confrontation, which is often avoided, he argues, because "dialogue, negotiation, and tolerance" are the preferred methods of engagement. In a reality of division between the oppressor and oppressed, however, Sobrino argues that anything less than confrontation is inadequate. He writes: "Of course, we must avoid and control violence as much as possible, but an option for the poor that fails to be dialectical, that is not an option against oppression, is not the option of Jesus; in the long run it leaves the poor at the mercy of the oppressor."[41] Sobrino's point about the necessity of confrontation for justice resonates closely with what I have been suggesting, namely that justice demands opposition, deciding *for* and *against*.

Sobrino's second element is "partiality." Appreciating and anticipating the nervousness that accompanies this language, Sobrino insists on retaining it "because it has been said, fallaciously, that 'equality' (or at least a gentler inequality) is possible, a sufficiently human 'universality,' and that this miracle would come about through neoliberal globalization." He goes further: "The flaw in the metaphor is that there's room for 'everyone' on the globe, which is an obvious lie. We mention this to emphasize that if the goal is salvation for the poor of this world, they must be explicitly placed at the center."[42] Here is the pinch that Sobrino so deftly highlights: anything less than partiality or "explicitly" placing "the poor . . . at the center," will not achieve the liberation intended. The real pinch, however, is that "the poor" cannot encompass all forms of oppression or exclusion. So Sobrino's point is accurate, but once we recognize that such partiality might also run up against other forms of injustice, oppression, and exclusion, the problem becomes more complex. Again, *if* liberation is the goal, which requires partiality and preference in order to disrupt the status quo, it appears a kind of strategic exclusivity is required. The reason for this, as I have stated, is because discussion of universality, inclusion, "all," etc., is not radical or particular enough. In fact, these modern universalities were the very thing that funded and perpetuated oppression, marginalization, exclusion in the first place; "that is why a contrary thesis is needed, and a willingness to take sides," writes Sobrino.[43]

To use a pertinent illustration of what is at stake here, we should consider the debate between "black lives matter" and "all lives matter." If liberationist work has taught us anything, then we should (and likely have come to) recognize that claiming "all lives matter" will never achieve justice, and thus it is necessary to protest "*black* lives matter," precisely because the status quo, the current situation and reality, indicates that they do not. But protesting "black lives matter" might also be problematic, as the issues raised in Chapter 3 identify, precisely because of what the category or identifier "black" entails. It can be understood as too exclusive or particular; for instance, it does not name *other* lives that unfortunately do not matter in our society: LatinX, LGBT, poor, immigrant, non-human lives, etc. Additionally, it is also not broad, expansive, or inclusive enough of all the injustices in our present society if it does not take into account how the category/label "black" is constructed, who is included/excluded in that category, its stability, complexity, and lack of intersectionality. And, as we have seen, this can mean that taking a stand for racial solidarity might mean marginalizing other issues of injustice. Although protesting "black lives matter" does not necessarily imply that other lives do not, what liberationist work reveals is that in a racist society we have to declare explicitly and protest, "*black* lives matter," even as we recognize that this does not include all forms of injustice, which means that it might further the exclusion and oppression of those others. Such is the double-bind of in/decision in liberationist work that I have tried to highlight: a necessity to make difficult decisions for the liberation of particular oppressed groups, while recognizing the impossibility of avoiding perpetuating exclusion and oppression for others.

"WE MUST MAKE DECISIONS"

If the work for liberation requires that we must choose and prioritize, even when such decisions might be problematic, what conclusion might we reach? Similar to Part I, I am not suggesting that there could ever be one answer, conclusion, or solution to this dilemma that avoids all the landmines. In fact, drawing on the notion of the *pharmakon*, my argument is precisely the opposite—there is no remedy that is not also itself poisonous. But returning to one of the earliest voices in this conversation might shed some insight into how to best navigate this dilemma transparently and vigilantly.

As we have seen, in the 1986 preface to *A Black Theology of Liberation*, James Cone admits limitations to his exclusive preference for African-Americans. At the same time, however, he also affirms that his "view of white theology is generally the same today as it was in 1970."[44] Cone writes:

> I was determined to speak a liberating word for and to African-American Christians, using the theological resources at my disposal. I did not have time to do the theological and historical research needed to present a "balanced" perspective on the problem of racism in America. Black men, women, and children were being shot and imprisoned for asserting their right to a dignified existence. Others were wasting away in ghettoes, dying from filth, rats, and dope, as white and black ministers preached about a blond, blue-eyed Jesus who came to make us all just like him. I *had* to speak a different word, not just as a black person but primarily as a *theologian*. I felt then, as I still do, that if theology had nothing to say about black suffering and resistance, I could not be a theologian.[45]

Cone's reflection upon the exigency of the situation facing the black community, which compelled him to "speak a different word"—i.e., "a liberating word" in the midst of oppression—reflects the sentiment that liberation demands an urgent, radical break from the status quo. Unfortunately, some thirty years later, the situation of racism in the United States is not drastically different than what Cone depicts here; in which case, we should genuinely ask whether there is not still a similar kind of exigency to (continue to) "speak a different word." Such exigency reflects, in fact, what Derrida described as the experience one encounters in the face of the undecidable.

Cone acknowledges that the situation was so dire that he did not have the luxury or time to present a "balanced" perspective on racism. Although, upon further reflection, he can admit some limitations to this earlier work (i.e., that racism was not the only form of oppression in the United States), he stands by the fact that he felt an obligation to "speak forcefully and truthfully" about the realities of racism and the hope of God's empowerment for those who resist it, especially because "theology" (i.e., *white* theology) was tacitly endorsing and perpetuating racism and *its* unjust exclusivity. He stands by the fact that he had to make a difficult decision. Clarifying that his goal was never to make black theology "acceptable to white racists and their sympathizers," he maintains the task of theology is not intended to be merely "a rational discourse about ultimate reality," it is also, and should be, "a prophetic word" that must be spoken in "clear, strong, and uncompromising language."[46] For Cone, this prophetic word included speaking truth to white theologians who had defined the discipline of theology, reinscribing the centrality of liberation in Christianity, pointing out the heresy of racism, and exposing the fact that (white) theology was nothing more than a "racist, theological justification of the status quo."[47] In his estimation, only a radical break with the status quo (i.e., "white theology") can begin the necessary work for liberation and justice. As Cone says, the exigency of the situation meant that "it was not time to be polite, but rather a time to speak the truth with love, courage, and care for the masses of blacks."[48] The "truth," for Cone, is the content of black theology, namely "that the liberation of the black community *is* God's liberation," meaning that theology is the process of interpreting God's liberating activity, which concerns, in the context of the United States, racism and the reality of the oppressed black community.[49] And Cone is uncompromising in maintaining that preference for the oppressed excludes the oppressor or oppressive situation, e.g., "white theology."

Moreover, Cone, anticipating an obvious reaction to his bold, particular, definitive—seemingly exclusive—claims about preference for African-Americans, expects that some will inevitably ask: "Why *black* theology?"[50] What about other injustices? Don't others also suffer under oppression? Don't even whites suffer from (certain forms of) oppression, especially in light of more recent work that identifies the multiplicity, hybridity, and complexity of identities and experiences, including the fact that race is not the only category by which people are oppressed? Cone offers several responses to these questions, including his claim that "in a revolutionary situation there can never be nonpartisan theology," that "God is never color-blind" or indifferent to injustice, and even an admission that "there are, to be sure, many who suffer, and not all of them are black."[51] But in the midst of these comments, Cone offers a telling response that might be insightful given the terrain we have just covered: "We must make decisions about where God is at work so we can join in the fight against evil." Cone is clear—in the end, we *must* make decisions, even if/when such decisions are problematic, limited, unbalanced, exclusive—perhaps even when they cannot account for, or include, other peoples, perspectives, and forms of injustice. Although he recognizes the problematic exclusivity of his claims, the alternative is itself problematic, i.e., the illusion of indecision, because of his concern about how that merely serves to perpetuate the oppressions and exclusions that are already so firmly in place. In other words, it might not be a matter of avoiding problematic decisions, but *which* decisions are we going to make? Cone, reflecting upon this precarious predicament, admits that the unjust status quo and task of theology places each of us in "an existential situation" where there is a burden "to make decisions without a guaranteed ethical guide." He calls this "the risk of faith." And indifference is not an option: "Either God is for blacks in their fight for liberation from white oppressors, or God is not. God cannot be both for us and for white oppressors at the same time."[52]

For Cone, it is clear that systemic racism ineluctably places each of us in a difficult, problematic situation wherein we cannot remain neutral: either we (tacitly) support racism, or we fight against it. And indifference or indecision is support because anything less than focusing explicitly on racial injustice is merely standing on the conveyor belt of racism. On the one hand, this seems to be reiterating what liberationists have said all along; on the other hand, Cone seems to suggest that the explicit focus on *racial* injustice might run up against *other* injustices. And this is where the critiques in Chapter 3 have entered the conversation, recognizing the way competing interests among oppressed groups is problematic for the work of liberation, and thus critiqued exclusive preference for one (oppressed group, injustice) at the expense of others. But it is Cone's transparency here about the inescapability of such limited decisions that is most insightful; he is not unaware about the problematic nature of his particular focus and emphasis on racial injustice, but he nevertheless appears to be acutely aware of the necessity for such.

THE PRIVILEGE OF INDECISION

Although Cone recognizes the problematic predicament of difficult decisions, he seems to be suggesting a kind of inability to escape it. Put simply, Cone suggests we cannot focus on *all* forms of injustice, oppression, exclusion; we do not inhabit that privileged position. And "privilege" might have a lot to do with the predicament I have been trying to sketch. In *God of the*

Oppressed, just after he had made a thorough argument for the blackness of Jesus Christ, Cone finds it necessary to meet his critics head on: "I realize that my theological limitations and my close identity with the social conditions of black people could blind me to the *truth* of the gospel. And maybe our white theologians are right when they insist that I have overlooked the *universal* significance of Jesus' message." In the 1970s Cone was already being critiqued for his over-emphasis on particularity, and while he admits his limitations and the lack of "universality" in his approach, he also quickly adds: "But I contend that there is no universalism that is not particular." Every standard of universality—Cone presciently argues as a forerunner to many similar post-structuralist responses—will always bear the marks of particularity. "Indeed their insistence upon the universal note of the gospel arises out of their own political and social interests" as well, Cone argues; white theologians just couldn't see that.[53] They believed they were merely just doing theology, universal Christian theology, and so when Cone argues that Jesus was black—even though his "whiteness" is purely a product of Western, European influence in an attempt to make Jesus reflect the dominant identity—it sends a shockwave through their theological frameworks. Besides revealing an implicit racism that would be so scandalized by the blackness of Jesus, the fact that white theologians struggled to see that their theologies were also particular, and that even their "universal notes" were always *from* particular locations, experiences, and identities, is a reflection of their power and privilege.

Privilege, e.g., white privilege, is a product of structural supremacy and dominance in a society or culture; in a sense, it is the inverse experience of oppression. When one group is targeted as "defective or substandard," then the rest—which is the dominant group—"is seen as the norm for humanity."[54] In a racist society, then, "white privilege is a concrete manifestation of how whites benefit from white supremacy."[55] As the dominant perspective, which is the norm, it is rarely identified by the one who inhabits and privileges from this position—and even more so, rarely recognized and acknowledged. When it is the accepted norm, there is no need to acknowledge and identify that part of one's identity. For instance, white people rarely mention their race, heterosexuals rarely mention their sexuality, able-bodied individuals rarely mention their abilities, etc. Moreover, society does not identify people this way either. When was the last time you heard someone refer to someone as "my white doctor," "my heterosexual brother," or "my able-bodied friend"? In a society where whiteness, heterosexuality, and certain standards of ability are the norm, there is no need to mention this fact, whereas you might often hear someone's race, sexuality, ability, religion, etc., be mentioned as an important identifying factor if they fall outside of the culturally dominant norm.

In an evening lecture at Drew Theological School in 2016, Thandeka told a story about her experience with a fellow faculty member as a young assistant professor. This woman anxiously came up to Thandeka in the cafeteria, flagging her down and explaining that she always wanted to know what it felt like to be black. Thandeka agreed to answer, but only if the woman agreed to a game of sorts: Thandeka challenged the woman to use the word "white" as an identifier every time she referred to someone of that race, e.g., "I'm going to pick up my white kids now." After a week of doing this, Thandeka would agree to meet with her and discuss what it was like to be black. Not surprisingly, that discussion never took place; in fact, Thandeka never heard from this woman again. Thandeka challenged all those attending the lecture to the same game, but quickly added that it will be very difficult to do as you will not only feel awkward and strange, but you might be surprised at the hostile reactions you will receive by pointing out whiteness.[56] This reveals that whiteness is not just hidden and unspoken because it is the norm, but that any mention of it will bring race into a situation that white people would not expect, causing them to reflect on their own racial identity, which is something whites do not do because they often do not have to.

Beverly Tatum describes the machinations of (white) privilege: "That element of the person's identity is so taken for granted that it goes without comment. It is taken for granted by them because it is taken for granted by the dominant culture."[57] If it is difficult for the dominant perspective to notice that they do indeed inhabit the dominant position, it is even more difficult to acknowledge the benefits and privileges that go along with that. In what is by now an oft-cited and well-known article, Peggy McIntosh's "White Privilege: Unpacking the Invisible Knapsack" gives a laundry list of societal privileges and advantages she daily experiences by being identified as white.[58] The entire impetus and motivation for the article, however, is in an attempt to think deeply about and reflect upon these privileges that often go unnoticed. McIntosh had to work hard to identify the ways in which society simply "worked" for her, gifting her with a host of advantages that she hadn't asked for and rarely noticed. In this way, privilege operates surreptitiously in the smog of domination and oppression (e.g., racism). Just as we do not often notice the smog of racism, those who benefit from it do not often notice the privilege that accompanies it. This is why Cone's critics could not see the particularity of their own perspective, because they assumed they were inhabiting an objective, universal perspective, which reflects their inherent (white) privilege.

Returning again to critiques of Cone's exclusive preference *for* African-Americans and *against* the injustice of white/black racism, we sharpen our focus on a more thorough analysis of how power and privilege impacts this issue. As we have seen, Cone admits in the 1986 revised edition of *A Black Theology of Liberation* that he did not have the time "to present a 'balanced' perspective on the problem of racism in America" when he first wrote about it in 1970.[59] We have already teased out the temporal part of what Cone means here, that the exigency of the situation demanded a decision here-and-now. But there is another aspect to this issue, more spatial than temporal, that also requires unpacking—and it has to do with the machinations of privilege.

In *The Cross and the Lynching Tree*, Cone offers a theological reflection on the history of lynching in the United States and explores the symbolic connections between Jesus's death on the cross and the death of thousands of black men and women who also hung on trees. Cone insists that the lynching tree is a metaphor for race in America and assures us that we will not overcome this terrible reality, nor make any significant progress in the struggle against racism, unless we acknowledge its presence: "The lynching tree is the most potent symbol of the trouble nobody knows that blacks have seen but do not talk about because the pain of remembering—visions of black bodies dangling from southern trees, surrounded by jeering white mobs—is almost too excruciating to recall."[60] In the second chapter of *The Cross and the Lynching Tree*, Cone turns to the question of the silence among white religious leaders about Christians who permitted such atrocities. Focusing specifically on twentieth-century theologian Reinhold Niebuhr, Cone wonders how "even the most progressive of America's white theologians and religious thinkers" failed to see the striking similarities between the lynching tree and the cross on Golgotha—or at least failed to recognize and speak explicitly about this reality.[61] Niebuhr, a noted theologian concerned with issues of social justice in his time, not only focused a lot of attention on the cross but was also particularly sensitive to racial issues, often writing and speaking explicitly about the plight of African-Americans. Yet Niebuhr, like every other white theologian, Cone argues, failed to connect "the crucifixion of Jesus by Romans in Jerusalem and the lynching of blacks by whites in the United States."[62] The reason, Cone argues, is the distance that these white theologians' power and privilege provided them from the realities and everyday experiences of racism. It is "one thing to teach theology in the safe environs of the classroom and quite another to live one's theology in a situation that entails the risk of one's life."[63]

Contrasting Niebuhr's approach with that of Martin Luther King, Jr., Cone points out how the former was too "balanced" and measured in his response because of his privileged position. Despite Niebuhr's focus on Christian realism (i.e., the "facts of experience") and the tragic nature of the cross, Cone wonders: "was there not a limit to Niebuhr's imagination . . . was he ultimately blind to the most obvious re-enactment of the crucifixion in his own time?"[64] Even though Niebuhr was at times honest about the realities of racism and seemingly radical in his approach for justice, Cone still points out Niebuhr's blindness and the limits of his imagination. And the real edge of Cone's critique is directed at Niebuhr's "call for gradualism, patience, and prudence," especially while "Willie McGee, Emmett Till, M.C. 'Mack' Parker and other blacks" were being lynched. Cone goes on to reference Niebuhr's employment of notions like "wisdom" and "fairness" so as "not to push the southern white people 'off balance.'"[65] Cone draws on responses to the "tranquilizing drug of gradualism" by civil rights leaders like Dr. Martin Luther King, Jr., who replied to such calls for gradualism, patience, and prudence: "It is hardly a moral act to encourage others to patiently accept injustice which he himself does not endure."[66]

Cone argues that Niebuhr's contradictory stance on the injustice of racism was a product of his vantage point as a white man, drawing on Niebuhr's own analysis of this dilemma in *Moral Man and Immoral Society*, "that groups are notoriously selfish and have limited capacity to step outside their interests and see the world from another group's standpoint."[67] Thus Cone points out, "rather than challenging racial prejudice," Niebuhr "believed it must 'slowly erode.'"[68] And for Cone, it is clear that Niebuhr's identification with "the powerful white majority" is what led him to be so "calm and dispassionate" about the injustices of racism.[69] Recalling an interaction between author James Baldwin and Niebuhr, Cone points out how the exchange reveals "Niebuhr was speaking with a 'rationality' that 'belongs to cool observers,'" while "Baldwin was speaking what 'ought to be true; and may become true if its truth is not doubted.'"[70]

On the one hand, Cone's critique of Niebuhr merely points out the limits of each and every perspective. As a white theologian it was extremely difficult for Niebuhr to fully grasp the experiences "regarding black suffering in the white community."[71] But I think there is a deeper insight that Cone is teasing out. It is not just a matter of difference among perspectives, but of the power and privilege that accompanies the dominant perspective. Simply put, Niebuhr had the privilege of not having to be passionate and radical, because he was too far removed from the situation. His balanced, patient, prudent response was merely a product of his privileged position. In short, despite all his writings against injustice, he was lured into the illusion of the safety of indecision, of not having to make decisions that cut and divide. This is the real target, and edge, of my argument: to incite us to consider the power and privileged position we inhabit when we (merely) critique, and thus claim to avoid, decisions that cut and divide. When we do so, are we, like Niebuhr, retreating to "a 'rationality' that 'belongs to cool observers'"? To what extent is the safety of indecision not only problematic because it forestalls justice, but also because how it might reflect our own power and privilege?

If intersectionality has taught us anything, it means that none of us inhabit a stable position of oppressor or oppressed, dominant or targeted category. Recent scholarship on the complex nature of such domination also reveals that working against one form of injustice might mean participating in another. And while this might leave us wanting to retreat to a space of indecision, we have, by now, recognized that it is equally problematic. We are left in the predicament wherein we must be transparent and vigilant in reckoning with the inescapability of difficult decisions. As Jarune Uwujaren and Jamie Utt frankly remind us:

> Intersectional feminism is difficult. If you're doing it right, it should be challenging you, stretching you, and making you uncomfortable. But feminism isn't here to make anyone comfortable. Quite the contrary, intersectional feminism should be making everyone uncomfortable because we never grow or progress when we are comfortable. . . . The difficulty of intersectional feminism is a difficulty and discomfort that is meant to inspire change. Thus, we have to be willing to take up the critical thinking and self-work necessary to push back against our privileges and to create an intersectional ethic and lens through which our feminism is crafted.[72]

What Uwujaren and Utt are calling a willingness to do the *"critical thinking and self work* necessary to push back against our privileges," I have been referring to as *transparency* and *vigilance* in the face of the undecidable. To what extent is the lure of indecision a reflection of such power and privilege? Given the intersectional nature of identity, the imbricated reality of various forms of injustice, might we always be called to critically analyze our power and privileged position, especially when we can so easily identify the limits of decisions that cut, divide, and exclude? Again, this is not meant to suggest that these critiques are invalid—they have advanced the conversation in important ways, and continue to do so. But, as the above quotation suggests, this kind of intersectional analysis is meant to continue to advance the conversation and inspire change. Such a recognition might mean that we also have to turn as critical an eye back on our own positions and complicity in injustice—to be more transparent about our inescapable decisions, our various forms of privilege, and the illusion of avoiding such that we have been complicit in. And, consequently, to be even more vigilant in our struggle against them. This is one of the central insights of intersectionality and analyses of privilege. None of us safely inhabit any stable position of oppressor/oppressed. And in contrast to those who use this insight to justify continued oppression, my suggestion is that it should cause us to continue to scrutinize and be vigilant about the variegated and complex nature of injustice, resisting the temptation to retreat to a space of indecision in the midst of the impossible decision.

JUSTIFYING DECISIONS

In *Womanist Ethics and the Cultural Production of Evil*, Emilie Townes maintains: "Evil does not . . . come in pristine forms. Like goodness, it is messy and rather confusing."[73] In this chapter I have tried to show how the evils of injustice, oppression, and exclusion do not come in "pristine forms," and, consequently, that any attempts to subvert, dismantle, and work toward liberation will always be "messy and rather confusing." More specifically, this chapter has explored a depth and complexity to the problem of in/decision, i.e., its "evil-ness," in order to uncover its messiness. In the spirit of the work with deconstruction in Part I, my concern is that if/when we avoid difficult decisions that cut and divide, we might rest assured that we have accurately identified the problem and begun our good, responsible, ethical work of solving or remedying this problem. But the problem might not lend itself to such a simple analysis, identification, and remedy. It is much thornier, complicated—i.e., more *problematic*—than that. In the specific context of liberationist discourses, such an analysis, identification, and remedy might actually undercut this work, if/when it leads us to a state of indecision on such complicated matters. In other words, priority, choice, preference might be inevitable and necessary—even when recognized as problematic—for liberation. And thus the liberationist is left having to "make the journey on [his/her] own," as Townes reveals, discerning between *which* injustice and *whose* liberation.[74]

We have discovered that intersectionality continues to complicate the work for justice. While it can serve to reveal the limits of any decision *for* particular groups and *against* particular forms of injustice, it can also reveal how indecision can be a by-product of power and privilege. In this way, intersectionality is "always already an analysis-in-progress," mimicking the movement of deconstruction one might say, revealing the limits of any approach or assured destination. "All intersectional moves are necessarily particularized and therefore provisional and incomplete. This is the sense in which a particularized intersectional analysis or formation is always a work-in-progress, functioning as a condition of possibility."[75] Although we might redact the last word of this quotation to "im/possibility," this is precisely the reading of Derrida I have been endorsing, urging us to consider the issue of in/decision as it relates to issues of justice. In my continued desire to not rest easy in a state of indecision, it is always with the acknowledgment that all decisions will be "provisional and incomplete." Again, the goal is to build upon the insights of more recent discourses, including intersectionality, not undo them or work against them. And if injustice demands explicit attention for liberation, because anything less will leave the status quo intact and perpetuate injustice, then "we must make decisions" about which injustice to focus on.

Angie Pears critiques the tendency of theologies of liberation "to interpret and represent context in a narrow way," and, when combined with the preferential option, has led to further exclusion of other oppressed groups. She goes on to argue that "these theologies have failed to recognize the ongoing impact of hierarchies of oppression because of their concern to present a unified liberation theology."[76] Pears goes on to suggest "fluidity and reflexivity" with regard to context, and this very well may be a viable way forward. But my concern is less with coming up with an overarching, meta-analysis of how to work for liberation and more simply, and humbly, to highlight a tendency to move away from the radical emphasis on particularity and context that earlier liberationists pointed out; especially because of how this leads to a tendency to move away from the difficult decision point, retreating to a space of indecision as a reflection of power and privilege. As Petrella summarizes: "Here lies the famous epistemological break: liberation theologies—whether Latin American, black, womanist, African, feminist, queer etc.—realize that theology has traditionally been done from the standpoint of privilege."[77] And I am concerned that the further we move away from this insight, even in the midst of advances and progress, the more in danger we might be.

While I have been arguing throughout this chapter about the inescapability of making difficult decisions for the achievement of justice, there has been a consistent worry about misinterpreting what I am suggesting. To begin with, I am *not* seeking to propose that in the midst of these difficult decisions that one form of justice takes priority over another in any kind of normative way. It is these kinds of claims that one must decide *against*. Rather, in the pursuit of particular forms of justice, it is always enfolded within the hope that "justice for all" will eventually be realized. It is in the spirit of Martin Luther King, Jr.'s point that "injustice anywhere is a threat to justice everywhere" that I am attempting to make my point.[78] My emphasis has been on the first part, arguing that "injustice anywhere" is exigent enough to warrant here-and-now decisive action, even if and when that cannot account for all forms of injustice or may even be in conflict with them. But my argument is not at the expense of the latter part of King's point, "justice everywhere." It is the hope and dream of a world without any injustice that motivates the work against particular forms of injustice. In the midst of this work, however, I want to offer a reminder about certain limitations—that no one ever inhabits the bird's (or God's) eye perspective, such that they could see the whole and work it all out. In fact, my argument *for* confronting difficult decisions has always been directed at deconstructing such a perspective, such that the work for justice everywhere necessitates decisive action for particular forms of justice anywhere.

As we have seen in our overview of the emergence of dalit liberation theology in the previous chapter, the need for a radical theology of liberation emerged *in the midst of* so-called progress. It was then that the recognition of something more radical emerged. This chapter has attempted to revisit a similar sentiment. I am not suggesting that progress has not been made or mitigating the insights and advances of work that leads us to be nervous about priority, preference, and even more so about decisions that cut, divide, and exclude. I am merely suggesting a similar nervousness about stopping there by highlighting the problematic nature of indecision. And my argument intends to build upon these recent discourses, not reverse course. If the insights of intersectionality and the complicated nature of injustice are valid, then it means that none of us safely inhabits any stable or monolithic identity, experience, or perspective. That certainly means identifying the limits of approaches that are too narrow and particular as well as the unjust, exclusive implications of doing so. But if intersectionality "isn't here to make anyone comfortable," then it also means there needs to be transparent, vigilant, pervasive reflection on our inescapable decisions and the kinds of power and privilege that each of us complexly inhabit, especially when that leads to resting assured that a critique of definitive decisions about issues of justice is all the work we need to do. And that might mean confronting and discerning difficult decisions with regard to particular, specific, concrete injustices, *especially* for those of us who occupy positions of power and privilege.

NOTES

1. Derrida, "Force of Law," 28.
2. Derrida, "Plato's Pharmacy," 68.
3. Ibid., 75.
4. Ibid., 76.
5. Ibid.
6. To be clear, Derrida does not pin a metaphysics of presence, and a denigration of writing to speech, all on Plato: "Not that this happens especially and exclusively in Plato" (p. 76).
7. Derrida, "Plato's Pharmacy," 97.
8. Ibid., 99.
9. Ibid., 109.
10. Ibid., 77.
11. Patricia McAuliffe, *Fundamental Ethics: A Liberationist Approach* (Washington, D.C: Georgetown University Press, 1993), ix.
12. Ibid., x.
13. Ibid., 62.
14. Beverly Tatum, *Why Are All the Black Kids Sitting Together in the Cafeteria? And Other Conversations about Race*, Twentieth Anniversary Edition (New York: Basic Books, 2017), 86.
15. Ibid., 84.
16. Ibid., 85.
17. Ibid., 86.
18. For recent in-depth explorations of white reactions to anti-black racism, see: Carol Anderson, *White Rage: The Unspoken Truth of Our Racial Divide* (New York: Bloomsbury, 2017); Robin DiAngelo, *White Fragility: Why It's So Hard for White People to Talk about Race* (Boston: Beacon Press, 2018); Reni Eddo-Lodge, *Why I'm No Longer Talking to White People about Race* (London: Bloomsbury Circus, 2017).
19. Tatum, *Why Are All the Black Kids Sitting Together in the Cafeteria?*, 86.
20. *Kirwan Institute for the Study of Race and Ethnicity*, "State of the Science: Implicit Bias Review 2014," http://kirwaninstitute.osu.edu/.
21. Ibid., 16.
22. Tatum, *Why Are All the Black Kids Sitting Together in the Cafeteria?*, 91.

23. Ibid., 86–87.
24. Ada Maria Isasi-Díaz, *Mujerista Theology*, 7.
25. McAuliffe, *Fundamental Ethics*, 67.
26. Miguel A. De La Torre, ed., *Handbook of U.S. Theologies of Liberation* (St. Louis, MO: Chalice Press, 2004), 2.
27. Traci C. West, "Is a Womanist a Black Feminist? Marking the Distinctions and Defying Them," in *Deeper Shades of Purple: Womanism in Religion and Society* (New York: NYU Press, 2006), 294.
28. Andrea Smith, "Heteropatriarchy and the Three Pillars of White Supremacy: Rethinking Women of Color Organizing," in *Color of Violence: The INCITE! Anthology*, ed. INCITE! Women of Color Against Violence (Cambridge, MA: South End Press, 2006), 66.
29. Ibid., 67.
30. Ibid., 69.
31. Traci C. West, *Disruptive Christian Ethics: When Racism and Women's Lives Matter* (Louisville, KY: Westminster John Knox Press, 2006), xi.
32. Ibid., xv.
33. Ott, "Feminism and Justice: Who We Are, What We Do," 38.
34. Ibid., 42.
35. Ibid., 38.
36. Jon Sobrino, *No Salvation Outside the Poor: Prophetic-Utopian Essays* (Maryknoll, N.Y: Orbis Books, 2008), ix.
37. Ibid.
38. In my experience teaching undergraduate courses in philosophy, theology, and contemporary ethical issues, Sobrino's words are hauntingly all too familiar. Especially in the United States, there is an eerie tendency for college students to appear apathetic and indifferent to issues of justice, which might have some connection to issues of "political correctness," as Sobrino surmises. When pressed on why they do not take firmer stances or recognize the problem more clearly, many admit a fear of saying the wrong thing, appearing politically incorrect, etc., which results in a refusal to engage these issues. In light of what this book intends to explore, I wonder to what extent these students—like most of us—have become so convinced of the "problem" of exclusion that we are afraid to say anything (exclusive), which might only serve to further perpetuate the injustice of the status quo by luring us into a state of indecision.
39. Sobrino, *No Salvation Outside the Poor*, 19 (emphasis mine).
40. Ibid., 21.
41. Ibid., 31.
42. Ibid.
43. Ibid., 32.
44. Cone, *A Black Theology of Liberation*, xix.
45. Ibid., xvi.
46. Ibid.
47. Ibid., xvii–xviii.
48. Ibid., xix.
49. Ibid., 5.
50. Ibid., 6 (emphasis mine).
51. Ibid., 6–7.
52. Ibid., 7.
53. Cone, *God of the Oppressed*, 126.
54. Tatum, *Why Are All the Black Kids Sitting Together in the Cafeteria?*, 104–15.
55. West, *Disruptive Christian Ethics*, 117.
56. See: Drew University, "Tracing the History of Racial Abuse in America," drew.edu, https://www.drew.edu/news/2016/03/29/tracing-the-history-of-racial-abuse-in-america.
57. Tatum, *Why Are All the Black Kids Sitting Together in the Cafeteria?*, 102.
58. Peggy McIntosh, "White Privilege: Unpacking the Invisible Knapsack," *Peace and Freedom*, July/August 1989.
59. Cone, *A Black Theology of Liberation*, xvi.

60. James H. Cone, *The Cross and the Lynching Tree* (Maryknoll, NY: Orbis Books, 2011), 3.
61. Ibid., 32.
62. Ibid., 31.
63. Ibid., 70.
64. Ibid., 37–38.
65. Ibid., 39.
66. Martin Luther King, Jr., *A Testament of Hope: The Essential Writings and Speeches of Martin Luther King, Jr.*, ed. James Washington (New York: Harper Collins, 1991), 80.
67. Cone, *The Cross and the Lynching Tree*, 40.
68. Ibid., 48.
69. Ibid., 54.
70. Ibid., 56.
71. Ibid., 57.
72. Jarune Uwujaren and Jamie Utt, "Why our Feminism Must be Intersectional (And 3 Ways to Practice It)," www.everydayfeminism.com/2015/01/why-our-feminism-must-be-intersectional/.
73. Townes, *Womanist Ethics and the Cultural Production of Evil*, 9.
74. Ibid.
75. Carbabo et al., "Intersectionality: Mapping the Movements of a Theory," 304.
76. Pears, *Doing Contextual Theology*, 170–171.
77. Petrella, *Beyond Liberation Theology*, 134.
78. Martin Luther King, Jr., *A Testament of Hope: The Essential Writings and Speeches*, 147.

Part III

Deconstructing Divine Undecidability

Chapter Five

Un/Avoidable Divine Decision

> *What makes us tremble in the* mysterium tremendum? . . . *knowing all along that it is God who decides: the Other has no reason to give to us and no explanation to make, no reason to share his reasons with us.*
>
> —Jacques Derrida, *Gift of Death*

> *Once I say I know the name of the event, once I can say, this is God . . . then the event ceases to be an event and becomes something that I have added to my repertoire, brought within the horizon of my experience, knowledge, belief, identification, and expectation, whereas the event is precisely what always and already, structurally, exceeds my horizons.*
>
> —John D. Caputo, *The Insistence of God*

There is one final context that this book intends to investigate with regard to the aporia of in/decision and my argument about discerning difficult decisions in the midst of undecidability: theological negotiations of divine decision. In fact, it might be the most dangerous and problematic aspect of in/decision, if not downright terrifying. It is, as Derrida notes, that which "makes us tremble . . . knowing all along that it is *God* who decides."[1] The theological notion (let alone the possibility or reality) that God—a being, an agent, entity, "Other"—might decide, without our consultation, with no reason or explanation, or at least "no reason to share such reasons with us," should make us tremble. This is the problem, as well as the attempted remedy to said problem, that Part III intends to investigate, namely, how to negotiate divine decision(s). Traditionally understood as "divine election," this theological notion has always been considered inherently problematic: even John Calvin himself—the preeminent figure in the history of the doctrine—referred to the doctrine of divine election as the *decretum horribile*.[2] It should come as no surprise that in contemporary, progressive theological contexts, one of the most pervasive critiques of divine decision is its inherent exclusivity. Whether in terms of predestination where some are eternally chosen and others are not for eternal salvation (or some are chosen for salvation and others are chosen for damnation), or even in more broader understandings of divine decision, the critique of divine decision's inherent exclusivity is one of the reasons many theologians avoid such a theological notion.

In this chapter we will begin our exploration of negotiations of divine decision by exploring the issues that arise with the attempt to remedy or avoid the problem of exclusive divine choice, continuing to affirm its exclusivity as thoroughly problematic. It will identify how avoiding a theology of divine decision is predicated on an attempt to remedy a double-edged problem of exclusivity and human mastery over divinity. However, avoiding divine decision in an attempt to remedy this double-edged problem which it entails, such theologies do not—and cannot—in fact, escape certain forms of that double-edged problem. As has been the format throughout this project, we will explore the double-edged problem that divine decision entails in order to gain a clearer picture of the complexity of the problem. Thus, in the following chapter we will explore the issues facing the theologian who decides to confess or include a notion of divine decision, revealing a no less precarious predicament. The overall goal of Part III, therefore, is to demonstrate how the problem of in/decision as manifested in divine decision is more complex, and thus more problematic, than it initially appears. And as was the case with the argument put forward in Part II regarding the role privilege plays, Part III will hone in on the way power is a fundamental aspect of divine undecidability that warrants continual critical analysis.

One of the primary arguments of this chapter will therefore focus on limits to attempts to remedy the problem wherein there is a desire to avoid a notion of divine decision. If and when the remedy to the problem of divine decision is that the theologian chooses the kind of God who chooses (or not), or the content of such a choice, then said remedy is trafficking in the very thing it has attempted to avoid or remedy. The theologian who avoids or excludes divine decision must reckon with the notion that any remedy to (exclusive) divine decision necessarily entails a form of (exclusive) human decision—by being the one who decides to exclude such a possibility—thus reducing God to an object of human decision, and trafficking in a version of what he or she has tried to avoid or remedy. Additionally, for those with a theological commitment to a divine reality beyond, apart from, or at least not beholden to the control of the human being, such a move reduces God to nothing more than human theological ideas, language, concepts. Even if one does not share a commitment to such a divine reality—i.e., whose concern is not (or never was) to maintain a notion of a divine reality beyond theological language and concepts—there might still be an expressed ethical concern about human mastery over divinity, wherein it is the human who can declare who/what God is/does, even if those ends appear ethical at first glance. If there is any concern about human mastery over divine mystery—as "when an embodied creaturely reality identifies itself with and so presumes to grasp and control an infinite mystery"—then the theologian who tries to avoid a notion of divine decision must also recognize that in said remedy God has been reduced to an object of human mastery, a God of their choosing.[3] In so doing, one would fall prey to John D. Caputo's critique of a "strong theology" that "belongs to the sovereign order of power and presence," wherein God becomes "something I have added to my repertoire, brought within the horizon of my experience, knowledge, belief, identification, and expectation."[4]

This chapter argues that a more thorough exploration of a theology of divine decision reveals an impossibility to avoid this double-edged problem of human mastery over divinity and exclusivity, wherein the theologian cannot escape trafficking in exclusive decision—the very thing intended to be remedied—as well as a theo-ethical betrayal of human mastery over divinity, wherein "God" has become the object of human choice/decision. A more thorough analysis of the problem of divine decision deconstructs any remedy, revealing an aporetic double-bind, and the rupture of the impossible necessity, and necessary impossibility. Critically engaging the problem of divine decision is therefore needed in order for Christian theology to be more rigorous and transparent about identifying and engaging the depth of the problem, in all its complexity and thorniness.

In an essay entitled "'Chosen by Grace': Reconsidering the Doctrine of Predestination," Margit Ernst-Habib critically engages the theological notion of divine decision and asks:

> Why should a feminist theologian be interested in this subject? Why should a feminist theologian . . . spend time and energy re-discovering this doctrine, which seems to work against some of her core concerns? Why not deposit it on the dumping ground of those theological doctrines that have proved to be destructive not only for women but for all people who do not fit into the definition of the "chosen race" because of their gender, race, class, or sexual orientation?[5]

While Ernst-Habib does in fact go on to make a case for retrieving a doctrine of divine election as a resource for "reassurance and empowerment for the marginalized," for the most part I think her initial, rhetorical question has actually been answered—contemporary theologians (not just feminists) have deposited a notion of divine decision on the dumping ground, and for good reason.[6] Divine decision has been destructive, precisely because it is exclusive. And as we have seen, in the wake of modernity, theologians and scholars of religion have reckoned with the problem of exclusivity and attempted to reconceive, if not purge, the exclusive elements of religion.

Given the fact that exclusion is such a primary concern—for which the goal is to remove or limit Christian theology's exclusive elements—a notion of divine decision, with its explicit form of exclusion, is often avoided, again for good reason. But how do we avoid—or more precisely can we avoid—the pitfalls associated with a theological notion of divine decision? Can we avoid that which leads us to avoid divine decision? In this chapter, I want to take a trip to the dumping ground, dust off this antiquated notion, uncrumple the paper that it was once written on, and just take another peek. Perhaps the motivation is similar to the character who slowly creeps up to the villain that was just shot multiple times, to ensure that he is actually dead. My goal is not to attempt to recover a notion of divine decision or make some sort of a pitch for it. It is more of a Derridean instinct to go to the trash-bin and see what turns up, an irresistible desire to take a second look at what has been discarded and why. In so doing, I discovered that what was seemingly discarded is the very thing we cannot escape; what appeared dead at first glance is very much alive and well in an even more insidious manner.

More specifically, the desire for avoiding divine decision is predicated on an attempt to remedy a problem, which reveals itself to be unavoidable in the remedy itself. Merely tearing out and crumpling up the theological page on which divine decision was written, violently tossing it in the bin, perhaps even setting it on fire in some sort of ritualistic pyre to cleanse religion of this reprehensible claim, does not solve it, or the problems associated with it, once and for all. There is no moving beyond, excluding, avoiding it. In fact, the move toward a pure remedy or solution might be the very thing that keeps the problem(s) alive. Such a move only replays the dynamic; it does not—because it cannot—escape the problem, and therefore the move to avoid divine decision carries with it theo-ethical issues of its own that need to be reckoned with, including a certain kind of inescapability to purge theology of an identified problem, an inability to offer a remedy without poison.

HERESY OF A DIFFERENT KIND

For the sake of clarification, I want to draw attention to the fact that the issue I am raising here about human theological choice and decision is one that has been continually addressed throughout the history of Christian theology, particularly in the premodern orthodoxy/heresy debates. Yet, at the same time, I want to clearly distinguish how my argument differs. From early Christian authors—such as Ignatius of Antioch, Irenaeus of Lyons, and Tertullian—who wrote against heretics and heresies, to the conciliar and doctrinal debates in the fourth and fifth centuries and beyond, Christianity has repeatedly attempted to define and defend "orthodoxy" over and against "heresy."[7] As Clayton Crockett points out, given that "the etymology of heresy can be traced to the Greek word *hairesis*, which means to choose . . . the implication is such that choice is in itself wrong and to be condemned."[8] In other words, defense of orthodoxy was predicated on a notion that the problem was with choice itself, i.e., with any human, theological decision. Since it was believed by orthodox theologians that the truth of Christianity was revealed, and thus established and confirmed beyond human control in an absolute sense, any picking and choosing on the part of the human theologian would always amount to error and lead to untruth. As Crockett argues, the conclusion was: "I choose and therefore I am a heretic. I choose and it's necessarily the wrong choice . . . because the problem is with choice itself, the presumption that one could choose."[9] Similarly, Justo González highlights how early Christian theologians like Tertullian (and subsequent generations of theologians who mounted the accusation of heresy) believed that "once one had found the truth of Christianity, one should abandon any further search for truth," which includes further human speculation. González quotes Tertullian's "Prescription Against Heretics": "You are to seek until you find, and once you have found, you are to believe. Thereafter, all you have to do is to hold to what you have believed. Besides this, you are to believe that there is nothing further to be believed, nor anything else to be sought."[10] For Tertullian, philosophical inquiry, based on human logic and reasoning, was the most dangerous of all speculation. Because God has revealed "the truth," any human speculation, or picking and choosing, would only amount to merely human projections and be led astray from the truth of divine revelation.

Although my own inquiry in this chapter shares a similarity with theologians who define orthodoxy over against heresy—in terms of highlighting the theological problem of human decision—there is certainly a clear point of departure in the goal and motivation for such. As has been convincingly pointed out, "the habit of producing heretics as outer boundary markers for orthodox identity . . . exposes a repressive evasion of evident Christian complexity."[11] In other words, the pursuit of orthodoxy has rejected or excluded, often violently, any alternative, defining itself in relation to (the) Other/s, and thus repressed an inescapable complexity that has always been part of the Christian tradition. My goal, however, is precisely the opposite: to expose a greater complexity within Christian theology, revealing the limitations of any proposed answer or final solution to the problem of divine decision. Thus, while the locus of problematic human theological decision is similar, the goal could not be more different. In fact, part of what I intend to show is the way in which the critique of orthodoxy—as a totalizing discourse that operates on a power dynamic, embedded within a logic of the One,[12] with excluding tendencies[13]—emerges from a theological location that is also nervous about human choice, control, and mastery over divinity.

In other words, I will argue that the problem of human theological decision, which is what drove the orthodox theologians to define heresy, is something that the progressive theologian—who critiques orthodox theologians for defining heretics—also believes to be problematic. Moreover, the remedy to the problem of exclusive divine decision cannot escape navigating some form of exclusive human theological decision, which is precisely what it defines as problematic and has attempted to remedy. Therefore, in direct contrast to any attempt at presenting an "orthodox" theological position here (in contrast to a "heretical" one), I aim to expose a greater complexity to the problem of divine/human decision, an impossibility and inescapability revealing no adequate, final, definitive solution or answer for the theologian who attempts to remedy it. In so doing, it will destabilize any orthodox position or stance with regard to the problem of in/decision as manifested in negotiations of divine decision, even as we gain a clearer picture of it. A clearer understanding of the problem of divine/human choice is not intended to render the problem unproblematic, nor to make a case *for* exclusion or any kind of exclusive divine/human choice, but to raise the stakes about just how problematic they are by revealing the limits of any attempt to remedy the problem(s).

AVOIDING DIVINE DECISION TO REMEDY EXCLUSIVITY AND HUMAN MASTERY OVER DIVINITY

As I have intonated, contemporary remedies to the problem of divine decision are predicated on an identification of exclusivity as the problem. As you may recall from our previous explorations of this consensus, an awareness of the problem of exclusivity has become increasingly demonstrated since the Enlightenment. In one of the landmark works in the dawning of modern theology, Immanuel Kant zeroes in on the problem of exclusivity in religion: "far from establishing an age suited to the achievement of the *church universal* . . . Judaism rather excluded the whole human race from its communion, a people especially chosen by Jehovah himself, hostile to all other peoples and hence treated with hostility by all of them."[14] For Kant, it is the Jewish theological notion of chosenness that is problematic for a modern, universal religion because of the former's inherent exclusivity. Of course, for Kant, the universal religion within the bounds of reason that he envisions is indeed Christianity, as we can only "begin the universal history of the Church . . . from the origin of Christianity, which, as a total abandonment of the Judaism in which it originated, grounded on an entirely new principle, effected a total revolution in doctrines of faith."[15] Apart from the glaring Christian supersessionism and disturbing anti-Semitism, Kant's point about the problematic nature of exclusivity in religion has been almost universally accepted and confirmed in modern (and "postmodern") Christian theologies. A thoroughly modern, universal religion must begin with a "total abandonment" of exclusive doctrines and dogmas, and because divine decision represents the problem *par excellence*, it should be one of the first to go.[16]

We also explored how in the wake of modernity, a sustained analysis and critique of religion's problematic exclusivity has continued, across various theological discourses, even if the goal is no longer to establish a "universal religion." Even when we have come to recognize the limits of any kind of Kantian, Hegelian, or modern notion of universality, there is still an acute concern about vestiges of exclusivity—as we have seen. In fact, more recent discourses are keen to point out the inherent exclusivity of modern universality itself, highlighting "how modernity's internal dynamics and factors operate 'discursive[ly to exclude].'"[17] From an ethical perspective, exclusion "names what permeates a good many of sins we commit against our neighbors"[18] and thus the focus has been on the "struggle to do away with faith structures of exclusion" that continue to privilege white, male, Western, Eurocentric, anthropocentric images, symbols, and perspectives to the exclusion of all others.[19] Contemporary theologians have also critically examined the preeminent instantiation of Christian exclusivity, namely Christo-centric claims about Christ as the exclusive path to salvation. Such "conservative exclusivistic claims for 'one and only'" no longer seem tenable given the reality of, and growing appreciation for, present-day religious pluralism.[20] As Martin Hägglund puts it, the consensus seems to be that "'good' religion . . . welcomes others and 'bad' religion . . . excludes," and thus the focus should be on avoiding or remedying exclusion as much as possible.[21]

However, contemporary remedies to the problem of exclusive divine decision, as found in the Christian theological tradition, that amount to a situation wherein the theologian chooses, more wisely, reasonably, and, often, in a way that *seems* less exclusive, cannot avoid certain forms of a double-edged problem of exclusion and human mastery over divine mystery that is the very motivation for avoiding divine decision in the first place. The task that I have set out before us is to highlight precisely how or why they cannot, drawing out the implications and issues that arise if and when divine decision—and perhaps even God more generally—is reduced to (nothing more than) an object of human decision. More importantly, because the move to remedy divine decision runs up against other expressed concerns within the very same corner of theological discourse, a sharper analysis of the attempted remedy to divine decision reveals a predicament wherein the theologian will need to discern between two versions of the same problem, as opposed to a clear identification of the problem (of divine choice) with a clear solution. Taking a lead from Chris Boesel, I am framing the goal of this engagement as an attempt to "get some clarity on the complexity of the limits" of attempts to remedy the problem of divine decision, "such that our decisions . . . become more informed, more responsible, and more difficult."[22] Building upon previous analyses offered above, a more thorough exploration of the problem of divine decision reveals that all we are left with, as I will argue, is a poisonous remedy, another illustration of Derrida's *pharmakon*, "that dangerous supplement that breaks into the very thing that would have liked to do without it."[23]

It is quite fitting then, that the focus of my analysis will be poststructuralist engagements with Christian theology, especially the former's attraction to the apophatic or negative theological tradition. Within such theo-ethical engagements with poststructuralism, one finds not only an acute concern about exclusivity and human mastery over divinity, but also an aversion to theological notions of divine decision, which make it a fitting focus for our analysis. In the opening pages of *Apophatic Bodies: Negative Theology, Incarnation, and Relationality*, the issue of human mastery over divinity is sketched quite clearly. Recounting the danger of too firm a relationship between human language, concepts, ideas and the divine, the editors of this volume write:

> The problem arises when the difference and distance between divine and creaturely reality is not big or radical enough; when creaturely finitude assumes too cozy a relation with the divine infinite, as if the former—creaturely concepts, categories, languages, texts, persons, communities—could comprehend and so contain divine reality. And when an embodied creaturely reality identifies itself with and so presumes to grasp and control an infinite mystery, it is time to start passing out the crash helmets and flak jackets to protect the bodies of neighboring but differing creatures. Mastery over divine mystery routinely results in a body count.[24]

Here we see the problem of human "mastery over divine mystery" clearly illustrated: whenever divinity is reduced to human "concepts, categories, languages, texts, persons, communities," there is ample reason to worry about too much power in the hands of the human theologian to comprehend, contain, and control the divine. As Boesel's chapter in this volume goes on to point out: "isn't human mastery of divine mystery always precisely ethically problematic, in that, in whatever form, it always puts the neighbor at risk?"[25]

This risk is what Letty Russell calls the "power quotient," the ability to enlist divine reinforcement and justification for human desires and ideals; and, unfortunately, history has proven that such power commonly translates into domination. Russell goes further in arguing that this sorted history has often been linked with a theological understanding of divine decision, especially when powerful communities, peoples, nations have (coincidentally) claimed chosenness: "divine election and its subsequent use in nation building and colonialism have often become a screen for imperialism and racial domination."[26] Drawing on the work of Renita Weems, Russell identifies the reification of divine election for colonialism, imperialism, and racism: "a people who consider themselves special in the eyes of God have the power and privilege to dominate others."[27] Kelly Brown Douglas highlights how such problematic notions of divine chosenness play out in the United States, where racial domination is predicated on a theological understanding of "the Anglo-Saxon myth of America's exceptionalism," which leads to a "stand-your-ground culture . . . that protects the supremacy of whiteness . . . to insure that nothing nonwhite intrudes on white space."[28] Historically, when humans have had the ability to claim and control divine power (including chosenness), it has typically meant "bad news" for others.[29] Russell captures the essence of the problem: "[divine] election helped provide divine reinforcement of racism and imperialist expansion in the United States, South Africa, and elsewhere."[30] The ways in which divine chosenness has been used to justify and validate oppression, domination, colonization, etc., are precisely why many contemporary theologians have abandoned a notion of divine decision.

Such concerns about human mastery over divinity are thus also found in the work of liberation theologians like Jon Sobrino, who has always had a healthy desire to secure theology from our "expectations regarding God." Matthew Lundberg hones in on the problematic nature of the theological endeavor for liberation theologians: "Human god-talk in natural theology is directed by a sinful and manipulative self-interest that grasps the positive features of created reality in an attempt to create an image of the divine that justifies and legitimizes human projects in the world." Drawing on Karl Barth's denunciation of "natural theology," Lundberg affirms the problem of "too cozy a relation" between creaturely finitude and the divine infinite because of how it can fund human, "sinful" endeavors. As Sobrino points out, "the sinful tendency to manipulate the idea of God" has material ramifications, translating into the historical sin of structural oppression.[31] In an attempt to respond "theologically to the oppression and poverty that has been tacitly and sometimes overtly supported by the Christian church and its theology since the 15th-century conquest," particularly in Latin America, Sobrino highlights and critiques the problems that arise when humans have control and mastery over divinity.[32] In other words, for liberation theologians such human control over divinity is not merely a theological *faux pas*, or sin against divine infinity, but problematic precisely because of how it "justifies and legitimizes human projects in the world," including colonialism, domination, and oppression. The problem, it seems, stems from the ability to "manipulate the idea of God," and the way that enlists too much power in the hands of the human theologian.

While the theo-ethical concern about too much power in the hands of humanity is widespread—as is concern about its connection to divine decision—I want to resharpen the focus of our analysis on poststructuralist theological engagements, particularly through the locus of Christian apophatic discourses. Part of the so-called *tournant théologique* included a revisiting of the Christian apophatic tradition because of how its "unsaying" resonates with poststructuralist discourses that acknowledge "the radical limits of finitude with regard to knowledge, language, and meaning."[33] Despite repeated contestations from such central figures as Derrida that "no, what I write is not negative theology,"[34] even "the most negative of negative theologies,"[35] Mary-Jane Rubenstein highlights how there is still "an uncanny relationship . . . between the deconstruction opened by the death of God and the *via negativa* guided by the living one."[36]

In the last few decades, there has been an "emerging arena of postmodern discourse" that engages "the theme of incomprehensible divine mystery and the critical-constructive readings of the apophatic tradition."[37] Part of Derrida's so-called "turn to religion" included significant engagement with—and at some points fervently distancing himself from—the apophatic tradition that has sent Christian theologians reeling ever since. Rubenstein reflects on this: "One wonders why, after thirty-five years, the question of 'apophaticism's' relation to 'deconstruction' has not been put to rest. After all, the author himself has issued the final word: 'No what I write is not 'negative theology.'"[38] Yet, theologians continue asking themselves: "Why does this not satisfy us? Why are we not satisfied with this 'not' . . . . Why do we keep asking him?" Perhaps it is because "both negative theology and deconstruction witness—and, in fact, catalyze—the failure of language to circumscribe an alterity that enables and exceeds linguistic determinations."[39]

In theological engagements with deconstruction and its relation to apophaticism, the motivation to maintain such an alterity is one of its driving forces. As we saw in Chapter 1, Derridean-inflected theological engagements with apophaticism express concern about reducing divine alterity, letting it seep into the grasp of human hands, because of how this kind of an ontotheological collapse into sameness can—and often does—spell bad news for the human Other on the receiving end of such a power trip. We explored Caputo's work in this area, which has shone a bright spotlight on the theo-ethical landmines of a "strong theology . . . in love with strength, right from the gate,"[40] and suggests a "weak theology . . . content with a little adverb like 'perhaps.'"[41] For Caputo, deconstruction helps apophatic theology resist such a desire to close, to encapsulate, to name, to disclose the secret, to answer the question. As Derrida notes in *"Différance,"* although apophatic theology gestures toward the impossible and unknowable, it is really "only in order to acknowledge [God's] superior, inconceivable, and ineffable mode of being."[42] There is an acute concern about the way in which, despite claims to the contrary, "negative theology drops anchor, hits bottom, lodges itself securely in pure presence and the transcendental signified." Caputo explicates the concern, that, in his reading, Derrida mitigates against: "Deconstruction saves negative theology from closure. Closure spells trouble . . . closure spells exclusion, exclusiveness; closure spills blood, doctrinal, confessional, theological, political, institutional blood, and eventually, it never fails, real blood."[43] Closure has wide-ranging ethical dangers, as Caputo deftly points out, including a collapse into a system of sameness that results in an "identity that nation-states build to defend themselves against the stranger, against Jews and Arabs and immigrants . . . against all the others, all the other others."[44] Any such collapse into presence would destroy the "otherness" of the *tout autre*, and thus Caputo reads deconstruction as aiding us in that process by allowing the *tout autre* to remain "wholly other" in order to respect the difference. "The whole point of the *tout autre* in deconstruction," Caputo argues, "its burning passion, is a messianic one, to keep the system open, to prevent the play of differences from regathering and reassembling in a systematic whole with infinite warrant."[45]

In addition to the collapse of difference-into-sameness that is destructive to the human Other, Caputo has also critiqued the tendency of theology to do the same to the divine Other, which goes hand-in-glove with the above ethical concerns. Reducing divinity to human control and mastery funds the violence of closure and exclusion by enlisting far too much power in the hands of humanity over divinity. In *Prayers and Tears*, Caputo advances a "religion without religion," echoing and channeling Derrida to sketch out the religiosity of deconstruction: "Deconstruction repeats the structure of religious experience. . . . Deconstruction regularly, rhythmically repeats this religiousness, *sans* the concrete historical religions; it repeats nondogmatically the religious structure of experience, the category of the religious."[46] Caputo argues the *sans*—i.e., "religion *without* religion," or religiousness *sans* determinate dogmas, doctrines, etc.—"differentiates the 'determinable' faiths, which are always dangerous,"[47] precisely because the latter places themselves (mistakenly) in the dangerous, dominant position of determining and deciding. For Caputo, part of the problem with determinable, dogmatic faiths is the mistaken illusion of the power to choose.

This kind of a divine-human power struggle is what Caputo names, in other contexts, "strong theology," and offers the alternative of a "weak theology." In *The Weakness of God: A Theology of the Event*, Caputo reflects further on the misplaced power that theology has desired, arguing that "theology has always been strong theology and religion has been strong religion, in love with strength, right from the gate."[48] Though he seeks to find in the theological tradition the places that gesture toward "the weakness of God," he laments theology's denial of such weaknesss because "it is too much in love with power, constantly selling its body to the interests of power, constantly sitting down to table with power in a discouraging contradiction of its own good news."[49] In opposition to a tradition that can (and often does) "accumulate an army and institutional power, semantic prestige and cultural authority," Caputo seeks to sketch a theology that unleashes the name of God as a "weak force."[50] For those keenly aware of the dangers of power, especially divine power in human hands, Caputo offers an alternative: "In a strong theology, the name of God has historical determinacy and specificity—it is Christian or Jewish or Islamic, for example—whereas a weak theology, weakened by the flux of undecidability and translatability, is more open-ended."[51] For Caputo, (part of) the problem with strong theology is its misplaced desire and claim to name something determinate and specific, thus reducing God to "an object of conceptual analysis."[52] Put differently, it appears that strong theology is ethically problematic because of its claim to put itself in the divine driver's seat, endowing it with a (desire for) power that is always dangerous.

At first glance it might appear, very clearly in fact, that a theology that takes Caputo's critical analysis seriously would indeed reject something determinate—and exclusive—like a theological notion of divine decision. A doctrine, notion, or theological claim of divine decision is ethically problematic, and epitomizes that which is or should be deconstructed, because it identifies a transcendental signified that declares something definitive about God, which, according to Caputo's reading of Derrida, is impossible. Additionally, the content of this theological notion is a determinate choice, i.e., divine decision for this/that. As we have seen, Caputo focuses on how Derrida continually disrupts and unsettles any absolute declarations about finality (religious and ethical), revealing the ways in which determinate forms of religion and justice are limited, always fall short, and are, by extension, themselves unjust. This includes, most especially, decisions that cut and divide. A theological claim of divine decision, especially with its unique presentation of the problem of exclusion, represents the problem *par excellence*. It is a messianism with a messiah. It is a determinate, exhaustive, definitive choice. It is closure. It is no longer awaited, for it *has* come, happened, arrived, been decided. It lodges itself securely in presence and the transcendental signified, which would betray the deconstructive movement of the impossible.

On the one hand, this is certainly true; Caputo's strident critique of determinate, exclusive doctrines and dogmas would undoubtedly apply to theological claims about divine decision. As I have maintained all along, theological claims for (exclusive) divine choice would definitely be ethically problematic along these lines of thinking. On the other hand, Caputo's critique might *also* be problematic for any attempt to remedy this problem. Theologians who reject, avoid, or exclude such a theological notion encounter a new set of issues that, ironically, fall prey to the same critique. Caputo's theo-ethical concern—about determinate religion, doctrines, dogmas—is directly related to the one that I am raising about attempts to remedy such, namely the problem of human mastery over divinity in any attempt to remedy the problem of divine decision. And because "mastery over divine mystery routinely results in a body count," this is a concern that needs to be taken seriously.[53]

To the extent that this is the case, a weak theology would also be subject to the same critique that Caputo marshals against a strong theology, navigating a similar kind of ethical danger, especially if/when it is decided that God does not decide. And if so, it begs the question as to whether a weak theology can safely avoid the problem. In fact, a weak theology can actually serve to *strengthen* the hand of the human theologian, which is the very thing Caputo is critiquing and trying to remedy. More importantly, any remedy to divine decision wherein the human theologian decides or chooses that God does not decide or choose, would be subject to the same critique marshalled against the "'determinable' faiths, which are always dangerous."[54] A God of undecidability—if/when that means a God who cannot, does not decide—can only be arrived at, or secured, through the *decision* of the theologian. Therefore, when the theologian chooses the kind of God who chooses (or not)—or even attempts to avoid such a notion—such a move reduces God to "an object of conceptual analysis," something the human theologian can choose (or not), and enlists the human (theologian) with a dangerous power supply—the very thing Caputo critiques about "determinate faiths." So while I very much agree with Caputo's ethical concern about enlisting the human theologian with a dangerous "power supply," I also want to raise the concern about how attempting to avoid a God who chooses does just that.[55] Furthermore, if exclusive decision—or a divine decision that excludes—is *the problem*, the remedy to divine decision that entails *excluding* such a possibility cannot avoid that which it has tried to remedy. In other words, such an analysis reveals that the remedy to (divine) exclusive decision is (human) exclusive decision—another instantiation of the *pharmakon* that I have tried to highlight throughout this book.

Caputo does not ever directly address a theological notion of divine election or decision.[56] However, he does explicitly express a similar concern about a God of *our* choosing. In *The Weakness of God*, Caputo further sketches out some of these theological concerns that lead him to construct a "theology of the event," wherein "the name of God is an event, or rather that it *harbors* an event, and that theology is the hermeneutics of that event, its task being to release what is happening in that name, to set it free, to give it its own head, and thereby to head off the forces that would prevent this event."[57] Caputo repeatedly emphasizes how the event continually evokes a sense of rupture, in-breaking, surprising, overflowing, releasing, etc. "There is always something uncontainable and unconditional about an event,"[58] Caputo argues, something that betrays any attempt to name it completely, which means that "the name can never be taken with literal force, as if it held the event tightly within its grip, as if it circumscribed it and literally named it, as if a concept (*Begriff*) were anything more than a temporary stop and imperfect hold on an event."[59] Thus theology should recognize that "an event cannot be held captive by a confessional faith or creedal formula," which is why Caputo contends that theology's task is to release and set free, rather than foreclose or hold captive, as in a doctrine of divine decision (for this or that).[60]

Again, it is fairly clear that a "concept (*Begriff*)," confession, or "creedal formula" of divine decision would seemingly betray the uncontainable and unconditional nature of the event. And for theologians who resonate with these theological concerns, a notion, concept, or doctrine of divine decision would be problematic because it attempts to circumscribe, name, and contain the eventive nature of the divine. Caputo continues:

> Events happen to us; they overtake us and outstrip the reach of the subject or the ego. Although we are called upon to respond to events, an event is not our doing but is done to us (even as it might well be our undoing). The event arises independently of me and comes over me, so that an event is also an *advent*. The event is visited upon me, presenting itself as something I must deal with, like it or not . . . the event is not necessarily good news.[61]

This language continues to cut against theological notions of divine decision for the very same reasons noted above. However, if one were to simply exchange "event" for "divine decision" here—which would undoubtedly do violence to Caputo's intention (despite any "death-of-the-author" claims)—this language would sound eerily familiar to the stalwarts of doctrines of divine decision in the Christian theological tradition like Augustine and Calvin. For these theologians, divine decision "happens to us . . . is not our doing but is done to us . . . arises independently of me and comes over me . . . presenting itself as something I must deal with, like it or not." Augustine and Calvin, for instance, would certainly agree that divine decision "is not necessarily good news," or does not always appear that way and is not always experienced as such. Calvin surely had ample reason to call divine election the *decretum horribile* (especially given his understanding of double predestination).[62]

When pressed to the limits of *why* God chooses or has chosen some, Augustine appeals to the mystery of God in an attempt to be faithful to the notion that divine decision is fundamentally about God's choice, not a human choice. While discussing God's mercy and judgment as it pertains to divine decision, Augustine defers to the inscrutability of God and God's ways as he cannot help but wonder about those who are not chosen, and interrupts his analysis of divine election by stating: "But His ways are unsearchable. Therefore the mercy by which He freely delivers, and the truth by which He righteously judges, are equally unsearchable."[63] In the midst of this treatise on divine decision as predestination, Augustine, who is never short on words, analysis, declarations, etc., makes a strangely *apophatic* gesture in the midst of his strongly *kataphatic* assertion of God's sovereign, free, gratuitous decision for desperate, dependent, despondent humanity. Augustine, who in the preceding—and subsequent—pages expressed full certainty, confidence, and clarity about who/what God has chosen, and how that is genuinely good news, now appeals to mystery when he cannot figure out or reconcile why a seemingly gracious God has chosen to condemn some human beings to eternal damnation of "His" own free will. In an attempt to maintain a notion of divine decision as truly divine—i.e., keep it out of the grasp and control of humanity— Augustine appeals to mystery when the human cannot understand, make sense of, explain, or justify what God has chosen not to reveal.

Calvin also appeals to the mystery (and beneficence) of divine will in his doctrine of divine election in order to assert that it is primarily God's decision and not ours. Before beginning to explicate his doctrine of predestination, Calvin addresses the danger of human curiosity and its wanderings into "forbidden labryrinths, and soaring beyond its sphere, as if determined to leave none of the Divine secrets unscrutinzed or unexplored." He thus admonishes the curious—and arrogant—seeker to remember "that when they inquire into predestination, they penetrate the inmost recesses of Divine wisdom, where the careless and confident intruder will obtain no satisfaction of his curiosity, but will enter a labyrinth from which he will find no way to depart." Thus the curious human inquirer should recognize that "it is unreasonable that man should scrutinize with impunity . . . and investigate, even from eternity, that sublimity of wisdom which God would have us to adore and not comprehend, to promote our admiration of his glory."[64] Calvin is suggesting that it is unreasonable to think that the human being could not only understand, but actually investigate with scrutiny, divine decision, as if the human being could attain the "sublimity of wisdom" that is only reserved for divinity. Again, like Augustine—and Caputo, for that matter—Calvin makes a similar appeal to the unconditional and uncontainable nature of divinity in order to keep it out of the grasp and control of humanity. Although for Calvin, this is less of an overtly apophatic move because he is more explicit in maintaining that the only way we can know the secrets of divine wisdom is through the testimony of Scripture, he does admit a certain unknown with regard to the mystery of divine division—a mystery that the human being is incapable of understanding or comprehending, and thus grasping and controlling.

What are we to make of this strange, shared resonance between those who confess a robust theological concept of divine decision and Caputo, who we might readily assume does not? While the resonance might not center on the theological content of whether or not God chooses, there is a shared concern about theology being reduced to something that is entirely up to the theologian. All three worry that divinity collapses into something that is within the grasp and control of the human "subject and ego," something that is merely the result of human theological desires and decisions. In short, the concern is that there is something inherently dangerous, both theologically and ethically, about reducing God to an object of human choice or decision. Caputo seems intent on maintaining the uncontainability of the event that happens to us, to "head off the forces that would prevent this event," that happens "independently of me and comes over me."[65] But if/when the theologian chooses to exclude the possibility of a God who chooses, the "event" (i.e., "God") is contained, prevented, is no longer independent of me, but very much dependent upon the decisions and choices that I make. Just as Caputo is arguing that "a confessional faith or creedal formula" forecloses, holds captive, or prevents the event (of God), the same is true for the exclusion of even the possibility that God might choose (or not). Pressed to the limits of their understanding about divine choice, Augustine and Calvin appeal to mystery, inscrutability, and unknowing. If one were to take seriously Caputo's apophatic stance with regard to the divine event, if one genuinely inhabited a space to let divinity be divine, then this would mean that one would need to reckon with a theological possibility of divine choice.

As we have seen, Caputo continues his theological project in a more recent work, *The Insistence of God: A Theology of Perhaps*, where he attempts to further distance his "weak theology" (a continuation of his theology of the event) from "strong theology," by drawing on a theological notion of "perhaps." Caputo insists: "One must, it is absolutely necessary, always say 'perhaps' for God: God, perhaps (*peut-être*). Whenever and wherever there is a chance for the event, that is God, perhaps."[66] In contrast to "theology in the strong standard version" that employs "omni-nouns and hyper verbs" to establish power and presence, "weak theology . . . is content with a little adverb like 'perhaps,'" which interrupts and intercepts, disrupts and deflects.[67] Proposing a weak theology of "God, perhaps," Caputo writes:

> Once I say I know the name of the event, once I can say, this is God, the event is God, then the event ceases to be an event and becomes something I have added to my repertoire, brought within the horizon of my experience, knowledge, belief, identification, and expectation, whereas the event is precisely what always and already, structurally, exceeds my horizons. What I mean by the event is the surprise, what literally over-takes me, shattering my horizon of expectation.[68]

Caputo continues his critique about definitive claims about God because of how they collapse divinity into "something I have added to my repertoire, brought within the horizon of my experience, knowledge, belief, identification, and expectation." Rather, Caputo proposes a more open-ended notion of divinity, a theology of "perhaps" that appreciates the surprise of the event that will always shatter my horizons and expectations.

Suppose one approached the issue of divine decision taking Caputo's critique seriously—what would be the responsible approach to this dangerous notion of divine choosing? If and when the theologian has decided that it is best for him or her to decide, when one has come to the conclusion (not surprisingly) that a God who chooses is far too violent, offensive, problematic (i.e., exclusive), has one not fallen prey to what Caputo is railing against here? If so, then perhaps excluding a notion of divine decision might actually be a denial of the "perhaps," because such a decision reduces God (even as "event") to something that consequently does not exceed my horizons of expectation. Could one even safely avoid such problematic decisions, both divine and human, even if one claimed a certain apophatic stance toward them? To the extent that this is the case, it would mean a precarious predicament wherein either we decide, and thus make God an object of our decision and, ironically, fall prey to the "strong" theology Caputo critiques here; or we leave room for a God who chooses (or not), perhaps.

Now, of course, Caputo (and others) might argue that a God who chooses—especially when connected to traditional understandings of divine election—is merely the work of a strong theology of absolutes, closure, dogmas, etc. And, on the one hand, this might be an accurate accusation. But what I am arguing, or attempting to problematize, is the way in which any definitive exclusion or denial of a God who chooses is subject to the same critique. In fact, critiques about definitive claims about God (e.g., a God who chooses) are definitive claims themselves. In an attempt to leave room, open up space, with "a little adverb like 'perhaps,'" does one inevitably close the gap?[69] How far does the "perhaps" go, especially when Caputo's theology of the "perhaps" insists that "God does not exist," but rather, "God insists"?[70] How apophatic are we really being if we have made decisions about God's decisions? Isn't a God we choose very much the product of our expectations, a God who has been "added to my repertoire, brought within the horizon of my experience, knowledge, belief, identification, and expectation"? And, if so, shouldn't that recognition be "what makes us tremble in the *mysterium tremendum* . . . knowing all along that it is God who decides," or not?[71]

At the very least, for those of us who have heard Caputo's clarion call about the problems of human mastery over divinity, a sharper awareness of the predicament that divine decision presents should cause us a great deal of trouble. Further along, Caputo writes: "If the name of God is not causing us a great deal of difficulty, it is not God we are talking about."[72] This is precisely what I am arguing here, by highlighting how the problem of divine decision should (continue to) cause us a great deal of difficulty, and if it is not, then perhaps we have not understood the problem in all its fullness and complexity. Any attempt to avoid the problem of divine decision can result in a God of our own choosing, along the way leading us to believe that we have solved the problem, and hence no longer causes us a "great deal of difficulty"; in so doing, that might mean "it is not God that we are [now] talking about." If we have begun to think we can do away with a God who chooses, safely avoid it, quickly dispose of and exclude such an antiquated, obsolete notion, then perhaps we were never talking about God to begin with. Caputo maintains that "God's problem"—or the problem with God, including and especially a God who chooses—"is that God *insists*, is an insistent problem that won't go away."[73] I am suggesting that this includes, most especially, a theological notion or possibility of divine decision. It is a problem that "*insists*, is an insistent problem that won't go away."

One might also argue that the problem of divine decision is a "non-problem" because it assumes, first, the existence of God, and additionally, a God who could, might, or would decide.[74] It is only a problem because it mistakes, in Caputo's words, "an event for a being, or a Super-being, a ground of Being, beyond or without being, a mighty being that does things, or mysteriously decides not to, an agent-being in the sky."[75] As Caputo continually argues, "God is not an agent who does things," and thus to suggest or even consider a God who chooses means one has not allowed the full weight of the "perhaps" to take hold.[76] Again, such a critique is not without warrant. But, yet again, I would also argue: the "perhaps" has already been collapsed into concluding that the existence of God is not even a possibility, much less the possibility of a God who can, does, might choose—and might make decisions that are not beholden to human decisions. And in so doing such a conclusion would deny and abrogate the "perhaps" altogether, turning "God" into "something I have added to my repertoire, brought within the horizon of my experience, knowledge, belief, identification, and expectation." In that case, such a denial would fall prey to Caputo's own critique. Put differently, excluding the possibility that God chooses (or not) not only traffics in the very thing attempted to be remedied, i.e., exclusive decision and choice, but also becomes something "I know . . . once I can say, this is God."[77]

UN/AVOIDABLE DIVINE DECISION

The larger point of this chapter is to unearth the problems that arise with divine decision and attempted negotiations of it, especially as that relates to the overall problem of in/decision that this book has been attempting to highlight. More specifically, we have been tracking the issues that arise when the theologian attempts to remedy exclusive divine decision by choosing the kind of "God" who chooses (or not) in an attempt to avoid the problem altogether. What I have argued, however, is that such a move is impossible because the attempt to remedy the double-edged problem of human mastery over divine mystery and exclusion—as manifested in divine decision—cannot escape some version of that problem. Again, we see the deconstructive *pharmakon* at work. Divine decision is an insistent problem that won't go away, that troubles even when we think we have safely escaped or remedied it, even when we convince ourselves that the thorn has been removed; I believe Caputo's theology of perhaps highlights this problem nicely, mostly because I think it shares a similar concern: the problem of reducing God to an object of human decision, control, and mastery. To the extent that Caputo's critique is accurate, however, it would mean that a "weak theology" might actually, unexpectedly, strengthen the hand of the human theologian, and be just as dangerous as a "strong theology"—or at least be unable to rid itself of the poison of "strong theology," continuing to traffic in what it has attempted to remedy. Additionally, unless the "perhaps" allows room (perhaps) for at least the possibility of a God who might choose, then it too would be subject to the same critique. More importantly, any remedy to the problem of divine decision that includes the human theologian being the one who makes (all) the choices and decisions, should also make Caputo—and anyone concerned about human mastery over divinity—nervous. Thus, a more thorough analysis of the problem of divine decisions reveals that any attempt on the part of the theologian to remedy it—by choosing an alternative—results in a betrayal of the very same ethical intentions to remedy that which is poisonous, including trafficking in some version of exclusive decision and human mastery and control over divinity.

Given my attempt to expose an inability to avoid the problem(s) of divine decision, how might we proceed? Given that the impossibility I have sketched is *impossible* precisely because the problem is *unavoidable*, what is the way forward? As I have maintained all along, an appreciation for this impossibility is not intended to leave us in a state of nihilism or apathy regarding the problem, quite the contrary. My motivation all along throughout this book, my sole intention, is to heighten our vigilance in dealing with the "violence" entailed in any approach or engagement with the problem of decision, especially divine decision(s). Borrowing once again from Derrida: "In saying this I am not advocating that such violence be unleashed or simply accepted. I am above all asking that we try to recognize and analyze it as best we can in its various forms . . . And if, as I believe, violence remains (almost) ineradicable, its analysis and the most refined ingenious account of its conditions will be the least violent gestures, perhaps even nonviolent."[78] If the violence of divine decision (i.e., the theo-ethical issues entailed in attempts to navigate it) is unavoidable, I am arguing that the way to be "least violent" in relation to the problem is to "try to recognize and analyze it as best we can." This includes being transparent about how it is unavoidable, and being as rigorous as possible in our "analysis and the most refined ingenious account of its conditions." In so doing, I agree with Derrida that this "will be the least violent gestures."

Additionally, the issue of in/decision manifested in our exploration of the problem of divine decision relates to the overall argument of this book about the role that power plays in these contexts. Here, the stated desire for avoiding the notion of divine decision is that it enlists the human theologian with a dangerous power supply, by being the one who could name, disclose, and determine who/what God has chosen or decided. But as I have tried to demonstrate in this chapter, this concern cannot be purely remedied by avoiding divine decision. Thus, the structural dynamic of in/decision manifests itself in this context as revealing an impossibility of safely avoiding the problem of divine decision altogether.

Returning again to "How to Avoid Speaking: Denials," when Derrida finally comes to grips with the realization that he must finally "stop deferring" and "try to explain [himself] directly on the subject, and at last speak of 'negative theology,'" he begins by asking: "How is it possible to avoid speaking about negative theology?" In a discourse that by definition intends to unsay, and avoid speaking, "how, if one speaks of it, to avoid speaking of it? How not to speak of it?"[79] Derrida realizes that perhaps he was unable to avoid it, that he can no longer defer, because in not speaking (about negative theology), was he not engaging in some sort of negative theological mode of discourse (about negative theology) all along? "Is there ever anything other than a 'negative theology' of negative theology?"[80] Like Derrida, we come to a similar realization with the problem of divine decision, that we were never able to avoid the problem in the first place, that our reasons for avoiding it as a way of avoiding a double-edged problem have resurfaced, that we have always already been in its midst.[81] Derrida reminds, and performs, the deconstructive predicament that I have tried to sketch: an inability to find safe ground or escape the problem, especially one that we would like to avoid. This chapter has tried to confront us with the reality of a denial, that to avoid divine choice as a way of avoiding its dangers—or worse, to think we have succeeded in avoiding such—is impossible. So how to avoid the God who chooses? Perhaps it is time we stopped deferring.

The goal of my argument in this chapter is neither to endorse a notion of divine decision nor collapse into a nihilistic approach to the problems it raises. To the contrary, the very insights of such a deconstructive analysis should heighten our vigilance in dealing with these theological and ethical problems. Deconstruction reveals that the stakes are higher than we even imagined: we are trapped in a situation with no pure or good solution—every attempt carries its own set of issues or problems. And as we will see in the next chapter, the problem gets no less complicated for those who decide to endorse or include a theological notion of divine decision. The analysis of in/decision in this book—and chapter—is intended to gain appreciation for, and recognition of, the fact that our best attempts are always limited, and yet we are trapped in a situation in which we cannot avoid, remedy, or escape them. This includes (most especially) those attempts to remedy the problem of decision—especially divine decision, as this chapter has argued. And as we will see, those who decide to include or endorse a theological notion of divine decision cannot escape this problem either.

NOTES

1. Derrida, *The Gift of Death*, 56–57 (emphasis mine).
2. Calvin, *Institutes of the Christian Religion*, 207.
3. Boesel and Keller, eds., *Apophatic Bodies: Negative Theology, Incarnation, and Relationality*, 4.
4. Caputo, *The Insistence of God*, 9–10.
5. Ernst-Habib, "'Chosen by Grace': Reconsidering the Doctrine of Predestination," 80.
6. Ibid., 81.
7. See: Ignatius and T. W Crafer, *The Epistles of St. Ignatius* (London: Society for Promoting Christian Knowledge, 1919); Irenaeus, *The Third Book of St. Irenaeus, Bishop of Lyons, Against Heresies* (Oxford: Clarendon Press, 1874); Tertullian and T. Herbert Bindley, *Tertullian On the Testimony of the Soul and on the "Prescription" of Heretics*, Early Church Classics (London, New York: Society for Promoting Christian Knowledge, 1914).
8. Clayton Crockett, "Polyhairesis: On Postmodern and Chinese Folds," *Modern Theology* 30, no. 3 (July 2014): 34.
9. Ibid., 35.
10. Justo L. González, *The Story of Christianity: The Early Church to the Dawn of the Reformation*, Volume 1 (San Francisco: Harper & Row, 1984), 75.
11. Catherine Keller and Laurel Schneider, eds., *Polydoxy: Theology of Multiplicity and Relation* (New York: Routledge, 2010), 2.
12. See: Laurel C. Schneider, *Beyond Monotheism: A Theology of Multiplicity* (Milton Park, Abingdon, Oxon; New York: Routledge, 2008).
13. See: Margaret R. Miles, *The Word Made Flesh: A History of Christian Thought* (Malden, MA: Wiley-Blackwell, 2004), 65–114.
14. Immanuel Kant, "Religion within the Boundaries of Mere Reason," in *Religion and Rational Theology*, ed. Allen W Wood, trans. George Di Giovanni (Cambridge: Cambridge University Press, 1996), 155.
15. Ibid., 156.
16. For Kant, this would also include an abandonment of all doctrines and dogmas that necessarily conflict with practical reason and human freedom.
17. Carter, *Race: A Theological Account*, 45.
18. Volf, *Exclusion and Embrace*, 72.
19. Isasi-Diaz, *Mujerista Theology: A Theology for the Twenty-First Century*, 65–66.
20. Heim, "Differential Pluralism and Trinitarian Theologies of Religion," 122.
21. Hägglund, "The Radical Evil of Deconstruction: A Reply to John Caputo," 127.
22. Chris Boesel, "Divine Relationality and (the Methodological Constraints of) the Gospel as Piece of News: Tracing the Limits of Trinitarian Ethics," in *Divine Multiplicity: Trinities, Diversities, and the Nature of Relation*, eds. Chris Boesel and S. Wesley Ariarajah (New York: Fordham, 2014), 257.
23. Derrida, "Plato's Pharmacy," 110.
24. Boesel and Keller, *Apophatic Bodies*, 3–4.
25. Chris Boesel, "The Apophasis of Divine Freedom: Saving 'the Name' and the Neighbor from Human Mastery," in *Apophatic Bodies: Negative Theology, Incarnation, and Relationality* (New York: Fordham University Press, 2009), 325.
26. Letty M. Russell, "Postcolonial Challenges and the Practice of Hospitality," in *A Just & True Love: Feminism at the Frontiers of Theological Ethics: Essays in Honor of Margaret A. Farley*, ed. Maura A. Ryan and Brian F. Linnane (Notre Dame: University of Notre Dame Press, 2007), 115–16.
27. Ibid., 118–19.

28. Kelly Brown Douglas, *Stand Your Ground: Black Bodies and the Justice of God* (Maryknoll, NY: Orbis Books, 2015), 44.

29. We should always be aware of, and note, the hidden supersessionism and anti-Semitism that might be at work in critical analyses of divine election, wherein we might easily slip into identifying Abrahamic election as *the* problem, thus adding a further layer to the problem. As Boesel writes: "Contemporary remedies applied to the imperialism of Christian faith . . . often seem to entail the assumption (for *contemporary* remedies, usually unstated) that Christian faith is imperialistic in the first place precisely to the extent that it is too Abrahamic" (12). In other words, the problem with Christian theology is that "it is too Jewish" (15). Such an awareness further illustrates the kind of complexity to these problems that I have intended to highlight. See: Chris Boesel, *Risking Proclamation, Respecting Difference: Christian Faith, Imperialistic Discourse, and Abraham* (Eugene, OR: Cascade Books, 2008).

30. Russell, "Postcolonial Challenges and the Practice of Hospitality," 119.

31. Matthew Lundberg, "Echoes of Barth in Jon Sobrino's Critique of Natural Theology: A Dialogue in the Context of Post-Colonial Theology," in *Theology as Conversation: The Significance of Dialogue in Historical and Contemporary Theology* (Grand Rapids, MI: William B. Eerdmans, 2009), 92.

32. Ibid., 84.

33. Boesel, "The Apophasis of Divine Freedom: Saving 'the Name' and the Neighbor from Human Mastery," 310–11.

34. Derrida, "How to Avoid Speaking: Denials," 77.

35. Derrida, "Différance," 6.

36. Mary-Jane Rubenstein, "Dionysius, Derrida, and the Critique of 'Ontotheology,'" *Modern Theology* 24, no. 4 (2008): 727.

37. Boesel, "The Apophasis of Divine Freedom: Saving 'the Name' and the Neighbor from Human Mastery," 307.

38. Mary-Jane Rubenstein, "Unknow Thyself: Apophaticism, Deconstruction, and Theology after Ontotheology," *Modern Theology* 19, no. 3 (July 2003): 387.

39. Ibid., 387–88.

40. Caputo, *The Weakness of God: A Theology of the Event*, 7.

41. Caputo, *The Insistence of God*, 9.

42. Derrida, *Margins of Philosophy*, 6.

43. Caputo, *The Prayers and Tears of Jacques Derrida*, 6.

44. Ibid., 231.

45. Ibid., 246.

46. Ibid., xxi.

47. Ibid., 47.

48. Caputo, *The Weakness of God*, 7.

49. Ibid., 8.

50. Ibid., 7.

51. Ibid., 8.

52. On the opening page of *The Weakness of God*, Caputo confesses "a weakness for theology," despite his attempts to avoid it, especially in *Prayers and Tears* where he is more comfortable talking in terms of "religion." Now, however, he admits that he can no longer "deny that what I am doing here is theological." In the footnote to this statement, he argues that his desire to avoid "theology" was because it "suggests the onto-theological project, which takes God as an object of conceptual analysis" (p. 301).

53. Boesel and Keller, *Apophatic Bodies*, 3–4.

54. Caputo, *The Prayers and Tears of Jacques Derrida*, 47.

55. Caputo, *The Weakness of God*, 13.

56. Although he does explicitly argue, in his more recent work, that "God is not an agent . . . [or] a being who does things," *The Insistence of God*, 31ff.

57. Caputo, *The Weakness of God*, 2.

58. Ibid.

59. Ibid., 3.

60. Ibid., 4.

61. Ibid., 4–5.
62. Calvin, *Institutes of the Christian Religion*, vol. II, 207.
63. Augustine, "On the Predestination of Saints," in *Four Anti-Pelagian Writings*, trans. John A. Mourant and William J. Collinge (Washington, DC: Catholic University Press, 1992), Chapter 11.
64. Calvin, *Institutes of the Christian Religion*, II:172.
65. Caputo, *The Weakness of God*, 2.
66. Caputo, *The Insistence of God*, 9.
67. Ibid., 9.
68. Ibid., 10.
69. Ibid., 9.
70. Ibid., 13.
71. Derrida, *The Gift of Death*, 56–57.
72. Caputo, *The Insistence of God*, 28.
73. Ibid., 29.
74. Caputo might also, likely, situate (and reduce) this kind of argument to the "Kantian version" of postmodernism, or "thin postmodernism," as he calls it in his description of "two types of Continental philosophy of religion" in *The Insistence of God*, 87ff. He attempts to advance a more "Hegelian version" of postmodernism, a "radical theology" of the event, where "God" too is a *Vorstellung*, where God does not exist, but insists.
75. Ibid., 30.
76. Ibid., 31.
77. Ibid., 10.
78. Derrida, "Afterword: Toward an Ethic of Discussion," 112.
79. Derrida, "How to Avoid Speaking: Denials," 82.
80. Ibid., 83.
81. Derrida performs the "always already" in the postscript to this engagement with negative theology, where he begins the essay with an ellipsis. See: *"Sauf le nom (Post-Scriptum)"* in *On the Name*, ed. Thomas Dutoit, trans. David Wood, John P. Leavey, Jr., and Ian McLeod (Stanford: Stanford University Press, 1993).

Chapter Six

Un/Avoidable Human Decisions about Divine Decision

> *All theology is* theologia viatorum. . . . *It does not exhibit its object but can only indicate it. . . . It is broken thought and utterance. . . . It can never form a system, comprehending and as it were "seizing" the object.*
>
> —Karl Barth, *Church Dogmatics*, III.3

> *For it would be a highly refined way of becoming master of God's Word to think we could put ourselves in a position in which we have securely adopted the right attitude to it, that of servant and not master. Would this not be the loftiest triumph of human certainty? But would it not be a confirmation and a fall into the temptation?*
>
> —Karl Barth, *Church Dogmatics*, I.1

Having identified how a more thorough analysis of the problem of divine decision presents an impossibility for any attempt to avoid or exclude it in Chapter 5, the goal in this chapter is to explore the way that divine decision also presents a theological impossibility for the theologian who chooses to confess or include it. In so doing, this chapter will accomplish the task of seeing the double-bind of in/decision at work as it manifests in divine decision. The theologian who decides to confess, discuss, or include a notion of divine decision must reckon with a divine decision that was never theirs, revealing an impossibility to discuss, understand, and confess such (even on the basis of divine revelation), while also reckoning with the necessity and inescapability of doing so, since the theologian cannot choose otherwise, as it was never their decision to make. But the theologian always runs the risk of conflating or confusing divine decision with their own, and thus reducing

God to an object of human theological choice. Thus, divine decision reveals an inescapable human choice, which always runs the risk of collapsing *divine* decision into merely *human* decision, the very thing one has tried to avoid. In conjunction with the argument above, what divine decision reveals, therefore, is a kind of deconstructive impossibility (that always already carries a structural inescapability and necessity, as I have demonstrated in Part I) for the task of theology. It is both *impossible* for the human theologian to confess or declare it, yet also *impossible* to avoid, limit, or exclude it (in other words, *inescapable*). This chapter intends to explore how a genuine, radical understanding of divine decision "deconstructs" theological negotiations of it, revealing an aporetic double-bind, and the rupture of the impossible necessity and necessary impossibility.

In order to accomplish the task at hand, we will take a close look at the doctrine of divine election (and divine revelation) in Karl Barth's theology, which is paradigmatic in many ways, including the way he takes "traditional" theological concepts, ideas, and doctrines, and amplifies them to their limit. And in our discussion of the emphasis on *divine* decision in divine election, Barth does not disappoint. Perhaps more so than any other theologian, Barth is adamant about maintaining an emphasis on theology's proper "object," i.e., God, that can only be known by appreciating the "subject" of divine action (e.g., revelation, election, etc.). This means that he consistently worries about theology collapsing into merely a human enterprise that privileges human knowledge, logic, reasoning, etc., when speaking about God, and thus reducing "God" to an object of theological analysis and decision. In the case of divine election, Barth similarly wants to maintain that it is, and remains primarily, *God's* decision, and not ours, such that we do not lose sight of the One who decides.[1] As is well known, for Barth this results in a radically Christocentric theological methodology wherein everything we say or know about God must always begin and end with Jesus Christ.

However, it is Barth's recognition of the inescapable fact that theology is, must be, and cannot help but be a human enterprise (i.e., spoken, written, confessed, proclaimed by humans) that makes it precarious and puts it in the impossible predicament. For Barth, as we will see, the "best" way to navigate such a predicament—especially in something thoroughly problematic like divine decision—is to fully ground theological discourse in divine revelation, as much as possible. Barth therefore represents the preeminent example of the theological impossibility I am highlighting in this chapter, namely the risk of reducing and collapsing divine decision to the discussion of the theologian's decisions, even if/when the theologian decides to include or confess it.

Consequently, this chapter argues that the predicament is no less precarious for the theologian who decides to confess a God who decides. In Barth we find a stated commitment—i.e., a human, theological decision—to maintain that it is primarily God who decides, not the human theologian, in divine election. As we will see, Barth's doctrine of divine election is grounded in his prior doctrine of divine revelation, which also adds to the impossibility. Although in Barth, human choice is not abrogated, there is still a commitment to the notion that divine election—especially because of how he bases it on a doctrine of divine revelation—is fundamentally about God's decision and not a human one. Thus there is the sense that God is responsible, for better or worse, for the problem of exclusive divine election; "in other words, don't blame Barth, blame God."[2] It is both Barth's desire to affirm divine decision as truly *divine*—i.e., God's choice, not the human theologian's—as well as his admission of the precarious position for the theologian, that makes his doctrine of divine revelation especially pertinent to our discussion. Barth acknowledges that divine decision places the human theologian in an impossible, yet necessary predicament: a necessity to confess God's decision (as God's, not ours), while recognizing the impossibility that accompanies doing so. Not only does Barth acknowledge that the human theologian cannot prove that God does actually decide—in the way Barth confesses and tries to explicate—nor even that God revealed such a decision (since he bases the former on the latter). Barth also recognizes that even the confession of such, based on divine revelation, can still result in a "God" of our own choosing, which is the very thing Barth (and any theologian who desires to confess and remain true to *divine* decision) has tried to avoid. Thus, Barth's doctrine of divine election highlights the impossibility and necessity, the necessary yet impossible predicament facing the theologian who confesses, chooses, includes a notion of divine decision.

The overall goal of this chapter will be to probe deeper into the remedy to the problem of divine decision by exploring what issues arise when the theologian attempts to navigate the perennial issue of divine decision—even while trying to be "faithful" to it—in order to reveal a complication to any attempted remedy of the problem. The chapter therefore concludes by pointing to the impossible predicament that divine decision presents wherein every attempt to remedy the problem engenders problems of its own, revealing an inescapability to the problem(s) that one attempts to remedy, and again brings us to the thesis that there is no remedy without a poison. The analysis of this chapter will build upon previous analyses, including the deconstructive insights of Part I, and, more explicitly, the conclusion about the problem of divine decision in the previous chapter. Moreover, as we already began to see in Chapter 5, the issue of power is part and parcel of the problem of divine decision. There, as Caputo argued, we saw that one of the reasons for avoiding a notion of a God who chooses is the way in which such a move enlists the human theologian with a dangerous power supply, collapsing the eventive nature of the divine into a doctrine, dogma, or theological concept at our disposal. Here, as we will see, there is a shared concern about too much power in the hands of the human theologian. For Barth, it is the theological confession of divine decision that mitigates against that. However, just as the argument in Chapter 5 proceeded to highlight the inability of avoiding divine decision to remedy the problem completely, here too I will argue that confessing or including a notion of a divine decision cannot escape the problem, or provide a pure remedy to it, either. Thus, Part III presents the aporetic double-bind of an impossibility for the human theologian to confess or include divine decision, yet also an impossibility to avoid or exclude some form of it (in other words, an inescapability). In short, it highlights a predicament wherein the theologian cannot avoid the problem, but must discern between various forms of it, revealing the inescapability of difficult decision(s). Similar to the argument in Part II, the culprit of in/decision is power; in this case, too much power in the hands of the human theologian leads one to believe that they can safely avoid the predicament of the difficult (divine/human) decision.

BARTH: DIVINE DECISION AS TRULY DIVINE (NOT HUMAN) DECISION

Throughout Barth's massive corpus, he tenaciously insists that "Christian theology" is only possible *if and when* God reveals Godself, which means that theology—i.e., the human witness to the divine event and action—must begin and end with God's self-revelation, not human ideas about "God" or any human capacity for knowledge about God.[3] Whether it was his critique of Friedrich Schleiermacher's desire to "validate the potential for religion" by making the human being and its capacity for religion the starting point,[4] or his accusation that theology had fallen prey to Ludwig Feuerbach's claim that "theology is anthropology" (i.e., "talk about God is in the end only talk about humanity"),[5] or even his famous *Nein!* to Emil Brunner who wanted to establish a human capacity for revelation,[6] "Barth was convinced that God could be known by God alone."[7] In other words, Christian theology needs to not only ensure that God remains its proper object, but also be radically dependent upon God as the free subject of divine action. In other words, theology must always and consistently listen to, respond, and speak only on the basis of divine self-revelation. For Barth, "in the event of revelation God himself is both the object of our knowing, and yet mysteriously the subject. He is the one who initiates and brings to completion the act of knowing."[8] As Barth consistently argues, it is crucial that we let God (as the subject of divine action) define Godself (as the object of theology) and be vigilant in not imposing human definitions upon God, which he believed theology had succumbed to in his context.

Here we see an immediate (ironic) resonance between Barth's concern, and the concerns expressed in the previous chapter, about human mastery over divinity. As a result of such a concern, however, for Barth it is imperative that the object of theology, God, is only possible if and when God, as subject, reveals Godself—which marks a clear departure from the apophatic tradition and Caputo. As Boesel points out, however, such a departure might actually function apophatically in its own way. "In the free event of divine self-giving," i.e., in Barth's doctrine of divine revelation that radically depends on God's self-revelation, what is revealed "never passes over into our possession, never becomes our own, even when given to us." Thus while the apophatic tradition—as well as postmodern engagement with it—attempts to "'save the name' of God from human mastery" by un-saying, Barth's notion of the divine freedom of God as subject of revelation can function similarly.[9] We will revisit the relation between Barth's theological move and an apophatic approach below, but it is important to note a shared resonance, and nervousness, between Barth and Caputo about too much power in the hands of humanity vis-à-vis divinity.

CONTEXT OF NINETEENTH AND EARLY TWENTIETH CENTURY: BARTH'S CONCERN ABOUT POWER

In order to gain a fuller appreciation for Barth's radical, methodological move throughout his theological oeuvre—as well as his reasons for doing so as it pertains to power and authority—it is important to get a sense of the theological climate that he was responding to and concerned about. For Barth, what happens in the nineteenth century is directly related to the issues that emerge in the early twentieth century, especially with the First and Second World Wars. By briefly surveying the theological movements and sociopolitical events of that context, the significance of Barth's theology, and why he was so concerned, will stand out most clearly—and part of the issue is power, especially human power and control with regard to divinity.

While it would be reductionistic to claim that after the (so-called) Enlightenment, Kant's "Copernican Revolution in thinking," and the French Revolution that secularization ruled and Christianity was relegated to the margins, "if not entirely irrelevant," in Western Europe and the Americas, these events certainly did have tremendous impact that led to significant paradigm shifts in Christian theology in the nineteenth century. In fact, Christianity's response to this crisis and shift, which allowed it to endure "as a vibrant intellectual tradition" and contribute "decisively to a wide range of conversations, movements, and transformations across all spheres of modern intellectual, cultural, and social history," was part of what Barth was concerned about.[10] Reverberations were still being felt from Kant's attempt to understand religion within the bounds of mere reason, with an emphasis on morality and an imperative of duty as a way of reconciling Christianity with an Enlightenment emphasis on rationality through transcendental idealism. These responses included Hegel's absolute idealism and panentheistic metaphysics, as well as Left-Wing Hegelian advances from Feuerbach and Marx who distilled the theological from Hegel's system. A renewed interest in "history" and historical research also became significant in this time period, from Hegel's understanding of *Geist* working itself through world history to emerging quests of the historical Jesus in order to awaken this historical person from his ossified state. In the midst of all this stands Schleiermacher's valiant attempts to make religion, i.e., Christianity, palatable to the cultured despisers and detractors. All in all, such significant philosophical and theological approaches and breakthroughs led to the nineteenth century becoming "an unusually rich period of Christian thought."[11]

While much has been made of Barth's critique of these approaches and his denouncing charge of liberalism, it is worth noting that he did in fact commend much to the richness of theological work in this time period. In his *Protestant Theology in the Nineteenth Century* he reflects upon its legacy: "They made in their time the same contribution to the task of the Church that is required of us today. As we make our contribution, we join in with theirs, and we cannot play our part today without allowing them to play theirs."[12] In a short address given just a few years later, Barth surveys, with deference, nineteenth-century theology and describes how these theologians were faced with a uniquely secular and an extremely cultured situation, commending them for fruitfully engaging their contemporary context.

Of course, Barth also laments the fact that such engagement with society became theology's "*decisive* and *primary* concern"; and the consequences of this going "overboard" were, for Barth, tragically disastrous. By opening itself up in this way, and making engagement with an increasingly secularized society its primary goal, theology lost sight of its own boundaries and limits. Its outward hypersensitivity meant that it "never failed to react . . . to impulses from outside," and Barth saw this as a crucial loss of identity. The permeable boundary where theology sought to engage culture, history, philosophy, and science disappeared: there became no distinction between what was particularly and distinctly Christian or theological and what was heretofore "outside." As Barth saw it, theology lost sight of its own task, commitments, and "truth," and consequently, through these "open windows and doors . . . fatal errors blew in, were admitted, and made themselves at home."[13] For Barth, issues, perspectives, and claims that were once alien—and often opposed—to Christian theology now enjoyed fruitful authority within its abode. As a result of this new occupation, theology's own organic voice was subdued, and this was nothing short of tyranny for Barth. The costs of favorable reception came at a high price: "What if acceptance was so eagerly sought that Christian faith ceased to be Christian faith?"[14]

According to Barth the results had further repercussions, beyond the realm of theological disagreements and approaches—which, for Barth, was no small matter in and of itself. Because theology was now like a "ship without a rudder," it could make no positive (or negative) contribution, could offer no resistance to the impulses, patterns, and movements of society. Ironically, Christian theologians' desire to fruitfully engage with culture and society had the unintended result of actually silencing theology's own voice in the process. Theology forfeited the ability to call society into account because it was no longer distinguishable—it had nothing unique to say. In his context as a pastor in Safenwil in the early part of his career, Barth experienced firsthand the inability of Christianity to speak to the Swiss proletariat because Christian theology was so bent toward intellectual, cultural, and socioeconomic elites. While there was an increasing desire to make Christianity more culturally acceptable by stressing its universal access and availability, in the early part of his career Barth focused his attention on the way theology informed "radical politics."[15]

Worst of all, Barth felt a growing reception of "natural theology"—a catch-all phrase that became an umbrella for any reliance upon human knowledge, means, and understanding that does not recognize theology's appropriate origin in divine self-revelation—provided no checks to claims about God (a uniquely tremendous authority indeed), which Barth understood as one of theology's central tasks. For Barth, the sociopolitical implications of power and authority were directly related to theological discourse. As Barth saw it, the consequences of nineteenth-century theology's merging with and reliance upon natural theology were continuing to reverberate in problematic ways into the 1930s. Barth witnessed firsthand the developments and conflict in the crisis between the "Confessing Church" and the "German Christians" to be symptoms of the problem of natural theology. As is well known, Barth's critique was politically motivated by Hitler's rise to power in 1933 and the support of many German Christians. In the midst of otherwise dense theological treatise, Barth offers a surprisingly personal reflection in *Church Dogmatics* and recalls the dilemma theologians felt at that time:

> The question became a burning one at the moment when the Evangelical Church in Germany was unambiguously and consistently confronted by a definite and new form of natural theology, namely, by the demand to recognize in the political events of the year 1933, and especially in the form of the God-sent Adolf Hitler, a source of specific new revelation of God, which, demanding obedience and trust, took its place beside the revelation attested in Holy Scripture, claiming that it should be acknowledged by Christian proclamation and theology as equally binding and obligatory.[16]

Barth recounts how the German Church, allowing the "trojan horse" into its borders, met this newfound quest for sovereignty with naïveté. And when the totalitarian state became effective, the "Church stood entirely defenseless and simply had to succumb to it for the time being."[17] Vulnerable to this new source of authority that demanded obedience, Christianity was desperately in need of comfort and counsel; it needed somewhere to turn. As it became increasingly clear where the Nazi regime was heading, and how the Church had been implicated, where could be found someone in whom the Church could place its full trust and obedience? Barth testifies that its only option was to "confess this Word of God alone," and thus, in the first article of the Barmen declaration, we see a definitive move to position ultimate authority: "Jesus Christ, as He is attested to us in Holy Scripture, is the one Word of God, whom we have to hear and whom we have to trust and obey in life and in death."[18] Having lived through this time, Barth admits that this was a necessary move. Drastic times called for drastic measures; and for Barth and others in this context, this Confession was a matter of life and death. Not just for him and his colleagues—who were dismissed from their German teaching posts months after this Declaration—but Barth also took seriously the very real threat and action being taken against Jews at this time and the many lives that were at risk.[19]

The point here is to bring into sharp focus what was at stake for Barth: "the first article of Barmen was not merely a pretty little discovery of the theologians. The position of 1933 was not one in which a fortune could be made in Germany with little theological discoveries."[20] These theological moves were political, and for Barth they were a direct result of the mistaken authority and power that theology granted to that which stands outside its proper source and norm.

For Barth, this is why natural theology was such a threat: the notion that God could be known by natural, human means—by human reason, logic, or understanding, or by any capacity on the part of the human being. It is also why he found it necessary to distance himself from his otherwise close colleague Emil Brunner.

Though Brunner and Barth held much in common, they parted ways when Brunner wanted to establish a human capacity and responsibility for revelation, which Brunner conceptualized as a "point of contact" between the human and divine in his pamphlet *Natur und Gnade*, and to which Barth responded with his famous *Nein!* The content of Barth's response was as harsh as its title. In fact, in the "Angry Introduction" Barth immediately wants to distance himself from Brunner who, according to Barth, has unwittingly portrayed them as similar. Barth claims that this forced him to play the role of the "wicked man" as he must now show how far apart they truly are.[21] He makes every attempt to be clear and explicit in setting things straight: "Natural theology does not exist as an entity capable of becoming a separate subject within what I consider to be real theology—not even for the sake of being rejected. Really to reject natural theology means to refuse to admit it as a separate problem."[22] Nevertheless, vitriolic rejection is just what he goes on to do in a manner that becomes all too familiar for Barth at this time: "If you really reject natural theology you do not stare at the serpent, with the result that it stares back at you, but you hit it and kill it as soon as you see it!"[23] Let's be clear, says Barth: "Every attempt to assert a general revelation has to be rejected . . . there is no point of contact for the redeeming action of God."[24]

Barth's scathing reaction toward natural theology was not limited to his exchange with Brunner. It reverberated consistently throughout most of his work, including his multivolume *Church Dogmatics*. In fact, natural theology often seems to operate as a catchall phrase for everything that does not recognize its appropriate origin in God's self-revelation. Many interpreters of Barth have ventured to decipher the precise definition of natural theology. Barth himself writes, "by 'natural theology' I mean every (positive *or* negative) *formulation of a system* which claims to be theological, i.e., to interpret divine revelation, whose *subject*, however, differs fundamentally from the revelation in Jesus Christ and whose *method* therefore differs equally from the exposition of Holy Scripture."[25] Common to each of the interpretive definitions seems to be a concern for knowledge or claims about God independent of God's revelation. Barth spells out the issue that he finds with the growing reliance upon human foundations for knowledge of God: "Modernist dogmatics is unaware of the fact that in relation to God man has constantly to let something be said to him, to listen to something, which he constantly does not know and under no circumstances and in no sense can he say to himself. Modernist dogmatics hears man answer when no one has called him. It hears him speak with himself."[26] For Barth, the problem of natural theology is that it is a discourse that speaks with itself, that has no exchange with that which is Other to it, that it answers a call that is issued from within itself. In stark contrast, all throughout *Church Dogmatics* Barth insists that "theology must begin with Jesus Christ, and not with general principles"; it must also "end with Him" and not with any allegedly self-evident, general conclusions.[27] As we have seen, this is partly a matter of the proper method and approach of doing theology in order to be faithful to theology's task (as Barth understands it), but also a matter of concern about power—more specifically, about human mastery and control over divinity and the sociopolitical implications that result.

DIVINE DECISION GROUNDED IN DIVINE REVELATION

Again, in the context of late-nineteenth and early- to mid-twentieth century theology, Barth is responding critically to the growing tendency in modern, liberal theology to speak about God from the basis of human ideas, logic, reasoning, experience, etc. For Barth, theology must be beholden to the "if and when" of God's self-revelation, and not any capacity or knowledge on behalf of the human being. Since everything Christian theology says and does must begin and end with God's self-revelation, Barth methodologically begins *Church Dogmatics* with a "Doctrine of the Word of God," in which he develops the notion of divine self-revelation in the event and person of Jesus Christ. For Barth, one cannot begin to speak theologically with a doctrine of God, which at first glance might seem like the "best" place to start, especially since Barth is very concerned about theology becoming subsumed under some other discipline or being beholden to something like philosophy or culture. However, to begin with a doctrine of God is, for Barth, to always already begin with one's prior understanding of God. And as Barth is at pains to stress in his first major work *The Epistle to the Romans*: "To us God is the Stranger, the Other."[28] As a result of this kind of infinite qualitative distinction between God and humanity, one cannot presume to know, grasp, or understand God on one's own or through some natural human faculty. Therefore, any knowledge of God must come to the human being from without, from beyond. Consequently, theology must begin with God's revelation to humanity—which is the Word of God in Jesus Christ for Barth—or else theology becomes susceptible to Feuerbach's claim that theology is merely anthropology, i.e., human projection onto a transcendent screen. Moreover, the particular content of the Word of God must always be the source and norm of theology, must be what Christian theology continually refers back to and be cautious against moving away from. And that particular content is Jesus Christ, as the Word of God, attested to in Holy Scripture, and witnessed in proclamation. All throughout *Church Dogmatics* Barth continually reminds the reader of the conviction that "apart from and without Jesus Christ we can say nothing at all about God and man and their relationship one with another."[29] Thus we arrive at the Christocentric theologian *par excellence*, as Barth maintains that Jesus Christ is not only the center of Christian theology, but that everything that can or should be said theologically must begin and end here.

Barth rigidly maintains this strict Christocentric logic all throughout *Church Dogmatics*, and the determination of theology by Jesus Christ is perhaps no clearer than in Barth's doctrine of divine election (i.e., divine decision), where Jesus Christ is both the human object (who is chosen) and divine subject (who chooses). Unpacking not only the content, but also the method of Barth's doctrine of divine election—which will include its dependence on divine revelation—highlights how he attempts to maintain divine election as ultimately *God's* decision, and not a human one, despite the fact that emphasizing the former cannot avoid the latter.

Barth begins the second part of volume 2 of *Church Dogmatics*, his "Doctrine of God," by continually reminding the reader what has already been established in the previous two-thousand pages—in his "Doctrine of the Word of God" (volume 1) and first part of volume 2—namely the notion that Christian theology must begin and end with, and be continually beholden to, the event of God's self-revelation (i.e., Jesus Christ). As he continues to sketch a doctrine of God, Barth reflects upon, and reminds the reader of, his attempts to "learn the lofty but simple lesson that it is by God that God is known" and sticking with the methodological presupposition that the starting point for a doctrine of God was "neither an axiom of reason nor a datum of experience." If and when a doctrine of God is drawn from the latter, Barth argues, its subject is no longer God, "but a hypostatized reflection of man." And the risk of such a collapse is always present. "At more than one stage" in the development of his doctrine of God, Barth admits, "we have had to guard steadfastly against the temptation of this type of doctrine." Thus the goal and task was to stick as closely as possible to the starting-point of "what God Himself said and still says concerning God." Barth maintains that "as strictly as possible" he has tried to confine himself to this divine "self-testimony," letting even the questions asked "be dictated by the answers which are already present in the revelation of God attested in Holy Scripture."[30]

Barth, again, is very clear about his theological methodology: "it is by God that God is known." God is known only through divine self-revelation, which is "accessible and comprehensible" in the human form of that "self-testimony" (i.e., "Holy Scripture.").[31] For Barth, this is the "best" way to avoid collapsing theology into "a hypostatized reflection of man," which resonates with Caputo's concern about divinity becoming "something I have added to my repertoire, brought within the horizon of my experience, knowledge, belief, identification, and expectation."[32] And since, as we have seen, Barth is convinced that Jesus Christ is God's "self-testimony," then theology must always begin and end there.[33]

Because Jesus Christ is the source and norm of Barth's theology, it follows that Barth will attempt to describe divine election with Jesus Christ at the center. In fact, Barth believes that the main failure of previous attempts to understand divine decision, especially John Calvin's preeminent doctrine of divine election (i.e., double-predestination), was a direct result of Calvin attempting to understand and explicate divine decision apart from the Word of God in Jesus Christ. For Barth, all the "dubious" aspects of Calvin's doctrine of divine election are a result of the separation of God and Jesus Christ.[34] In Barth's estimation, understanding divine election apart from Jesus Christ led Calvin to erroneously conclude that humanity is the object of

God's choice, which resulted in Calvin's infamous double predestination: the human chosen by God for salvation or perdition. In his *Institutes of the Christian Religion*, Calvin describes his understanding of divine election: "In conformity, therefore, to the clear doctrine of the Scripture, we assert, that by an eternal and immutable counsel, God has once for all determined, both whom he would admit to salvation, and whom he would condemn to destruction."[35] For Barth, one can only reach the conclusion that divine election is (only) about a decision concerning the eternal destinies of human beings by attempting to understand divine election abstractly—in other words, attempting to understand divine election *apart from* God's self-revelation, which for Barth is the person and event of Jesus Christ.[36] As Barth has been at pains to stress all throughout *Church Dogmatics*, the Christian does not deal with an abstract concept of "God"—or even a "God" of the theologian's choosing—but who (he believes) God has revealed Godself to be.

In so doing, Barth maintains that in divine election "its direct and proper object is not individuals generally, but one individual—and only in Him the people called and united by Him." In the strictest sense, then, only Jesus Christ can "be understood and described as 'elected' (and 'rejected')."[37] Not surprisingly, for Barth, Jesus Christ is the object of the divine decision as the elected human being, through which all humanity participates in Jesus Christ's righteousness, glory, and exaltation. Therefore, the fellowship that Jesus Christ has with God as the perfect human being (who has accepted this fellowship) now becomes available to all humanity because Jesus Christ represents the human being elected by God. At the same time, however, Barth asserts that Jesus Christ also bears humanity's judgment because of sin. Jesus Christ is not only the human being chosen for fellowship with God, but is the human being chosen to bear the punishment, judgment, and wrath of God because of humanity's disobedience. Thus, part of Calvin's error is that he mistakes the object of the divine decision to be particular, individual human beings, when for Barth the object of divine decision could only be one particular human being, Jesus Christ.

But the present focus of this chapter should bring our attention to the other—in fact, more primary and primordial—aspect of Barth's twofold doctrine of divine election where Jesus Christ is not only the "object" of God's choice (as human being representative of all humanity), but the "subject," i.e., the God who chooses: "It is the name of Jesus Christ which, according to the divine self-revelation, forms the focus at which the two decisive beams of the truth forced upon us converge and unite: on the one hand the electing God and on the other elected man."[38] Highlighting Chalcedonian Christology's view of Jesus Christ as fully God and fully human, Barth also depicts Jesus Christ as the subject of divine decision: the electing God. With Jesus Christ as the electing God we see God's self-determination—or self-election—to be *this* way. In other words, Jesus Christ is not only the object of

God's choice or decision, but in Jesus Christ we see the very nature of God as God in relationship, fellowship, and communion with humanity because Jesus Christ is the very "concrete and manifest form of the divine decision."[39]

It is important to note, however, that Jesus Christ's electing—as the divine decision—also entails a *human* decision, which adds a fundamental aspect to Barth's understanding of divine election, especially with regard to our present focus. Since Barth subscribes to the traditional Christological understanding of the simultaneous full humanity and divinity of Jesus Christ "without division, without separation," the humanity of Jesus is not (just) elected, but also elects.[40] Barth clarifies that with so much focus on Jesus Christ as the electing God and elected human being, we must also not neglect the active, electing aspect of Jesus's humanity, i.e., how "as man" he also elects "God in faith."[41] For Barth, then, divine election—primarily as *God's* decision—always entails, involves, calls for *human* election, decision, choice in response. In Barth's understanding, God (in Jesus Christ) elects/chooses humanity (in Jesus Christ), and the human being (in Jesus Christ), in turn, elects/chooses God in faith. There is, therefore, always a necessary aspect of human decision involved in divine election for Barth, especially when one confesses or decides to include it theologically. The problem, as we will see, arises with the recognition that there is no safeguarding against the collapse or reduction of divine decision into merely human decision. This aspect of Barth's doctrine of divine election will be important for our present discussion of the "impossibility" of divine election as we move forward, namely how to confess, understand, or even *choose* a choice that is fundamentally "other," i.e., God's. The short "answer" for Barth—although even he admits there is no way to ultimately insure or protect against this—is only on the ground of divine revelation of said divine decision. But before turning more explicitly to that complexity (or impossibility/necessity), we should continue our exploration of Barth's attempt to assert that divine election is, or should be, ultimately, primarily about God's decision and not (merely) the theological decisions we make.

Part of Barth's concern about previous understandings of divine decision, including those of Augustine and Calvin, is the way in which an appeal to mystery or unknowability can actually mitigate against the very content of divine election by turning it into human speculation and reducing it to merely human choice or decision. In Barth's understanding, Jesus Christ, as both the subject and object of divine election—the electing God and elected human being—safeguards against any unknown mystery regarding divine decision, for if Jesus Christ is the elector and elected then we have the content of the very decision before us. Otherwise, for Barth, we might be concerned about what kind of God we are dealing with when discussing such a precarious topic as divine decision. The "good news," then, at least for Barth, is that in

Jesus Christ we are dealing with the very decree of God: the One who decides and the object of that choice. And it is the "certainty" of such (through faith) that permits Barth to declare that divine election—previously understood as *decretum horribile*—"is the sum of the Gospel because of all words that can be said or heard it is the best."[42] In other words, the fact that in divine election we have to do with Jesus Christ as the electing God (and elected human being), is what makes it "good news," in fact the "best" news humanity could ever receive, precisely because it reframes what was once a "horrible decree"—because of God's mysterious decision and choice of some over others—into the divine decision for all humanity, in the election of Jesus Christ.

Barth therefore marks a clear departure from an appeal to an unknown mystery in an attempt to ensure that divine decision does not collapse into human decision. As we have seen in Chapter 5, contemporary engagements with the apophatic tradition, including Caputo's "weak theology," emphasize unknowability in order to protect divinity from human mastery and control. In Augustine and Calvin's doctrines of divine election, we find a similar appeal to mystery and unknowability, for similar reasons.

As we gestured to in the preceding chapter, when pressed to the limits of "why" God chooses or has chosen some, Augustine appeals to the mystery of God in an attempt to be faithful to the notion that divine decision is fundamentally about God's choice, not a human choice. Although the point that Augustine is trying to make is that it is "good news" that God chooses any to be saved, he too cannot help but wonder about those who are not chosen, who are predestined to eternal damnation, and the ways in which that seems like very bad news (at least for some). For Augustine, this kind of apophatic stance with regard to divine decision is the best way of avoiding its collapse into merely human decision. Again, Augustine, in an attempt to maintain a notion of divine decision as truly divine—i.e., keep it out of the grasp and control of humanity—appeals to mystery when the human cannot understand, make sense of, explain, or justify what God has chosen not to reveal. Calvin also appealed to the mystery (and beneficence) of divine will in his doctrine of divine election, as we saw in Chapter 5, in order to assert that it is primarily God's decision and not ours.

As we can see, Augustine and Calvin's desire to maintain that divine election is truly about God's decision comes by way of an appeal to divine mystery in order to keep it out of the grasp and control of humanity. This appeal to mystery might be understood, in Caputo's language, as an attempt to let the divine event "happen to us . . . overtake us and outstrip the reach of the subject or the ego." "Although we are called upon to respond to events," as Augustine and Calvin seems to be doing here, they too must also admit that "an event is not our doing but is done to us (even as it might well be our undoing)" leaving us with "something I must deal with, like it or not," especially when "the event is not necessarily good news."[43]

But it is Barth's shared desire to keep divine decision truly *divine* that actually clears up some of the mystery, because Barth is convinced that God has indeed revealed Godself in Jesus Christ. "So much depends upon our acknowledgment of the Son . . . as the Subject of this predestination," Barth writes, because if Jesus Christ is not "primarily the Elector, what shall we really know at all of a divine electing and our election?" If we remove our focus from revelation of God in Jesus Christ when discussing divine election, Barth critically asks, then what are we left with? The result, Barth argues, is that we shall be driven to speculate about a *"decretum absolutum"* instead of affirming the good news of divine election.[44] And this is the real pinch, both for Barth and for our own inquiry into how much divine election truly is about God's decision (and not ours): on the one hand, to maintain the notion that divine election is ultimately God's decision led Augustine and Calvin to the point of mystery—if it is God's, then it is not ours to be analyzed, questioned, or scrutinized. Although not focused particularly on the topic of divine decision, Caputo (and others) also maintain that the best way to avoid collapsing divinity into human grasp and control is by appeal to a certain kind of mystery or "uncontainability" of the divine event. However, Barth questions whether or not appealing to mystery might have its own way of turning divine decision into a "God" of our own choosing. And, in fact, he argues that declaring quite the opposite—i.e., that there is no such *decretum absolutum*, no will of God "apart from the will of Jesus Christ,"[45] that in this divine decision we can know and trust with a certainty which "nothing can ever shake that we are the elect of God"[46] —is a surer way to maintain divine decision remains divine, because "He tells us that He Himself is the One who elects us."[47] In other words, as Barth sees it, what might seem like deference to mystery—as in the case of Augustine, Calvin, or Caputo—in order to safeguard against human mastery over divinity, might actually have the opposite result, namely running the risk of collapsing divine decision into human decision.

Let's dive deeper into this strange logic. Barth admits that his thesis, that divine election begins and ends with Jesus Christ, marks a significant departure from previous understandings of the doctrine in many ways, including its refusal to adhere to an unknown mystery of divine election. In these previous interpretations, Barth argues, both "the Subject and object of predestination (the electing God and elected man) are determined ultimately by the fact that both quantities are treated as unknown." As we have seen, both Augustine and Calvin appeal to mystery when (inevitable) questions are raised in light of the rationale or justification of God's choice; in other words, for them, this "unknown" protects the agency and subjectivity of God—since it is divine (and not human) decision, it makes sense for us to not know or fully understand it. Barth, who appreciates this desire to maintain the primacy of the divine in divine election, acknowledges the motivation to confess the electing God as an ultimately "supreme being" who can dispose freely of "His own omnipotence, righteousness and mercy," with absolute right, power, and lordship to "determine the destiny" of all things. But we must also acknowledge, Barth argues, that in so doing "the electing God" has become an "unknown quantity." And it is at this very point that "obscurity has undoubtedly enveloped the theories of even the most prominent representatives and exponents" of divine election in the history of Christianity. Indeed, Barth continues, "in the most consistently developed forms" of divine election we are told that "we have to do, necessarily, with a great mystery." In "the sharpest contrast" to these previous understandings of divine decision, however, Barth affirms that his own argument and discussion about divine decision—i.e., that "the eternal will of God is the election of Jesus Christ"—ineluctably means a denial "of any such twofold mystery."[48]

Barth clearly has a shared commitment with Augustine and Calvin to allow God to "dispose freely" in divine election; in other words, not to impose our decisions upon God but confess that God is the One who chooses in freedom in divine election, and has revealed this to us. However, in stark contrast to Augustine and Calvin, Barth finds it necessary to deny such an unknown mystery in order to do so. Part of Barth's issue—and what he understands as one of the main issues with any notion of divine decision—is "whether it is incomprehensible light or incomprehensible darkness."[49] In other words, is divine election "good news" or "*dusaggelion*" (i.e., bad news)?[50] Barth is convinced that divine election is, should be, and was always intended to be "the sum of the Gospel," and "not a mixed message of joy and terror, salvation and damnation."[51] But, according to Barth, such an affirmation of the good news of divine election, i.e., where all are chosen in Jesus Christ, "could not and cannot be made" without declaring that when dealing with divine decision "we have to do on both sides with only one name and one person . . . Jesus Christ."[52] Thus, part of Barth's problem with such an appeal to divine mystery is that it necessarily obscures the goodness of the news that divine election was (always) intended to be.

But more pertinent to our present focus is the other issue Barth takes with the appeal to divine mystery when discussing divine decision, namely the way in which it can actually, unexpectedly, collapse divine election into human decision. The way Barth sees it, "as long as we cannot ultimately know" what the content of this divine decision is, who this electing God is, or who or what is elected or chosen, then it does not in any way lead us to be silent and humble in the face of this mystery.[53] In other words, appeals to an "unknown" do not necessarily lead to humility, silence, and respect for the fact that this decision is God's and not ours, as perhaps it was intended; in fact, such appeals often have the opposite result. As Barth sees it, appeals to "mystery" or "unknown" routinely results in speculation, which is precisely what Augustine, Calvin, and others are trying to avoid. And when we speculate about what the content of this divine decision is or could (or should) be, the "mystery" or "unknown" does not stay that way, but becomes, in fact, a very known concept or idea. And such inescapable human speculation is what makes Barth nervous. In fact, Barth argues that "it is inevitable that we ourselves should try to fill in the gap" left by this mystery, and, in doing so, make known the supposed unknown, arbitrarily ascribing some name or concept to this unknown, and seeking "in Him this or that reality." In so doing, we would fall prey to one of Barth's chief concerns, no longer humbling ourselves before God, but to "this or that self-projected image of God." And while this is not the intention of previous exponents of divine decision "who plunge us into that obscurity," Barth admits that "we can hardly restrain ourselves as long as they refuse" to direct us more clearly and explicitly toward this "genuine form of mystery which we could and should approach with genuine silence, humility and adoration."[54]

For Barth, an appeal to mystery or unknown might not (always) have the desired effect of avoiding reducing divinity to human speculation, but actually increases the risk. Appealing to mystery can in fact open up the space for human speculation about the nature of this God, this divine decision, or its object(s), in which case it does not remain a "genuine . . . mystery." Moreover, this process is irresistible, Barth argues, because "we can hardly restrain ourselves as long as they refuse" to offer anything regarding this divine decision. It is inevitable that in the face of this so-called mystery, we should "fill the gap" by arbitrarily placing *some*-thing in its place to humble ourselves before, i.e., a "self-projected image of God." In Barth's estimation, then, genuine appreciation for the Subjectivity of God in divine decision—i.e., that in such a notion we are truly dealing with God's choice and not ours—comes only when we actually know who this God is and what this decision is, as revealed in Jesus Christ. In other words, affirming that God has indeed chosen means affirming what that choice actually is, not simply deferring to mystery or unknowability, because Barth believes that one cannot help but speculate and thus "make known the unknown," or at least attempt to do so. While deference to mystery might be intended to preserve divine autonomy when discussing divine decision, Barth argues that there is no guarantee that this is the case.

AN APOPHATIC CERTAINTY AND KATAPHATIC UNCERTAINTY

Barth's point about how appeals to mystery can inevitably result in declaring something known applies not only to Augustine and Calvin, but also the views expressed in Chapter 5. As I suggested, those concerned about human control and mastery over divinity should recognize the way such a concern is betrayed when the theologian chooses the kind of God who chooses (or not). Additionally, despite Caputo's attempt to keep "weak theology" free from determination, declaration, and decision and to remain content with "a little adverb like 'perhaps,'" he seems to make Barth's point when he writes that "one must, it is absolutely necessary, always say 'perhaps' for God."[55] Such an absolute necessity and demand seems contrary to "perhaps." And when Caputo declares that "God does not exist," but rather, "God insists,"[56] he seems to betray the "perhaps" by doing what he critiques "strong theology" for doing, such that instead of leaving room for "the event" he does indeed "fill in the gap" by declaring something definitive about "God," i.e., that "God does not exist." Perhaps, then, Barth was onto something when he suggested that appeals to mystery, unknowability, or uncertainty do not often remain that way, as it is inevitable that we would position something in this space to fill the void.

To the extent that this is the case, it would mean that there might not be any genuine or pure apophaticism that might be free of this kind of performative self-contradiction. Perhaps, then, Derrida's initial critique of apophatic theology was accurate—that although apophatic theology gestures toward the impossible and unknowable, it is really "only in order to acknowledge [God's] superior, inconceivable, and ineffable mode of being."[57] For Derrida, the negative theologian knows all along what they are (not) talking about—"even 'the most negative of negative theologies' knows where it comes from, where it is going, and how to get there."[58] In other words, an apophatic approach might not be able to insulate itself from a desire of knowability or certainty. Moreover, it would also lend veracity to Caputo's own critique of apophatic theology wherein he argues that it inevitably "drops anchor, hits bottom, lodges itself securely in pure presence and the transcendental signified." But it would also mean that there is no genuinely apophatic stance that could escape this dilemma either—including the "perhaps"—as I have tried to argue in the previous chapter regarding divine decision. And thus, rather than reading deconstruction as that which "saves negative theology from closure," as Caputo suggests, deconstruction reveals that the problem of closure and certainty can never be purely remedied.[59]

Of course, even Barth recognizes that "certainty" entails problems of its own as well—though certainly not to the same extent as Caputo—which points to the kind of aporetic double-bind of impossibility I have been alluding to all along. Barth admits that his certainty about the substance and content (or subject and object) of divine decision does not fully solve the problem either, at least epistemologically, and thus acknowledges the impossibility of the task at hand. In fact, such certainty still leaves very pressing questions, namely whether such an affirmation can be made, whether Barth is right to make it, or on what basis he can do so: "How do we know that Jesus Christ is the electing God and elected man? How do we know that all that is to be said concerning this mystery must be grounded in His name?"[60] It should come as no surprise that Barth addresses these questions by referring back to his initial premise, explicitly his doctrine of revelation, the Word of God revealed in and through Jesus Christ. What this means, for Barth, is that we "know" because this is who God has revealed Godself to be. This is, no doubt, circular reasoning; and according to George Hunsinger: "Barth was well aware of the circularity of this argument. He had in no way tried to prove that God has engaged in an act of self-revelation."[61] In other words, while Barth boldly confesses his understanding of divine self-revelation (and divine decision), his goal was never to prove that this was the case. And neither is it the intention of this chapter to seek after any such "proof" with regard to if God decides, who or what God chooses, or the nature of such decision. Rather the aim is merely to point to the issue that arises when discussing divine decision, namely the impossibility and problematic nature of negotiating, analyzing, choosing and making decisions about "divine" decision. That is precisely the issue that Barth's theology raises: How to ensure that divine decision remains truly *divine* decision? How to avoid a collapse into merely human decision, resulting in a god of our own choosing and turning a "divine" decision into what we desire, hope for, or discern as the best possible option? And Barth, perhaps more so than any theologian, attempts to resist this collapse as much as possible. The issue that remains, however, is not merely whether or not he succeeded in doing so—which would mean definitive, factual, certitude that Jesus Christ is indeed the electing God and elected human being (which is a futile inquiry because even Barth claims this can only be known through faith)—but how divine decision presents an impossibility by its very nature. This would mean that the response to the above questions of "how to ensure" or "how to avoid" can only be answered with a denial, like Derrida suggests—that divine decision causes us to reckon with the impossibility of knowing, confessing, declaring that God might choose (or not), while also an impossibility to avoid or remedy this dilemma by reducing divine decision to merely the theological discussion of what is most reasonable, ethically coherent, desirable, and viable according to the standards that we set.

Such impossibility was not lost on Barth either. For all his talk of certainty regarding divine revelation, divine decision, and Jesus Christ as the source and norm of both, Barth recognized that theology, by its very nature, presents an impossibility. In other words, it is futile to think we could ensure that we have succeeded in protecting theology from doing that which it is trying to avoid—either apophatically or kataphatically. Again, Barth arrives at certainty, methodologically, *because* he wants to affirm that Christian theology always begins and ends with God (through revelation, in Jesus Christ), and not human reasoning, experience, etc. Thus, Barth's attempt to maintain the subjectivity of God in divine election results in a necessity to speak about divine election in the way God has chosen, not the choices we make. Yet we also find Barth making strange, unexpected gestures in the opposite direction throughout *Church Dogmatics*, discussing "the speech of God as the mystery of God," in order to unsettle anyone who might rest assured in such certainty.[62] Speaking of the unavoidable limitations of theology, Barth writes:

> All theology is *theologia viatorum* . . . It does not exhibit its object but can only indicate it, and in so doing it owes the truth to the self-witness of the theme and not its own resources. It is broken thought and utterance to the extent that it can progress only in isolated thoughts and statements directed from different angles to the one object. It can never form a system, comprehending and as it were "seizing" the object.[63]

Again, Barth's real desire is to be as rigorous as possible "that in everything our concern is with *God's* speech and *God's* act," and not our own. Thus Barth must also be wary of the "continual temptation to think and speak of the Logos of God . . . in such a way that we think we know it . . . that we think we perceive its structure and understand its operation, so that in thought and speech we are its master, as well or as badly as man may become the master of any object of thought or speech."[64] In other words, if theology ever intends to be about a divine reality, and not merely the projection of human ideas such that its object (i.e., "God") comes under the control and mastery of humanity, then theology should always appreciate the precarious position it is in. Barth thus asks the reader whether or not they have sufficiently recognized "that the serious element in serious theological work is grounded in the fact that its object is never in any circumstances at our command, at the command of even the profoundest biblical or Reformation vision or knowledge, at the command of even the most delicate and careful construction?"[65]

Here Barth is also issuing a warning against resting too much in any kind of certainty—much like his warning against an appeal to mystery—over any theological notion, doctrine, or dogma because of the way it too might bring God under the command and mastery of human thoughts, ideas, and decisions. In fact, he goes so far as to admit that even in his own theology there is no way "we could and should prove that we have not deceived ourselves, that we have really been speaking of the Logos of God," because "thinking we can prove this in some sense, we should really betray the cause."[66] In other words, if all the talk about basing theology on divine revelation and not our own understanding meant anything, then "we must accept the fact that only the Logos of God Himself can provide the proof that we are really talking about Him when we are allegedly doing so." Going further, he writes:

> And we should have succumbed already to the afore-mentioned temptation if we were to look about for some means to ward it off, to secure ourselves against it, and to make ourselves immune to temptation. For it would be a highly refined way of becoming master of God's Word to think we could put ourselves in a position in which we have securely adopted the right attitude to it, that of servant and not master. Would this not be the loftiest triumph of human certainty? But would it not be a confirmation and a fall into the temptation?[67]

And here is the point in which we reach the pinnacle of the impossible predicament with regard to our present focus on divine decision. Barth acknowledges that the temptation to bring God (and "God's Word") under human control and mastery cannot be safely guarded against, even by doing what he has tried to do, i.e., recognizing the temptation, by trying not to do so, and rigorously maintaining that focus throughout. Because in so doing, even then we could fall prey to "the loftiest of human certainty" by thinking that we had "adopted the right attitude" theologically, and thus escaped the temptation or avoiding the danger. In fact, identifying the temptation at the outset and thus working hard to ward it off, might inevitably function in some kind of certainty or assurance itself that we have succeeded in doing so. In other words, the very attempt to accomplish the task at hand—especially when we rigorously work at it—might reveal the impossibility of securing ourselves against that which we have tried to avoid. Yet again, we stumble across another instantiation of the *pharmakon*.

To the extent that Barth is onto something here, it would mean a direct exposure and critique of the approaches highlighted in Chapter 5, including those that believe that they have been able to safely avoid human mastery over divine mystery, that they have succeeded in warding it off, secured themselves against it, and "adopted the right attitude to it." Moreover, it would also mean that there is no stance that one could take with regard to divine decision—including Barth's—that could safely avoid the pitfalls and dangers it presents. The goal in Chapter 5 was to illustrate how that is the case for avoiding a notion of divine decision. And here the problem is inescapable also, as Barth admits. When one decides to confess or include a notion of divine decision, there is no guarantee that it has not been reduced to a mere human decision, which is the very thing these theologians—like Barth—have tried to avoid.

Thus Barth seems to appreciate a theological impossibility, a danger that is inescapable, where he must admit: "All our delimitations can only seek to be signals or alarms to draw attention to the fact that God's Word is and remains God's, not bound and not to be attached to this thesis or to that antithesis."[68] And the theological commitment to divine subjectivity does not result in "an ultimate 'assuring'" of theology, "but always a penultimate 'de-assuring' of theology, or, as one might put it, a theological warning against theology."[69] Barth thus appreciates the precarious position divine decision (and the theological task writ large) presents, one in which the theologian finds himself or herself caught in an aporetic double-bind, this impossible, yet necessary predicament: a necessity to confess divine decision (as God's, and not ours), while recognizing the impossibility of doing so. Furthermore, as Barth suggests, there is no guarding or protecting against, no avoiding or escaping, the dilemma, the impossibility/necessity, even if/when one recognizes and attempts to avoid it, as he himself has tried to do.

This kind of "de-assuring" is precisely the goal of this chapter, and more generally, this book: that any attempt to remedy (divine) decision will be met by limits, by an impossible predicament, by an aporetic double-bind. In our discussion of this problem in Part III, I am drawing attention to the way in which that is highlighted by a notion of divine decision. Even more specifically in this chapter, I am highlighting how even a recognition of the problem, even an attempt to keep divine decision *divine*—and not merely *human* decision—cannot avoid the dilemma, such that there is no way "to look about for some means to ward it off, to secure ourselves against it" or "to think we could put ourselves in a position in which we have securely adopted the right attitude to it."[70] That would apply both to the theologian attempting to remedy divine decision (by trying to avoid it), as well as the theologian attempting to remain "true" to it (by deciding to include it).

In an essay entitled "The Need and Promise of Christian Preaching," Barth expounds even more upon the aporetic double-bind of theological impossibility and necessity that this chapter has tried to highlight. As intonated by the title, Barth's main focus is on the necessity facing the preacher. The need to preach the Gospel, for Barth, emerges from "God's promise, which lies behind it all." Yet this necessity carries with it a simultaneous (or even greater) impossibility as well. "But we must not stop here," Barth writes, speaking of the necessity of Christian preaching, "the Word of God on the lips of man is an impossibility."[71] Although the Christian preacher is called by God to preach the "Word of God"—ushering forth a necessity—for Barth doing so is simultaneously impossible. It should come as no surprise that the impossibility arises from Barth's conviction that "the word of God is and will and must be and remain the word of *God*," and there is always the danger in Christian preaching—and, in Christian theology, I would add—of confusing what is rightfully God's with what is ours, by collapsing it into something within our possession and control. Barth reflects on the "great peril" that the preacher, and theologian, faces:

> Is there not every likelihood that men will seem to have undertaken and—who knows?—accomplished the feat of taking God's word on their lips as their own? . . . What can it mean? It means above all that we should feel a fundamental alarm. What are you doing, you man, with the word of *God* upon *your*

lips? Upon what grounds do you assume the role of mediator between heaven and earth? . . . Did one ever hear of such overwhelming presumption, such Titanism, or—to speak less classically but more clearly—such brazenness! One does not with impunity cross the boundaries of mortality![72]

Although part of Barth's concern here is how the preacher can claim to "usurp the prerogative of God," ours is a little less ominous (i.e., I am not trying to invoke a concern about the wrath and vengeance of a punitive God)—though ominous nonetheless. As I have tried to sketch the problem in this chapter, I think Barth's concern over the peril of assuming to speak of, for, or even about divine decision is sound and sober. Thus, when Barth speaks about the perilous situation facing the one who claims to preach God's word, that "so far as *we* know, there is no one who deserves the wrath of God more abundantly than the ministers," we might also appreciate how divine decision reveals a similar kind of peril and danger in the predicament facing every theologian.[73]

Barth continues: "As a matter of fact, the church is really an impossibility. There can be no such thing as a minister. Who dares, who can, preach, knowing what preaching is? The situation of crisis in the church has not yet been impressed upon us with sufficient intensity. One wonders if it will ever be."[74] Through a similar kind of reasoning, I am arguing that the impossibility is equally as live for the theologian, such that what a more thorough analysis of divine decision reveals is that "there can be no such thing as a theologian," if being a theologian means safely navigating this impossibility/ necessity. If divine decision highlights this impossibility—in either speaking about a God who chooses or choosing not to—then the situation is certainly a "crisis," one in which I have tried in this chapter to impress "upon us with sufficient intensity." To make matters worse, for the theologian (and preacher), the impossibility is such that there is no safely escaping the problem, which highlights the inescapability I have tried to sketch as well. Remember, for Barth, the impossibility emerges in light of the necessity. As he says elsewhere, "We ought to speak of God. We are human, however, and so cannot speak of God."[75] To that end, this chapter has pursued the problem of divine decision wherein it is the theologian who faces the impossibility and necessity of deciding, either to confess, declare, or include divine decision, or to avoid, remedy, exclude it.

Before closing our exploration of Barth's theology of divine election, I want to highlight a dynamic in play that is particularly relevant to this project's overall aim. We have focused our attention explicitly in Part III on the methodological problem of excluding or including the notion of divine decision and the impossibility that emerges on both ends—but we must remember that the primary motivation for avoiding divine decision in the first place is because of its inherently exclusive decision or choice, i.e., God choosing this/that. And while Barth's theology certainly exemplifies the tension of the methodological impossibility (and necessity) of divine decision, it also exemplifies this latter issue of exclusivity—especially the kind of nuanced, specific exclusivity we have been seeking to highlight: the structural inescapability of exclusion inherent in divine decision, which does not necessarily entail God electing some to eternal salvation while excluding others in an absolute decision. Barth's doctrine of divine election surely gestures toward a more "universal" notion of divine decision, as all are chosen in Jesus Christ; yet it is still exclusive. Methodologically, Barth is certainly exclusive because divine election can only be properly understood in Jesus Christ. This is important to acknowledge because it "can pack a rather mean exclusionary punch" for anyone who does not affirm Jesus Christ as God's (primary, only, exclusive, once-and-for-all) revelation and decision, which might include not only practitioners of any other religious tradition, but Christians as well who do not share in this conviction.[76] Simply put, "the problem is obvious: God *only* in Jesus Christ," which *excludes* all other theological or religious understandings, traditions, beliefs.[77] Thus, even if *all* are chosen in Jesus Christ, which might seem to suggest that it is not exclusive, it is the fact that all are chosen *in Jesus Christ*, that is certainly exclusive. So Barth's doctrine of divine election can also serve to represent the main problem this project has been tracking all along: the inherent, structural exclusivity of decision, that is manifested in our exploration of divine decision. Of course, it is not the same kind of exclusivity found in "traditional" doctrines of divine election wherein some are elected to salvation while others are not; but the overall goal here has been an attempt to highlight an inevitable (form of) exclusivity, which Barth's theology also illustrates—especially this more nuanced form that need not be a once-for-all, absolute, eternal exclusion.[78]

THE IMPOSSIBILITY OF THEOLOGICALLY MAINTAINING DIVINE ELECTION AS TRULY DIVINE

Through our final exploration of the problem of in/decision here in Part III I have highlighted a more rigorously *theological* layer by exposing the deconstructive impossibility divine decision presents. As we saw in Chapter 5, for the theologian who is concerned about the exclusivity of divine decision, or even a notion of a "God" who chooses (at all), our exploration revealed a precarious predicament for any attempt to remedy, avoid, or exclude it. If the remedy to exclusive divine election is that the theologian chooses, or decides the kind of "God" who chooses (or not), what such choice might be, etc., then said remedy is trafficking in the very thing it has attempted to avoid or remedy, namely, exclusive election, choice, decision. Furthermore, for the theologian who is concerned about human mastery and control over divinity, the remedy to divine decision also reveals an impossibility to avoid that which is problematic. If there is a genuine concern about "God" (as a theological notion or idea) or even God (as a divine reality) becoming "something I have added to my repertoire, brought within the horizon of my experience, knowledge, belief, identification, and expectation,"[79] or human "mastery over divine mystery,"[80] then it is impossible to exclude (at least) the possibility, "perhaps," that God chooses. It might also be inevitable to say, name, or declare something about "God," even when one appeals to mystery, unknowability, or "perhaps." Additionally, our exploration of divine decision revealed the impossibility of guarding against human mastery over divine mystery, even if/when one believes to have adopted the right attitude toward it.

In this chapter we explored the problems that arise for the theologian who decides to confess, declare, include divine decision in said theology. In so doing, he/she must acknowledge the impossibility of avoiding a collapse into merely human decision, which is the very thing one is trying to avoid, because there is no avoiding the human aspect of confessing—or deciding to confess—such. Our foray into Karl Barth's theology revealed not only the impossibility of proving the reality or fact of divine decision, as only "God . . . can provide the proof that we are really talking about [God] when we are allegedly doing so,"[81] but also the impossibility of avoiding the risk of speaking about divine decision "in such a way that we think we know it . . . that we think we perceive its structure and understand its operation, so that in thought and speech we are its master."[82] And because even for Barth divine decision always entails (some form of) human decision, there is no escaping that which one has tried to avoid. Even Barth's appeal to the "certainty" (through faith) of divine revelation acknowledges there is no escaping this predicament.

Lest this chapter be read as an apologetic for Barthian theology as if he were able to solve the problem, it is important to clarify that I read Barth more as merely representing an attempt at negotiating the predicament divine decision presents, by at least acknowledging its impossibility. As we have seen all along throughout our engagement with the problem of undecidability, transparency about its difficulty (i.e., impossibility and inescapability) has been one of the main things I have been arguing for us to reckon with. As for Barth, he could very well fall prey to the target of his own critique, or at least the manifestation of the impossibility he acknowledges, simply by pointing out "Barth's own systematic blindness to his patriarchal context," which has been present through most of the quotations cited in this chapter.[83] This includes, not least, his exclusive use of and reference to the masculine, i.e., "He," "Him," "His," "man," etc., not to mention the patriarchal approach and overtones of his theology. Such blindness might lead us to ask how "His" decision(s) and choice(s) were impacted by "him," or vice-versa?

Part of what Part III—and the overall argument of this book—seeks is "truth in advertising." If the theologian is convinced that "God" is merely a function of human intentions, an object for our use, an entity, object, or symbol that we deploy for ethical, theological, or political ends, in which case a notion of a "God" who chooses is too violent, unethical, exclusive, then said theologian must recognize that they too fall prey to the critique of "human mastery over divine mystery," which is often marshaled against "traditional" theologies. The theologian cannot *both* remedy divine decision *and* avoid human mastery over divine mystery, as well as some form of exclusive decision (human or divine). At the same time, the theologian concerned about a "God" of our choosing, who desires or at least hopes for theology to be about something *beyond* human mastery, control, creation, or choice, should recognize that there is no way to safeguard against this kind of objectification. Furthermore, the theologian is always trafficking in human control, decision, choice, in "broken thought and utterance," even as one tries to remain true to divine decision.[84] A more thorough analysis of divine decision reveals the tension of this aporetic double-bind. As Boesel argues: "because this is *divine* activity, the measure of it—*ethically* and . . . *epistemologically*—is precisely that which is and always remains radically beyond our ken and so radically beyond our ethical as well as epistemological grasp, control, and mastery."[85] And thus any attempts to remedy this problem encounter strict limits, an impossibility, an impossible necessity—in short, an unavoidability. Thus, it is also inescapable, and the theologian is left to reckon with, confront, and acknowledge this difficult (divine) decision, with no guaranteed outcome.

NOTES

1. Karl Barth, *Church Dogmatics*, ed. G. W. Bromiley and T. F. Torrance, trans. G. W. Bromiley et al., vol. II.2 (Edinburgh: T&T Clark, 1957), 50–51.
2. Boesel, "Divine Relationality and (the Methodological Constraints of) the Gospel as Piece of News: Tracing the Limits of Trinitarian Ethics," 259.
3. I use the phrase "Christian theology" here to signal one of the primary points of Barth's theology, namely that theology is—or should be—about an actual, living, personal reality, and not merely human ideas, concepts, language, etc. From here on out, however, when discussing Barth's views, the term "theology" is meant to signify this understanding.
4. Karl Barth, "Evangelical Theology in the 19th Century," in *The Humanity of God* (Richmond: Westminster John Knox Press, 1960), 22.
5. Trevor Hart, "Revelation," in *The Cambridge Companion to Karl Barth* (New York: Cambridge University Press, 2000), 40.
6. Karl Barth, "No!: Answer to Emil Brunner," in Emil Brunner, *Natural Theology: Comprising "Nature and Grace,"* trans. Peter Fraenkel (London: The Centenary Press, 1946).
7. George Hunsinger, *How to Read Karl Barth: The Shape of His Theology* (New York: Oxford University Press, 1991), 36.
8. Trevor Hart, "The Word, the Words and the Witness: Proclamation as Divine and Human Reality in the Theology of Karl Barth.," *Tyndale Bulletin* 46, no. 1 (May 1995): 83.

9. Boesel, "The Apophasis of Divine Freedom: Saving 'the Name' and the Neighbor from Human Mastery," 320.
10. Joel D. S. Rasmussen, Judith Wolfe, and Johannes Zachhuber, eds., *The Oxford Handbook of Nineteenth-Century Christian Thought* (Oxford: Oxford University Press, 2017), 1.
11. Ibid., 7.
12. Karl Barth, *Protestant Theology in the Nineteenth Century* (London: SCM, 2001), 3.
13. Barth, "Evangelical Theology in the 19th Century," 19.
14. Ibid., 23.
15. See: George Hunsinger, ed., *Karl Barth and Radical Politics* (Philadelphia: Westminster, 1976).
16. Karl Barth, *Church Dogmatics*, ed. G. W. Bromiley and T. F. Torrance, trans. T. H. L. Parker et al., vol. II/1, 2nd ed. (Edinburgh: T&T Clark, 1964), 173.
17. Ibid., 174.
18. Ibid., 172.
19. This can be seen in a letter to Rabbi Emile Cohen in 1934 about the "shame and horror" Barth feels, as a Christian, for the "terror" befalling the Jewish people. See Paul S. Chung, *Karl Barth: God's Word in Action* (Cambridge: James Clark, 2008), 296.
20. Barth, *Church Dogmatics*, vol. II/1, 176.
21. Barth, "No!: Answer to Emil Brunner," 73.
22. Ibid., 75.
23. Ibid., 76.
24. Ibid., 74.
25. Ibid.
26. Karl Barth, *Church Dogmatics*, ed. G. W. Bromiley and T. F. Torrance, trans. G. W. Bromiley, vol. I.1 (Edinburgh: T&T Clark, 1975), 61–62.
27. Barth, *Church Dogmatics*, II.2, 4.
28. Karl Barth, *The Epistle to the Romans*, trans. Edwyn C. Hoskyns (London: Oxford University Press, 1933), 318.
29. Karl Barth, *Church Dogmatics*, ed. G. W. Bromiley and T. F. Torrance, trans. G. W. Bromiley, vol. IV/1, 2nd ed. (Edingburgh: T&T Clark, 1961), 45.
30. Barth, *Church Dogmatics*, II.2, 3.
31. In another context, it might be worth considering *this* methodological move, and exclusivism, on Barth's part, and to what extent it ensures knowledge of God.
32. Caputo, *The Insistence of God: A Theology of Perhaps*, 10.
33. Barth, *Church Dogmatics*, II.2, 4.
34. Ibid., 111.
35. Calvin, *Institutes of the Christian Religion*, 181.
36. Of course, Calvin (and others) have also based their doctrine(s) of divine election on revelation, as is evidenced by the quote above; it's just that Barth believed the content of divine revelation should be based solely on Jesus Christ.
37. Barth, *Church Dogmatics*, II.2, 43.
38. Ibid., 59.
39. Ibid., 105.
40. Henry Bettenson, ed., *Documents of the Christian Church*, 2nd ed. (London: Oxford University Press, 1963), 73.
41. Barth, *Church Dogmatics*, II.2, 102.
42. Ibid., 3.
43. Caputo, *The Weakness of God*, 4–5.
44. Barth, *Church Dogmatics*, II.2, 105.
45. Ibid., 115.
46. Ibid., 116.
47. Ibid., 115.
48. Ibid., 146.
49. Ibid.
50. Ibid., 18.
51. Ibid., 13.

52. Ibid., 146.
53. Ibid., 147.
54. Ibid.
55. Caputo, *The Insistence of God*, 9.
56. Ibid., 13.
57. Derrida, *"Différance,"* 6.
58. Rubenstein, "Dionysius, Derrida, and the Critique of 'Ontotheology,'" 726.
59. Caputo, *Prayers and Tears*, 6.
60. Barth, *Church Dogmatics* II.2, 148.
61. Hunsinger, *How to Read Karl Barth*, 36.
62. See, for instance, the subject heading "The Speech of God as the Mystery of God" in: Karl Barth, *Church Dogmatics*, ed. G. W. Bromiley and T. F. Torrance, trans. G. W. Bromiley, vol. I.1 (Edinburgh: T&T Clark, 1975), 162ff.
63. Karl Barth, *Church Dogmatics*, ed. G. W. Bromiley and T. F. Torrance, trans. G. W. Bromiley and R. J. Ehrlich, vol. III.3 (Edinburgh: T&T Clark, 1961), 293.
64. Barth, *Church Dogmatics*, I.1, 162.
65. Ibid., 163.
66. Ibid.
67. Ibid.
68. Ibid., 164.
69. Ibid., 164–165.
70. Ibid., 163.
71. Karl Barth, "The Need and Promise of Christian Preaching," in *The Word of God and the Word of Man*, trans. Douglas Horton (Gloucester, MA: Peter Smith, 1978), 124.
72. Ibid., 125.
73. Ibid., 126.
74. Ibid.
75. Karl Barth, "The Word of God and the Task of Ministry," in *The Word of God and the Word of Man* (Gloucester, MA: Peter Smith, 1978), 186.
76. Boesel, "Divine Relationality and (the Methodological Constraints of) the Gospel as Piece of News: Tracing the Limits of Trinitarian Ethics," 255.
77. Ibid., 258.
78. Given the inevitable, structural exclusivity this book has demonstrated, one might consider whether Barth's particular form of exclusion is more palatable than other forms, if the possibility of avoiding it altogether is no longer viable.
79. Caputo, *The Insistence of God*, 10.
80. Boesel and Keller, *Apophatic Bodies*, 4.
81. Barth, *Church Dogmatics*, I.1, 163.
82. Ibid., 162.
83. Keller, *On the Mystery: Discerning Divinity in Process*, 9.
84. Barth, *Church Dogmatics*, III.3, 293.
85. Boesel, "The Apophasis of Divine Freedom: Saving 'the Name' and the Neighbor from Human Mastery," 324.

Conclusion

The Decision Maker That Therefore I Am

> The vanity of scientists! My article, it is true, is an extremely important one, perhaps even epochal in its significance. With it, my little invention, in hand, any doctor can probe the very secrets of the soul, diagnose the maladies that poison the wellsprings of man's hope. It could save the world or destroy it—and in the next two hours will very likely do one or the other—for as any doctor knows, the more effective a treatment is, the more dangerous it is in the wrong hands.
>
> —Walker Percy, *Love in the Ruins*

In Walker Percy's *Love in the Ruins*, the protagonist, Dr. Thomas More, contemplates how his invention of the "ontological lapsometer" might be an effective treatment for the current state of things, which are not going so well. This novel of speculative fiction is set "at a time near the end of the world," where, among other things, people are divided along political, racial/ethnic, and ideological lines. Each side is experiencing extreme psychiatric maladies: "Conservatives have begun to fall victim to unseasonable rages, delusions of conspiracies, high blood pressure, and large-bowel complaints. Liberals are more apt to contract sexual impotence, morning terror, and a feeling of abstraction of the self from itself."[1] Dr. More believes that he has stumbled upon something that can not only diagnose, but also treat the ontological condition that ails society—while at the same time being potentially (and extremely) dangerous. "It could," he contemplates, very likely either "save the world or destroy it." "For as any doctor knows," Dr. More suggests, "the more effective a treatment is, the more dangerous it is in the wrong hands."[2]

Although I do not harbor any illusion—unlike our dear friend Dr. More—that I have found a "treatment" or remedy for the problem of in/decision, his reflection does resonate with my argument in a particular way. To the extent that decisions that cut, divide, and exclude are impossible to avoid and remedy, we can be assured that they are still—and perhaps now so more than ever—dangerous. As I have been trying to suggest all along, my goal has not been to give us a way out, an escape, a remedy, cure, or treatment to the problem that will result in a bill of clean-health. I have never been after any kind of assurance, "ethical certainty, good conscience, satisfaction of service rendered, and the consciousness of duty accomplished."[3] In fact, this book has tried, as much as possible, to push in the other direction by offering an understanding of undecidability that will always ruffle the feathers, disabuse, problematize, question our assurance, complicate our conscience, and render the task and duty of engaging the problem of in/decision un-accomplished. To the extent it has succeeded it would mean that no one will be able to walk away feeling "good" about what we have discovered. Put simply, my conclusion is that no approach to problem of in/decision can result in "an ultimate 'assuring' . . . but always a penultimate 'de-assuring.'"[4] Dr. More reflects on the vanity of scientists and scholars who are apt to believe their findings are "extremely important . . . perhaps even epochal."[5] And this "bad Catholic" who struggles with his own issues of grief, alcoholism, and a host of psychological issues, Dr. More himself is not immune from this temptation. While *this* book (and its author) might not be invulnerable to it either, the thrust of the argument throughout has been an attempt to force us to confront our misguided sense that we have rightly diagnosed and treated the problem.

To continue to play with Dr. More's reflection, my goal has been to demonstrate how the problem of in/decision is—and will always be—both "dangerous" and a "treatment." The backdrop for the argument of this book is the consensus about the problematic nature of decisions that cut, divide, and exclude. They are dangerous indeed—perhaps more so now than ever; and thus the treatment would be attempting to navigate them as responsibly as possible, which often means avoiding them. The substance of my argument, however, has revealed the impossibility of avoiding the cut of the difficult decision, leading to the conclusion that indecision is *as problematic* as any decision that cuts, divides, and excludes. In the two contexts explored, I have argued that claiming to retreat to a space of indecision is dangerous (because it is impossible) when it comes to issues of justice, as well as when attempting to theologically navigate divine decision. The implication would then be that decisions that cut and divide can and do function as an effective treatment—but we must not lose sight of the fact they are still very dangerous. In fact, they are more dangerous than we think, precisely because they can/do also function as treatment. As I have tried to demonstrate, they might best be referred to as a dangerous treatment, an illustration of Derrida's *pharmakon*—the remedy that is always itself a poison, or the poison that can also be a remedy.[6] And decisions that cut and divide are not just dangerous in the "wrong hands," as Dr. More suggests, for in our case there are no hands in which the treatment is not dangerous. There is no worthy physician to which we can entrust this prescription. And, again, continuing to illustrate how "in the ruins" we are, I have also tried to highlight an exigency to the situation, namely that we are not only faced with an impossible predicament—how (not) to decide—but the situation is such that we must do so now, because we are always already within this predicament. Thus, like Dr. More, "in the next two hours"—or even always already—our fate awaits us, and as we attempt to discern between that which "could save or destroy," we should also recognize the immediacy of how such decisions "will very likely do one or the other."[7] As James Cone admits, the situation is both dire and exigent, such that we do "not have time to do the theological and historical" (or ethical, philosophical, etc.) "research needed to present a 'balanced' perspective on the problem,"[8] but "we must make decisions," limited, problematic decisions. Our exploration of the problem of in/decision reveals that "we are thus placed in an existential situation . . . in which the burden is on us to make decisions without a guaranteed ethical guide."[9]

I have also tried to highlight the role that power and privilege plays in these contexts. In both of the above cases examined, I argued that power distorts one's relationship to the predicament of in/decision, leading one to believe that they could escape the impossibility of the difficult decision and retreat to a space of indecision. In the context of justice pursuits, I have highlighted the mistaken belief that one could safely avoid the cut of the decision of which a particular form of injustice takes priority, as a reflection of power and privilege to mistakenly stand outside, above, beyond the decision point. In the context of theological negotiations of divine decision, I have highlighted the mistaken belief that one could avoid the cut of the decision by deciding, implicitly, if and what kind of a divine decision has been made, as a reflection of too much power in the hands of the human theologian to mistakenly stand outside, above, beyond the decision point. While it may appear at first glance that I am arguing in two competing directions—*for* making decisions in one context and *against* making decisions in the other—in fact, the structure of the argument is intended to highlight an aporetic double-bind that inhabits each context, and the argument in these two particular discourses reflects the way that each has tried to escape the double-bind by collapsing the tension on one side or the other. There is thus no (one) answer or approach to the predicament. Moreover, this book attempts to reveal the deconstruction of any approach or response that would relax the tension, in either direction. Again, the argument in each discourse is radically and fundamentally related to the contexts explored (i.e., discourses about justice and theological negotiations of divine decision); *both* contexts have attempted to avoid the decision in seemingly different ways that nonetheless reflect a structural similarity of attempting to escape the double-bind. As I have argued, the illusion of power is the culprit in both.

All that remains now is for me to enter into these contexts myself and stake my own difficult decision(s). If the argument of this book has led us to the acknowledgment of the inescapability of the predicament of in/decision, then this analysis must also acknowledge my own presence in these contexts—otherwise, such an analysis will be subject to my own critique by assuming a non-position, or a position of indecision with regard to these issues, as a reflection of my own power and privilege. In other words, if the book were to merely end with this analysis and diagnosis of the problem, it would be yet another way of avoiding the problem by assuming some kind of stance outside or beyond it, which would instantiate a contradiction of the argument put forward here. If the argument of this book has led us to the point where we recognize an inability to avoid difficult decisions—if it has led us to the point of recognizing the double-bind of in/decision—then this certainly applies to me as well. There is no escaping the double-bind. In closing, therefore, I must reveal the dirt on my own hands in these messy contexts and not fall prey to my own argument by attempting to avoid the difficult decision. Or, perhaps more accurately, I must performatively *fall prey* to my own argument by revealing the way(s) I too am caught in this double-bind, lest this last admission also be read as a way out of the double-bind.

In the context of decisions for particular forms of justice, this predicament is especially pertinent, as my identity and experience as a white, Western, cisgender, heterosexual, over-educated male affords me a host of privileges and power. Thus, I must always consider and acknowledge my own identity, social location, and experience. How is it always "gendering," "whitening" or "straightening" what I am hearing, seeing, responding to, agreeing/disagreeing with? In what ways is it leading me to mistakenly inhabit some kind of an "objective," higher plane, outside or beyond the decision point, wherein I merely critique, analyze, and judge limited, difficult decisions? While I cannot make ultimate, once-for-all decisions about the complexity of such matters—and I am not advocating for this at all throughout this book—I must also be careful not to slip into the illusion that I can avoid making difficult decisions, in particular moments, that will always be limited and problematic.

However, even in pointing out my own context(s), identity, social location, privilege, etc., I must also be careful *not* to assume that somehow doing so has led me to some higher plane of understanding, some enlightened (e.g., "woke") perspective that allows an escape from the aporetic double-bind either, wherein I can offer a treatment that is not dangerous or a remedy without poison. The whole point of my argument has been to point out the impossibility of doing so. There is no escaping the messiness, difficulty, problematic nature of the decision that cuts, divides, and excludes. Although, as I have tried to argue, the whole point of this deconstructive insight is to increase our vigilance in dealing with the problem, such that acknowledging our sites of power and privilege and recognizing the decisions that we are always already complicit in is part of our responsible, transparent engagement with this problem. Yet such vigilance requires that we never slip into assuming that we have solved the problem either.

In order to sketch out the problem facing the decision maker, I will draw on contemporary examples—because again, this dynamic is only ever encountered in concrete contexts—that illustrate complicated issues of identity and justice, and provide an example of the double-bind at work: I cannot, but I must. In so doing, I leave myself open to critique by staking a difficult decision. Similarly, in the theological context of divine decision, I risk staking a difficult decision on the issue of divine decision, even as I recognize the problematic nature of doing so. I therefore close the book by illustrating the predicament and giving the reader an example of a deconstructing undecidability that requires discerning limited, problematic, difficult decision(s).

In a long address on the question of "the animal" published alongside other essays in *The Animal That Therefore I Am*, Derrida begins by stating: "I would like to entrust myself to words that, were it possible, would be naked."[10] As Derrida reflects on his own nakedness before the animal—in fact, a cat, his own cat—in Derridean fashion he causes each of us to reflect on our own nakedness as well and the call for each of us to respond in the face of the animal. Deconstructing undecidability has a way of stripping us bare, leaving us standing naked and vulnerable with the results of our choice, no longer clothed by the supposed security of indecision. Of course, some are not always afforded the opportunity and occasion of making decisions, which is surely a privilege in and of itself. Some are, unfortunately, stripped of that ability by circumstantial or societal situations. But the intended audience of this book is those of us who can wear the clothes of indecision, who have the opportunity and privilege of not deciding. In fact, it urges those of us with that privilege to make decisions that critically engage the circumstances and societal apparatuses that deprive certain individuals with the ability to make their own decisions. As Derrida reminds us: "No justice is exercised, no justice is rendered, no justice becomes effective . . . without a decision that cuts and divides."[11] Similarly, in this later work, Derrida reminds us each of our latent animality—or *divinanimality*—such that what we have always tried to remain separate and distinct from, i.e., the animal, is what founds our very humanity.[12] Just as Derrida realizes his humanity in the face of his cat, so too this book is an attempt to remind us of our reality of the decision maker that therefore I am in the face of the impossible decision. And it is now time for me to strip away my own indecisiveness, to bare my own vulnerability, to stare in the face of the undecidable, and decide.

UN/JUST DECISION: DECIDING FOR A PARTICULAR FORM OF JUSTICE

I have argued for the inescapability of making difficult decisions for particular forms of justice. What this means, first of all, is that decisions must be made *against* injustice. In the pursuit of justice, we must take stands against the unjust status quo, recognize the conveyor belts of racism, hetero-patriarchy, and other forms of ubiquitous injustice that we are always already complicit in.[13] While this insight is apparent in many liberationist works, the more complex situation that I have tried to highlight is the way in which such decisions for particular forms of justice might be in conflict with others. More recent work has highlighted the complex nature of various forms of injustice and identities that complicate such decisions. Against this backdrop I have argued that difficult decisions are still necessary, even if/when such conflict arises. In other words, even if/when pursuits of justice reveal a certain form of injustice.

There are many examples from which to draw on in order to highlight how deciding for one form of justice (which entails deciding against a particular form of injustice) exemplifies a difficult decision (i.e., a decision for justice that cannot escape some form of injustice). But in order to illustrate this tension, I have chosen to focus on the way it manifests with regard to issues of race and gender. Even more particularly, I will use a somewhat recent and seemingly insignificant example that arose in the context of the interplay between professional sports and music culture in the United States. Although not typically the subject of academic analyses, sports and music can be surprisingly incisive when it comes to issues like patriarchy, sexism, racism, and white privilege. These issues play out in arenas and stadiums, on airwaves and playlists, and in subsequent conversations and discussions, in ways that can sometimes cut through the morass of contentious political and academic discourse. To the extent that Beverly Tatum is accurate in her description of cultural racism (and sexism, homophobia, Islamaphobia, etc., I might add) being "like smog in the air," sometimes "so thick and visible, other times . . . less apparent, but always, day in and day out, we are breathing it in," then perhaps we need something to draw our attention to that which is always there but, as a result, is hard to discern.[14] That might just be part of sexism and racism's most insidious quality; they are—more often than not—furtive, surreptitious, clandestine. They often fly under the radar, are in the subtleties. No doubt, there are times when racism and sexism become explicit, conspicuous, or blatant. But I believe part of the real danger is how difficult they are to pinpoint, which is why we need something to help cut through the smog; and perhaps such help can come from the unlikeliest of places. Perhaps in the arena, or on the air, one catches a glimpse of the smog in a new light.

In May 2017, LaVar Ball, the outspoken father of highly touted college basketball player and prospect Lonzo Ball, made headlines yet again, this time for disparaging and aggressive comments made to a female sports reporter, Kristine Leahy. In the media backlash that resulted from this incident, especially on hip-hop radio stations in the greater New York City area, I spotted a particularly relevant issue that bears further analysis, namely the complex intersection of sexism and racism in the United States, and the difficult decisions that face those concerned about such realities and issues, including issues of injustice, violence, and (sexual) assault.

In order to tease out the thorniness of the issue I am trying to highlight, we need to understand a bit of the backstory and the nuances of the exchange between Ball and Leahy—as well as the media response that ensued—because of how they help illustrate this issue. LaVar Ball had already been labeled a polarizing figure by many sports analysts because of his antics, constant media appearances, and extensive over-the-top promotions of his son, Lonzo, who had (at the time) declared himself eligible for the 2017 NBA draft scheduled for late June.[15] LaVar Ball had continually made a series of bold claims about his son, including several comments about how he believed his son to (already) be "the best player in the world."[16] Such bold claims and ubiquitous appearances were deemed odious by a sports culture that typically turns up its nose at such self-aggrandizing and boastful behavior.[17] An article in *USA Today* in March 2017 called LaVar Ball a "one-man media tour" that was gaining too much attention for his "endless string of interviews full of cocky claims and premature promises, coupled with insults."[18] And after this recent incident with Kristine Leahy in May, some feel that LaVar's (and Lonzo's, by association) image had been tarnished even further. For instance, New York *Daily News* writer Seth Walder said what many had been writing and thinking: "We already knew LaVar Ball was loud and obnoxious. Add dismissive and disrespectful to the list."[19]

Now on to the incident that highlights the predicament: on May 17, 2017, LaVar Ball appeared on a popular sports radio show (also simulcast on the FoxSports1 television network), "The Herd with Colin Cowherd" to promote his "Big Baller" brand—that he himself created in order to market his son Lonzo—including the new line of basketball shoes that reportedly retail at $495.[20] The host of the show and well-known sports personality, Colin Cowherd, pried into the exorbitant cost of these shoes, asking LaVar Ball: "Have you sold any shoes yet?" To which Ball responded: "Yeah, I've sold a good amount, to me. There's different amounts." Kristine Leahy, a female "contributor to the program"—who is (literally) seated behind the guests on Cowherd's show—interjected from the rear and asked "how many?" [21] At this point, Ball placed his hand up in Leahy's direction, without turning to address her, and said "stay in your lane." Ball proceeded to try to continue his conversation with Cowherd, the male host, who initially chuckled at Ball's comment. A back-and-forth ensued between Ball and the female contributor to the program, with Leahy clearly feeling slighted by LaVar Ball's comment and gesture of dismissal. However, Ball continued to face the male host and place his hand up in Leahy's direction, as to not even acknowledge her presence, and said: "I don't even worry about her, she scares me." Leahy attempted to respond to Ball's comments, which were repeatedly unacknowledged by Ball, and finally declared to him: "I think that's kind of disrespectful." Ball, continuing to face Cowherd, said "I don't even look over there, because she scares me, I'm thinking assault right now.... Leave me alone." Cowherd addressed the increasingly awkward exchange that was developing in front of his very eyes, which is uncharted territory for a sports talk show. Perhaps in an attempt to stand up for his slighted female colleague and deescalate the situation, Cowherd replied: "She's a reporter, her job is to probe." Ball responded: "She can report to whoever she want behind her, I'm talking to you Colin." As the tense dialogue continued, Leahy asked: "Can you look me in the eye?" Never breaking eye contact with Cowherd, Ball retorted: "I don't want to look you in the eye, you scare me to death." Ball tried to get the conversation back on marketing his brand and his son, but Leahy continued to interject, at one point stating that big brand companies like Nike, Adidas, and Under Armour "wouldn't want to work with you because you don't respect women." Later on in the show Ball said: "I never disrespect women. But I'll tell you what, if you act like that, guess what? Something's coming to you, and it's okay." Without flinching, Leahy immediately responded: "Wait, are you threatening me?" To which Ball responded (still facing Cowherd): "See how she's trying to turn the words. I would never threaten you."

To the average watcher or listener with even the slightest sensibility toward equality, Ball appeared to be blatantly sexist, offensive, disrespectful, and exhibiting even threatening behavior. Here was a male, LaVar Ball, on a male sports show, dismissing and disrespecting a female and choosing to discuss exclusively "male matters"—i.e., sports, marketing, business—only with the male host, and then making vague, ominous comments. And, for the most part, this was the media response to this initial exchange. Charles Curtis of *USA Today* called Ball "completely disrespectful," stating that it was "undeniable" that he was threatening Leahy: "And it should be the last time he is allowed on the show—until at the very least he can look at Leahy, a respected reporter. And apologize."[22] Leahy, appearing on another sports show later that day, reflected on the exchange that was already receiving widespread media attention, saying that LaVar Ball responded to her initial question "in a very dismissive and inappropriate way, and I had two choices, I could either sit back and take it, or I could stand up for myself." While she admitted that Ball might have been upset at her pressing questions, she also said: "But you can't come at me and disrespect me and not look me in the eye and threaten me. That's just not okay."[23] An article for the website Complex explicitly called this exchange a "'sexist' rant" and stated: "Ball has said and done some off-the-wall things on live TV this spring, but this was easily his most uncomfortable—and sexist—moment yet."[24] MSN.com reported that in response to this tense exchange, Ball announced that "Stay in Yo Lane" t-shirts will now be sold by Big Baller Sports brand "to make money off the embarrassing exchange."[25] The article also mentioned that Leahy "took to Twitter . . . to ask her followers to donate money to the Support Girls Inc. organization, where Leahy tweeted: 'In lieu of shirts, join me in donating $50/60 or whatever you can to inspire all girls to be strong, smart and bold.'"[26]

In light of increasing movements that support women's full equality (which has not yet been fully realized in society), including encouraging women to stand up for themselves and realize their full potential, the above analyses and Leahy's response seem in line with these movements. Moreover, allegations by women of threats, sexual harassment, and sexual assault, sparking the #metoo movement, has made the issue of whether or not such allegations are credible, extremely contentious.[27] From a feminist perspective, it raises the issue of women's credibility and the way that has become the focal point of those who have come forward. Shouldn't we be inclined to believe these allegations, given the history of sexual assault and harassment, especially in how statistically underreported it is? Moreover, if a woman feels threatened—as Leahy did in this situation—shouldn't that be enough to take seriously and lead us to believe that there is indeed a genuine threat? Given the overwhelming statistics (that support the real, lived experience) of countless women being assaulted and harassed in our culture, blaming the victim and not lending credibility to such claims only further perpetuates the subjugation and objectification of women. Thus a firm stance *against* this tactic and a decision to endorse a #webelieveher movement as part of the #metoo campaign seems like an appropriate decision *for* women's rights and justice: Kristine Leahy was disrespected and felt threatened by LaVar Ball's comments and behavior, which were unacceptable. Anything less than this kind of stance or decision merely supports the status quo wherein women's wholeness has not been prioritized.

However, there is another analysis of this situation when race is considered. The day after this exchange between Leahy and Ball, and the social-media outpouring that erupted in its wake, hip-hop radio DJ Charlamagne Tha God approached the incident from a much different perspective. After initially tweeting in defense of LaVar Ball immediately following the incident, Charlamagne went a step further. The next morning Charlamagne made Leahy the "Donkey of the Day," a daily segment on his New York area morning radio show, "The Breakfast Club" on POWER 105.1, where he calls out something in the news that embodies foolishness.[28] Responding to claims in the media about Ball's comments and actions as disrespectful and threatening to Leahy, Charlamagne suggests there is a different way to understand what transpired on the set that day. And framing this exchange in a wider context is the key, he argued: "people see the clap back, but don't see the initial clap that caused the clap back, and this is the case here."

During the opening of the segment, Charlamagne tries to set the stage: "Before we get into LaVar and Kristine's exchange on FoxSports1 yesterday, let's put it into context. Kristine Leahy has been critical of LaVar Ball in the past, specifically questioning his parenting skills and even saying LaVar Ball's kids are afraid of him." Charlamagne then plays a clip of Leahy stating that Ball's sons are wrongfully "being forced" into a career in basketball against their will, with Leahy saying: "they are being told 'you will start basketball at age six.'" In the clip, she then goes on to say that Lonzo, the son who was being recruited by the NBA at that time, "looks terrified" in interviews, citing an exchange she had with Lonzo where she asked him if he ever had a disagreement with his father and he said "no." Leahy claims this is clear evidence that Lonzo, like the other Ball sons, are "genuinely afraid" of their father, because every child disagrees with their parent at some point. After the clip, Charlamagne comes back on air and suggests, firstly, that Leahy is out of line for criticizing the parenting relationship LaVar Ball has with his sons, especially when "their future's look bright" as up-and-coming NBA prospects. Moreover, Charlamagne points out the inherent contradiction when the common critique—most often of black men—is that there are not enough "fathers in kids' lives"; but here is a situation where the father is very much in his children's lives "as much as LaVar is, then you say 'he is doing too much.' I don't get it." Referring back to the incident on the day prior, Charlamagne argues that LaVar was merely giving "the same energy that Kristine was giving him."

Charlamagne then plays a clip of the exchange between Ball and Leahy on the Cowherd show and proceeds to "unpack that exchange" by arguing that Leahy should have known why Ball was angry at her—she had blatantly, and publicly, criticized his parenting skills. And if this exchange was so controversial, Charlamagne points out, then why didn't the host of the show, Colin Cowherd, say anything about it, such as "don't disrespect my co-host like that" (recall that Cowherd initially chuckled when Ball first responded to Leahy)—which suggests to Charlamagne that Cowherd "thought the exchange was fine." Second, Charlamagne says that Leahy "tried to play the gender-card," when in fact Ball "wasn't disrespecting all women, he was disrespecting [Leahy]," simply because she had already publicly disrespected him.

But most importantly (especially for our purposes), Charlamagne suggests that Leahy also "played the race card and didn't even know it." He points out: "If you [were] paying attention, you kept hearing LaVar Ball say 'Kristine, I don't want to talk to you because you scare me.'" The reason, Charlamagne argues, is because Ball understands the danger of the dynamic wherein a "big, scary black man going at a little white woman in America never ends well." One the "top three scariest things a black man can hear," Charlamagne states, "is 'are you threatening me?' from a white woman, especially when you are not even threatening her." According to Charlamagne, LaVar Ball clearly saw what was happening in that moment, which is why he kept saying "I'm scared of you." What we witnessed in this exchange, then, was not Ball disrespecting and threatening Leahy, but, in Charlamagne's words: "a classic, age-old example of a white woman demonizing a black man and it's that type of demonizing that led to Emmett Till getting killed." Charlamagne invokes "the kind of demonizing that black men have been dealing with for years," including the countless historical incidents in the United States where black men where publicly lynched for suspicion of threat or assault to white women—which was the case for Emmett Till in 1955. But this demonization is not merely historical, as black men are still under threat in the current criminal justice system where they are shot and assaulted with impunity and imprisoned at an overwhelming rate. Thus what Leahy did, according to Charlamagne, was "dangerous"; and Ball—who Charlamagne had previously referred to as a "revolutionary"—"handled that situation perfectly." The segment ends, as it always does, with Charlamagne saying "give Kristine Leahy the biggest hee-haw, please" and a donkey bray is played.

The media storm about this incident only further ignited after Charlamagne's segment. A colleague of Kristine Leahy's on FoxSports1, Jason Whitlock, responded to Charlamagne on a show with Leahy calling him "irresponsible" for drawing a connection with Emmett Till and falling prey to being "caught up in this social media era that we're in" where we "sensationalize," "exploit," and "demonize" people.[29] Whitlock defended Leahy's response by agreeing that Ball was indeed "inappropriate . . . dismissive, condescending" and "came off sexist," and he could understand why Leahy felt threatened. For Charlamagne to "analogize [this situation] to Emmett Till" was "way out of bounds" and "ridiculous" and "plays into a racial politics that has gotten way out of hand via social media." Whitlock then addresses Charlamagne directly, saying: "Stop it, cut it out, grow up, be a man." He goes on to say: "We're being racially divided for no reason, for the entertainment of people over Twitter and Instagram, this needs to stop." Leahy, who was sitting next to Whitlock during this segment, responds by saying: "This was never supposed to be a war and it's turned into it. It was never supposed to be a war between me and LaVar, between me and Charlamagne Tha God . . . it's not a war on race, it's not a racial discussion, it's not a feminist discussion, it was about respect, purely respect." She goes on to maintain that she did not know how else to interpret LaVar's comments and attitude toward her other than as disrespectful and threatening.

Of course, it did not stop there, as the next day Charlamagne made Jason Whitlock the "Donkey of the Day."[30] Charlamagne begins by refreshing the listeners as to what transpired in the past few days, including his giving Kristine Leahy the same tag because her response to Ball was a textbook example of "let me weaponize my whiteness to demonize the black man—anyone who can't see it, doesn't want to see it." He clarifies that he wasn't intending to compare LaVar Ball to Emmett Till, but merely suggesting that her reaction "was the same kind of energy that got Emmett Till killed," i.e., the weaponizing of whiteness to demonize the black man. He then addresses Whitlock directly, playing a clip of Whitlock also appearing on the Cowherd show (with Leahy present) where Whitlock says Charlamagne spun this "in a racial way that is difficult for white people to handle." To which Charlamagne responds, quite aggressively: "Do you know why it's hard for white people to handle? Because waste of good black skin like you, Jason Whitlock, get around these Caucasians in corporate settings and don't tell the truth. How are we going to make racial progress in this country if we don't communicate, tell them the truth?" Just as the focus had been on Leahy feeling uncomfortable as a woman by Ball's comments, Charlamagne argues: "I can point out, as a black man, what makes me uncomfortable. And Kristine Leahy demonizing LaVar Ball and weaponizing her whiteness by saying this man was threatening her when he clearly wasn't makes me uncomfortable." Furthermore, "news like that" wouldn't make white people uncomfortable and be hard for them to understand or handle, Charlamagne contends, "if Negroes in positions like you [Jason Whitlock] told them the truth . . . but you're too busy attacking black people and demonizing us that you don't seem to understand that." He then invoked Malcolm X's quote: "If you're not careful, the newspapers will have you hating the people who are being oppressed and loving the people who are doing the oppressing." And Charlamagne maintains that is what is happening here. Continuing to call out Whitlock, Charlamagne points out that Whitlock never "called out" Leahy for her demonization of LaVar Ball, even addressing the other two black commentators in that segment saying he is disappointed in them both for not speaking up and "explaining to the damsel in distress why she was in the wrong." Even if they think Ball was wrong, wasn't she also at fault also for suggesting she was in danger from "the big, scary black man"?

Charlamagne also points out that there is all this talk about Leahy being disrespected by Ball while she literally sits behind the guests on Cowherd's show, which is a sign of disrespect to her already as a woman. Charlamagne then highlighted contradictions in Whitlock's approach and analyses of other athletes, including his body-shaming of tennis star Serena Williams, suggesting that this is what Whitlock always does as he loves "tearing down black excellence and always strives to demonize black people in the media for absolutely no reason." Charlamagne also played clips where Whitlock compares Lebron James to Donald Trump because of their shared wealth and economic privilege, as well as Whitlock's critiques of NFL quarterback Colin Kaepernick's well-publicized kneeling during the national anthem in protest of the shooting of unarmed black men by police. All of this leads Charlamagne to continue going after Whitlock, who he claims always does "what you have to do to keep your white counterparts happy . . . and be the white man's watch dog; that's all you do is bark and try to bite black people, on behalf of the white man." Otherwise, Charlamagne insists, he would have at least tried to "school Leahy" on why her rhetoric was racially dangerous, "not just to LaVar Ball," but also "why that type of energy has been dangerous to black men in America" historically and continually.

Charlamagne's racial analysis of the incident between Ball and Leahy was corroborated by several other media outlets, including an article on bet.com (connected to the television network, Black Entertainment Television) that lists several social media responses claiming Leahy too quickly "assumed the victim role." That this was a "classic case of white privilege" by Leahy not being able to see her whiteness at play and the dynamic invoked when a white woman accuses a black man of threatening her.[31] Several tweets posted on this page discuss the danger that such a threat poses to black men, which is the very point Charlamagne was trying to make.

The reason I chose this incident as a concrete example of the dynamic I have been trying to highlight is because it has all the characteristics of the precarious predicament that various forms of systemic injustice highlight. It is not only complex and multi-layered, but there is also something about the seemingly insignificant nature of it playing out on airwaves, television screens, and social media outlets that demonstrates how it is so much more than that. Even though the mediums—sports, music, radio, social media—appear insignificant at first glance, the vitriolic responses illustrate that there are genuine issues and real lives at stake here. On the one hand, there is the issue of gender and women's experience, safety, and wholeness. As I stated above, given the recent movements (e.g., #metoo, #webelieveher) that have brought the subjugation, abuse, assault, disrespect, and harassment of women to greater public attention, Leahy's experience of disrespect and genuine threat should be taken seriously. And taking a stand for these issues, in the midst of a culture that still resists granting credibility to women and their experiences, blames the victim, or silences and marginalizes these voices, is necessary for any advancement in the struggle against these kinds of injustices. On the other hand, there is the issue of race and the demonization of black men in the United States. Given the recent movements (e.g., #blacklivesmatter, #sayhername) that have highlighted the shooting of unarmed African-Americans by police with impunity, the continued overpopulation of prisons that are statistically filled with black men between the ages of 18–30, and the history of lynching, murder, and oppression of the stereotypically aggressive, violent, and dangerous black man, Ball's own fear should also be taken seriously. And taking a stand for these issues, in the midst of a culture that still resists acknowledging these realities (both historical and contemporary), struggles to discuss anti-black racism in an open and honest way, and resists scrutinizing analysis of the function of white supremacy and white privilege, is necessary for any advancement in the struggle against these kinds of injustices. The responses on both sides of these issues demonstrate taking such a stand: on the one hand, defending Leahy's experience of disrespect and feeling threatened; on the other hand, defending Ball's fear of being demonized and threatened himself.

And as we have seen, there is no stance to take in this situation that can "have it both ways." As the arguments in Part II outlined, the imbricated nature of injustice reveals a complex predicament. That is, unfortunately, the way that these injustices function. To make matters worse, this situation—and my analysis of it up to this point—only highlights one small aspect of these much larger issues of racism and sexism (which again, are only two examples of injustice in our society). We have only been discussing anti-black racism and not other forms; we have not addressed the issue of intra-black prejudice, discrimination, and conflict, as it pertains to other factors like socioeconomics, gender, sexuality, etc.; we could also analyze the body-shaming issue that looms over the entire incident; we could scrutinize the other ways gender plays a role in sports, music, and pop-culture, including the exchange between Whitlock and Charlamagne and the latent image of masculinity that is lurking beneath the surface. All of this is to suggest, as I have been trying to do all along, that these issues demand discerning difficult decisions. Which form of injustice takes priority? Which side of these issues do we support? Who will we choose to be in solidarity with? I have, hopefully by now, demonstrated that *not* deciding in the midst of these impossible decisions is as problematic as choosing one or the other. There is no safe place to stand—we must make decisions, as Cone suggests, or else our indecision is merely tacit support for the injustices already in place. To not decide is to stand on the conveyor belt of the unjust status quo as it moves us along. In this incident it moves us in the direction of either silencing women's experience about being disrespected and threatened; or it minimizes the danger black men face by being demonized.

As promised, the goal of this section was not only to use a concrete example to highlight these issues, but to no longer stand outside of them—as a reflection of my own power and privilege in my experience as a white male—and make a difficult decision. In this case, I choose to take a stand against racism and the demonization of black men. I agree with Charlamagne's analysis of the situation about the racial dynamics that were at play in this situation. In so doing, then, this means that Ball's fear of demonization takes priority over Leahy's, that at this moment I have to choose between which form of justice to be in solidarity with. Of course, such a decision surely warrants critique from the other side. Moreover, it does not do *justice* to Leahy's experience and the issues associated with it, which means there is a certain form of *injustice* in said decision. There is no escaping the way this decision undercuts the solidarity I do have with women who experience subjugation, harassment, and assault (both threatened and actual) and my desire to support these movements as much as possible; in short, my desire for this kind of justice. And a similar dynamic would be in play if I had chosen in the other direction, wherein I would have had to neglect my antiracist commitments to support Leahy, neglecting to do justice to Ball's experience and perpetuating racial injustice. But to not decide would only be tacit support for both, which would also be unjust. And my argument all along has been focused on highlighting this form of injustice—i.e., the illusion of indecision—for fear that we have merely stopped at pointing out and criticizing the limits of any decision in the name of so-called pure justice. If we have learned anything from our exploration of the aporetic double-bind of justice, however, then we should have come to recognize that we are always navigating some form of injustice in our pursuit(s) of justice. Deconstructing undecidability is not remaining in indecision, but, in the moment of suspense of the undecidable, to (still) decide. Injustice demands concrete stances and decisions in order to rectify and liberate. There is no once-for-all decision on these matters, and I am not suggesting that any decision in the moment is more than merely that. But discerning, confronting, reckoning with such difficult decisions is necessary, even though—or perhaps more precisely *because*—they are so problematic.

Additionally, and relatedly, I think this issue is especially pertinent to those who find themselves in dominant positions and identities, like myself—in other words, those with power and privilege. My argument throughout this book always risks being misunderstood as an apology, defense, or excuse for continued injustice, exclusion, and oppression because it presents an "impossible" predicament. But my goal is quite the opposite: *unless* we recognize that difficult decisions are necessary and inescapable, the always already unjust status quo will remain intact. And the real problem, I believe, especially for those who do not have an affiliated identity with these kinds of injustices, is the illusion of indecision. Some might have no choice but to decide *which* problem, issue, injustice to work for/on; but the reality is that others do have that luxury, and if change is going to occur, we cannot avoid making difficult decisions. Simply put, indecision is the matrix of hegemony. There are those (with real power) who have decided, who continue to decide, who will decide, and that reality requires rigorous discernment and decisiveness in order to disrupt the unjust status quo.

DISCERNING DIVINE DECISIONS

The final decision that I must also risk pertains to the issue highlighted in Part III regarding divine decision. There I argued that there is no escaping navigation of the precarious position that the notion of divine decision puts us in theologically. In short, there is no avoiding the difficult decision as it pertains to divine decision. The double-bind I sketched is a predicament wherein there is no remedy to the problem of divine decision that does not collapse in either direction. The attempt to remedy divine decision by avoiding it cannot escape reinscribing the very problem it attempts to fix (e.g., exclusion and human mastery over divinity). While at the same time the attempt to remedy the problem of human decision with regard to divine decision by avoiding the former cannot do so in any pure manner either.

Rather than attempting to present an argument for staking a decision on these matters that might deftly and responsibly navigate this dilemma in a way that synthesizes the dialectic in anyway—i.e., avoids the double-bind I have sketched—my argument is that every decision regarding divine decision is thoroughly problematic. Thus, just as I did above concerning matters of injustice, here too I must simply assert a decision and accept the consequences and critiques it garners. Again, any decision in this predicament is always only an "in the moment" decision. Moreover, my analysis has tried to highlight the issue of power and privilege and how that functions in these two contexts. In the matter of divine decision, there is an acute concern—on both sides—about too much power in the hands of the human theologian to decide. But, as I have tried to argue, indecision is just as much a reflection of such power.

In the context of theological negotiations of divine decision, therefore, I choose to endorse a notion of a God who chooses. I agree with Barth's concern about how deciding to avoid or reject a notion of divine decision results in a God of our choosing, reducing divinity to an object of human decision. In so doing, then, this means that such a theological position would have to attempt to navigate the thorny dilemma of divine decision, not least addressing the matter of who or what God chooses in divine election. It would mean having to construct a theology of divine election that wrestles with the notion of exclusivity, persistently asking what results when God chooses *this* and not *that*?[32] Of course, such a theological decision surely warrants critique from the other side; and there is no escaping the way this decision undercuts my stance against exclusivity or the theological landmines associated with collapsing divinity into the grasp and control of humanity, and, consequently, undercutting the very desire to endorse a notion of divine decision in the first place. It might also fall prey to Caputo's critique of a strong theology of absolutes, assurance, closure, dogmas. It might be merely a manifestation of a lingering metaphysics of presence or onto-theology. It assumes the existence of a God who could choose, which means that might not have allowed the full weight of Caputo's "perhaps" to take hold and mistakes, in Caputo's words, "an event for a being, or a Superbeing, a ground of Being, beyond or without being, a mighty being that does things, or mysteriously decides not to, an agent-being in the sky."[33] And, just as I pointed out with the decision above, a similar dynamic would be in play if I had chosen in the other direction, wherein I would have had to neglect Barth's concerns and avoided speaking about a God who decides.

But, similarly, to not decide does not solve the problem either, because it assumes that there is a stance to take on this issue that could avoid the double-bind of undecidability. Just as there is no once-for-all decision on these matters, there is also no escaping the precarious predicament divine decision presents. Acknowledgment of this predicament also entails recognizing that there is no security in believing we have "adopted the right attitude to it."[34] Whether we choose to include or exclude it, divine decision reveals that there is no safe ground, no certainty to be had, theologically or ethically, with respect to how we approach it. Whether we take the more apophatic approach, like Caputo, and propose a "weak theology" that "is content with a little adverb like 'perhaps,'"[35] in order to prevent "God" from becoming "something I have added to my repertoire, brought within the horizon of my experience, knowledge, belief, identification, and expectation";[36] or whether we boldly declare, like Barth, a very particular kind of divine decision (e.g., that it "*is* the election of Jesus Christ"[37] that in this divine decision "we can know with a certainty which nothing can ever shake that we are the elect of God"[38]), neither can prevent or safeguard against human mastery over divine mystery, the exclusive cut of the decision, or collapsing it into merely human decision. As Barth admits: "And we should have succumbed already to the afore-mentioned temptation if we were to look about for some means to ward it off, to secure ourselves against it, and to make ourselves immune to temptation."[39] The "best" we can do, therefore, is to acknowledge the predicament and the decision(s) we make with regard to it. This kind of "truth in advertising" is the reality we must confront in deconstructing undecidability.

NOTES

1. Walker Percy, *Love in the Ruins* (New York: Avon, 1971), 20.

2. Ibid., 7.
3. Derrida, "Passions: 'An Oblique Offering,'" 17.
4. Barth, *Church Dogmatics*, I.1, 164–65.
5. Percy, *Love in the Ruins*, 7.
6. Derrida, "Plato's Pharmacy," 111.
7. Percy, *Love in the Ruins*, 7.
8. Cone, *A Black Theology of Liberation*, xvi.
9. Ibid., 7.
10. Jacques Derrida, *The Animal That Therefore I Am*, ed. Marie-Louise Mallet; trans. David Willis (New York: Fordham University Press, 2008), 1.
11. Derrida, "Force of Law," 28.
12. Derrida, *The Animal That Therefore I Am*, 132.
13. Derrida himself demonstrates this necessity in the short piece "Taking a Stand for Algeria" in *Acts of Religion*, ed. Gil Anidjar (New York: Routledge, 2002).
14. Tatum, "Defining Racism: Can we Talk?," 6.
15. Lonzo Ball was drafted in the first round of the NBA draft about a month after this incident, taken second overall by the Los Angeles Lakers.
16. Sean Gregory, "How One Family is Beating the NCAA at Its Own Game," CNN.com http://time.com/4699494/lonzo-ball-lavar-ball-ucla-ncaa-tournament/?xid=homepage (accessed May 20, 2017). See also: Ben Bolch, "LaVar Ball's Boasts about Sons, Including UCLA Star Lonzo, Draw Strong Reactions," LATimes.com http://www.latimes.com/sports/ucla/la-sp-lavar-ball-20170219-story.html (accessed May 20, 2017).
17. One could probe even further into this mindset in sports culture and tradition to find that such "boastful" behavior is often accompanied with racial connections and overtones, i.e., when NFL player Richard Sherman was called a "thug" for his boasting after a 2014 playoff game.
18. Sam Amick, "Could LaVar Ball Scare NBA Teams from Drafting Lonzo Ball?" USAToday.com, https://www.usatoday.com/story/sports/nba/2017/03/16/lavar-ball-hurt-lonzo-ball-nba-draft-stock-ucla-march-madness/99248918/ (accessed May 20, 2017).
19. Seth Walder, "VIDEO: LaVar Ball Tells FS1 Reporter Kristine Leahy to 'Stay in Your Lane,' says Big Baller Brand Isn't for Women" NYDailyNews.com, http://www.nydailynews.com/sports/basketball/lavar-ball-tells-fs1-kristine-leahy-stay-lane-article-1.3174194 (accessed June 1, 2017).
20. The full video interview can be seen here: https://www.youtube.com/watch?v=ho_50UbSn40
21. Lawrence Yee, "LaVar Ball Clashes with Female Reporter, Warns Her 'Something's Coming to You,'" Variety.com http://variety.com/2017/biz/news/lavar-ball-kristine-leahy-fight-herd-with-colin-cowherd-fox-sports-one-1202431029/ (accessed May 20, 2017).
22. Charles Curtis, "LaVar Ball Threatened 'The Herd' co-host Kristine Leahy," USAToday.com https://www.usatoday.com/story/sports/ftw/2017/05/17/lavar-ball-threatened-the-herd-cohost-kristine-leahy-when-she-dared-to-question-him/101795862/ (accessed May 20, 2017).
23. Ryan Gaydos, "LaVar Ball Under Fire for Remark to Female Fox Sports 1 Reporter," FOXNews.com http://www.foxnews.com/sports/2017/05/18/lavar-ball-under-fire-for-remark-to-female-fox-sports-1-reporter.html (accessed May 20, 2017).
24. Chris Yuscavage, "LaVar Ball Goes Off on Fox Sports Reporter in 'Sexist' Rant: 'Stay in Your Lane,'" Complex.com http://www.complex.com/sports/2017/05/lavar-ball-tells-fox-sports-1-kristine-leahy-stay-in-your-lane-cringeworthy-interview (accessed May 20, 2017).
25. Microsoft Network, "Kristine Leahy Classily Reacts to LaVar Ball 'Stay in yo lane' Shirts," MSN.com http://www.msn.com/en-us/sports/nba/kristine-leahy-classily-reacts-to-lavar-ball-'stay-in-yo-lane'-shirts/ar-BBBwHy6 (accessed May 20, 2017).
26. Ibid.
27. This was written during the Supreme Court nomination of Brett Kavanaugh and ensuing accusations of sexual assault by Kavanaugh of several women in the 1980s.
28. The full segment can be viewed here: https://youtu.be/ooOuywioQB4.

29. The full segment can be viewed here: https://www.youtube.com/watch?v=5XUgpNM7ywA.
30. The full segment can be found here: https://youtu.be/4TVvRqBvnys
31. Black Entertainment Television, "People Are Disgusted This Reporter Asked LaVar Ball 'Are You Threatening Me?'" BET.com https://www.bet.com/news/sports/2017/05/18/people-react-to-lavar-ball-s-comments-to-female-reporter.html (accessed May 20, 2017).
32. For a process-inflected constructive theology of divine election, see: Donna Bowman, *Divine Decision: A Process Doctrine of Election* (Louisville, KY: Westminster John Knox, 2002).
33. Caputo, *The Insistence of God*, 30.
34. Barth, *Church Dogmatics*, I.1, 163.
35. Caputo, *The Insistence of God*, 9.
36. Ibid., 10.
37. Barth, *Church Dogmatics*, II.2, 146.
38. Ibid., 116.
39. Barth, *Church Dogmatics*, I.1, 163.

Bibliography

Althaus-Reid, Marcella. *Indecent Theology: Theological Perversions in Sex, Gender and Politics.* London: Routledge, 2001.
Altizer, Thomas. *Deconstruction and Theology.* New York: Crossroad Pub Co, 1982.
Anderson, Carol. *White Rage: The Unspoken Truth of Our Racial Divide.* New York: Bloomsbury, 2017.
Armour, Ellen T. *Deconstruction, Feminist Theology, and the Problem of Difference: Subverting the Race/Gender Divide.* Chicago: The University of Chicago Press, 1999.
Ashcroft, Bill, Gareth Griffiths, and Helen Tiffin, eds. *Post-Colonial Studies: The Key Concepts.* 2nd edition. London: Routledge, 2001.
Augustine. *Four Anti-Pelagian Writings.* Translated by John A. Mourant and William J. Collinge. Washington, DC: Catholic University Press, 1992.
———. "On the Predestination of Saints." In *Four Anti-Pelagian Writings*, translated by John A. Mourant and William J. Collinge. Washington, DC: Catholic University Press, 1992.
Barth, Karl. *Church Dogmatics.* Edited by G. W. Bromiley and T. F. Torrance. Translated by G. W. Bromiley. Vol. I.1. Edinburgh: T&T Clark, 1975.
———. *Church Dogmatics.* Edited by G. W. Bromiley and T. F. Torrance. Translated by T. H. L. Parker et al. Vol. II.1. 2nd ed. Edinburgh: T&T Clark, 1964.
———. *Church Dogmatics.* Edited by G. W. Bromiley and T. F. Torrance. Translated by G. W. Bromiley, J. C. Campell, Ian Wilson, J. Strathearn McNab, Harold Knight, and R. A. Stewart. Vol. II.2. Edinburgh: T&T Clark, 1957.
———. *Church Dogmatics.* Edited by G. W. Bromiley and T. F. Torrance. Translated by G. W. Bromiley and R. J. Ehrlich. Vol. III.3. Edinburgh: T&T Clark, 1961.
———. *Church Dogmatics.* Edited by G. W. Bromiley and T. F. Torrance. Translated by G. W. Bromiley. Vol. IV.1. 2nd ed. Edinburgh: T&T Clark, 1964.
———. *The Epistle to the Romams.* Translated by Edwyn C. Hoskyns. London: Oxford University Press, 1933.
———. "Evangelical Theology in the 19th Century." In *The Humanity of God.* Richmond, VA: Westminster John Knox Press, 1960.
———. "The Need and Promise of Christian Preaching." In *The Word of God and the Word of Man*, translated by Douglas Horton. Gloucester, MA: Peter Smith, 1978.
———. "No! Answer to Emil Brunner." In *Natural Theology: Comprising "Nature and Grace."* Translated by Peter Fraenkel. London: Centenary, 1946.
———. *Protestant Theology in the Nineteenth Century.* London: SCM, 2001.
———. "The Word of God and the Task of Ministry." In *The Word of God and the Word of Man.* Gloucester, MA: Peter Smith, 1978.

Batstone, David, et al., ed. *Liberation Theologies, Postmodernity and the Americas*. London: Routledge, 1997.
Bell, Daniel M. *Liberation Theology after the End of History: The Refusal to Cease Suffering*. London: Routledge, 2001.
Bennington, Geoffrey. "A Moment of Madness: Derrida's Kierkegaard." *Oxford Literary Review* 33:1 (July 1, 2011): 103–27.
Bennington, Geoffrey, and Jacques Derrida. *Jacques Derrida*. Chicago: University Of Chicago Press, 1999.
Bettenson, Henry, ed. *Documents of the Christian Church*. 2nd ed. London: Oxford University Press, 1963.
Boesel, Chris. "The Apophasis of Divine Freedom: Saving 'the Name' and the Neighbor from Human Mastery." In *Apophatic Bodies: Negative Theology, Incarnation, and Relationality*. New York: Fordham University Press, 2009.
———. "Divine Relationality and (the Methodological Constraints of) the Gospel as Piece of News: Tracing the Limits of Trinitarian Ethics." In *Divine Multiplicity: Trinities, Diversities, and the Nature of Relation*. New York: Fordham University Press, 2013.
———. *Risking Proclamation, Respecting Difference: Christian Faith, Imperialistic Discourse, and Abraham*. Eugene, OR: Cascade Books, 2008.
Boesel, Chris, and Catherine Keller, eds. *Apophatic Bodies: Negative Theology, Incarnation, and Relationality*. New York: Fordham University Press, 2009.
Boff, Leonardo. *Jesus Christ Liberator: A Critical Christology for Our Time*. Maryknoll, NY: Orbis Books, 1978.
Bowman, Donna. *The Divine Decision: A Process Doctrine of Election*. Louisville, KY: Westminster John Knox Press, 2002.
Buber, Martin. *I and Thou*. Translated by Walter Kaufman. New York: Touchstone, Simon & Schuster, 1996.
Calvin, John. *Institutes of the Christian Religion*. Translated by John Allen. Vol. 2. Philadelphia: Presbyterian Board of Christian Education, 1936.
Cannon, Katie G. "Hitting a Straight Lick with a Crooked Stick: The Womanist Dilemma in the Development of a Black Liberation Ethic." *The Annual of the Society of Christian Ethics* 7 (1987).
Caputo, John D., ed. *Deconstruction in a Nutshell: A Conversation with Jacques Derrida*. New York: Fordham University Press, 1996.
———. "Hoping in Hope, Hoping against Hope." In *Religion with/out Religion: The Prayers and Tears of John D. Caputo*, edited by James H. Olthuis. New York: Routledge, 2002.
———. *The Insistence of God: A Theology of Perhaps*. Bloomington: Indiana University Press, 2013.
———. *The Prayers and Tears of Jacques Derrida: Religion without Religion*. Bloomington: Indiana University Press, 1997.
———. *Radical Hermeneutics: Repetition, Deconstruction, and the Hermeneutic Project*. Bloomington: Indiana University Press, 1987.
———. *The Weakness of God: A Theology of the Event*. Bloomington: Indiana University Press, 2006.
Carbado, Devon W., Kimberlé Crenshaw, Vickie M. Mays. "Intersectionality." *Du Bois Review: Social Science Research on Race* 10, no. 2 (2013).
Carter, J. Kameron. *Race: A Theological Account*. Oxford: Oxford University Press, 2008.
Chatterji, Saral K. "Why Dalit Theology?" In *A Reader in Dalit Theology*. Madras: Gurukul Lutheran Theological College, 1990.
Cheng, Patrick S. *Radical Love: Introduction to Queer Theology*. 1st edition. New York: Seabury, 2011.
Chung, Paul S. *Karl Barth: God's Word in Action*. Cambridge: James Clark, 2008.
Clarke, Sathianathan. *Dalits and Christianity: Subaltern Religion and Liberation Theology in India*. Delhi: Oxford University Press, 2000.
———. "Subalterns, Identity Politics and Christian Theology in India." In *Christian Theology in Asia*, edited by Sebastian C. H. Kim. Cambridge, UK; New York: Cambridge University Press, 2008.

Cone, James. *Black Theology & Black Power*. Second Edition. Maryknoll, NY: Orbis Books, 1997.
———. *A Black Theology of Liberation*. Fortieth Anniversary Edition. Maryknoll, NY: Orbis Books, 2010.
———. *The Cross and the Lynching Tree*. Maryknoll, NY: Orbis Books, 2011.
———. *God of the Oppressed*. Maryknoll, NY: Orbis Books, 1997.
Costoya, Manuel Mejido. "Rethinking Liberation." In *Rethinking Latino(a) Religion and Identity*. Cleveland: The Pilgrim Press, 2006.
Crenshaw, Kimberlé. "Demarginalizing the Intersection of Race and Sex: A Black Feminist Critique of Antidiscrimination Doctrine." *University of Chicago Legal Forum* (1989): 139–68.
———. "Mapping the Margins: Intersectionality, Identity, and Violence against Women of Color." *Stanford Law Review* 43, no. 6 (1991): 1241–1300.
Critchley, Simon. *The Ethics of Deconstruction: Derrida and Levinas*. Oxford: Blackwell, 1992.
Crockett, Clayton. *Derrida after the End of Writing: Political Theology and New Materialism*. New York: Fordham University Press, 2017.
———. "Polyhairesis: On Postmodern and Chinese Folds." *Modern Theology* 30, no. 3 (July 2014).
Cudney, Shane. "Religion without Religion: Caputo, Derrida, and the Violence of Particularity." In *Religion with/out Religion: The Prayers and Tears of John D. Caputo*, edited by James H. Olthuis. New York: Routledge, 2002.
De La Torre, Miguel A. *Doing Christian Ethics from the Margins*. Maryknoll, NY: Orbis Books, 2004.
———, ed. *Handbook of U.S. Theologies of Liberation*. St. Louis, MO: Chalice Press, 2004.
Derrida, Jacques. "Afterword: Toward an Ethic of Discussion." In *Limited Inc*, edited by Gerald Graff, translated by Jeffrey Mehlman and Samuel Weber. Evanston, IL: Northwestern University Press, 1988.
———. *The Animal That Therefore I Am*. Edited by Marie-Louise Mallet. Translated by David Willis. New York. Fordham University Press, 2008.
———. *Dissemination*. Translated by Barbara Johnson. First Thus edition. University of Chicago Press, 1983.
———. "Faith and Knowledge: The Two Sources of 'Religion' at the Limits of Reason Alone." In *Acts of Religion*, edited by Gil Anidjar. New York: Routledge, 2002.
———. "Force of Law: The 'Mystical Foundation of Authority.'" In *Deconstruction and the Possibility of Justice*, edited by Drucilla Cornell, Michel Rosenfeld, and David Gray Carlson. New York: Routledge, 1992.
———. *The Gift of Death, Second Edition and Literature in Secret*. Translated by David Wills. 2nd edition. Chicago: University Of Chicago Press, 2007.
———. *Glas*. Paris: Galilée, 1974.
———. "How to Avoid Speaking: Denials." In *Derrida and Negative Theology*, edited by Harold G. Coward and Toby Foshay. Albany: State University of New York, 1992.
———. *Limited Inc*. Edited by Gerald Graff. Translated by Jeffrey Mehlman and Samuel Weber. 1st edition. Evanston, IL: Northwestern University Press, 1988.
———. *Margins of Philosophy*. Translated by Alan Bass. Reprint edition. Chicago: University Of Chicago Press, 1984.
———. "Of an Apocalyptic Tone Recently Adopted in Philosophy." Translated by John P. Leavey, Jr. *The Oxford Literary Review* 6, no. 2 (1984).
———. *Of Grammatology*. Translated by Gayatri Chakravorty Spivak. Corrected edition. Baltimore: Johns Hopkins University Press, 1998.
———. "Passions: 'An Oblique Offering.'" In *On the Name*, edited by Thomas Dutoit, translated by David Wood. Stanford, CA: Stanford University Press, 1995.
———. *Psyche: Inventions of the Other*. Edited by Peggy Kamuf and Elizabeth G. Rottenberg. Volume 1. Stanford: Stanford University Press, 2007.
———. "Sauf le nom." In *On the Name*, edited by Thomas Dutoit, translated by David Wood. Stanford, CA: Stanford University Press, 1995.

———. *Specters of Marx: The State of the Debt, The Work of Mourning & the New International*. New York: Routledge, 2006.
———. "Taking A Stand for Algeria." In *Acts of Religion*, edited by Gil Anidjar. New York: Routledge, 2002.
Derrida, Jacques, and George Collins. *Politics of Friendship*. London: Verso, 2005.
Devasahayam, V. "Pollution, Poverty and Powerlessness—A Dalit Perspective." In *A Reader in Dalit Theology*. Madras: Gurukul Lutheran Theological College, 1990.
DiAngelo, Robin. *White Fragility: Why It's So Hard for White People to Talk about Race*. Boston: Beacon Press, 2018.
Douglas, Kelly Brown. *Stand Your Ground: Black Bodies and the Justice of God*. Maryknoll, NY: Orbis Books, 2015.
———. "Twenty Years a Womanist: An Affirming Challenge." In *Deeper Shades of Purple: Womanism in Religion and Society*, edited by Stacey M. Floyd Thomas. New York: NYU Press, 2006.
Dudiak, Jeffrey M. "Bienvenue—Just a Moment." In *Religion with/out Religion: The Prayers and Tears of John D. Caputo*, edited by James H. Olthuis. New York: Routledge, 2002.
Eddo-Lodge, Reni. *Why I'm No Longer Talking to White People about Race*. London: Bloomsbury Circus, 2017.
Ernst-Habib, Margit. "'Chosen by Grace': Reconsidering the Doctrine of Predestination." In *Feminist and Womanist Essays in Reformed Dogmatics*, edited by Amy Plantinga Pauw and Serene Jones. Louisville, KY: Westminster John Knox Press, 2006.
Fuss, Diana. *Essentially Speaking: Feminism, Nature and Difference*. New York: Routledge, 1989.
Garcia, Lorena. "Intersectionality." *Kalfou* 3, no. 1 (Spring 2016).
González, Justo L. *The Story of Christianity: The Early Church to the Dawn of the Reformation*, Volume 1. San Francisco: Harper & Row, 1984.
Goss, Robert. *Jesus Acted Up: A Gay and Lesbian Manifesto*. 1st edition. San Francisco: Harper San Francisco, 1993.
Gutiérrez, Gustavo. "Notes for a Theology of Liberation." *Theological Studies* 31, no. 2 (June 1970).
———. "Option for the Poor." In *Systematic Theology: Perspectives from Liberation Theology: Readings from Mysterium Liberationis*, edited by Jon Sobrino and Igna Ellacuria. Maryknoll, NY: Orbis Books, 1993.
———. *A Theology of Liberation: History, Politics, and Salvation*. Revised. Maryknoll, NY: Orbis Books, 1988.
Hägglund, Martin. "The Radical Evil of Deconstruction." *Journal for Cultural and Religious Theory* 11, no. 2 (Spring 2011): 126–50.
Hart, Kevin. *Trespass of the Sign: Deconstruction, Theology and Philosophy*. New York: Fordham University Press, 1989.
Hart, Trevor. "Revelation." In *The Cambridge Companion to Karl Barth*. New York: Cambridge University Press, 2000.
———. "The Word, the Words and the Witness: Proclamation as Divine and Human Reality in the Theology of Karl Barth." *Tyndale Bulletin* 46, no. 1 (May 1995).
Heim, S. Mark. "Differential Pluralism and Trinitarian Theologies of Religion." In *Divine Multiplicity: Trinities, Diversities, and the Nature of Relation*, edited by Chris Boesel and S. Wesley Ariarajah. New York: Fordham University Press, 2014.
Hibbert, Giles. "Gay Liberation in Relation to Christian Liberation." In *Towards a Theology of Gay Liberation*, edited by Malcolm Macourt. London: SCM Press, 1977.
Horn, Gerd-Rainer. *Western European Liberation Theology: The First Wave (1924–1959)*. Oxford: Oxford University Press, 2008.
Hunsinger, George. *How to Read Karl Barth: The Shape of His Theology*. New York: Oxford University Press, 1991.
———. *Karl Barth and Radical Politics*. Philadelphia: Westminster, 1976.
Ignatius and T. W. Crafer. *The Epistles of St. Ignatius*. London: SPCK, 1919.
Irenaeus. *The Third Book of St. Irenaeus, Bishop of Lyons, Against Heresies*. Oxford: Clarendon Press, 1874.

Isasi-Díaz, Ada Maria. *Mujerista Theology: A Theology for the Twenty-First Century*. Maryknoll, NY: Orbis, 1996.
Jantzen, Grace. "Contours of Queer Theology." *Literature and Theology* 15, no. 3 (September 2001): 276–85.
Jones, Serene. *Feminist Theory and Christian Theology*. Minneapolis: Fortress Press, 2000.
Kant, Immanuel. "Religion within the Bounds of Mere Reason." In *Religion and Rational Theology*, edited by Allen W. Wood and translated by George Di Giovanni. Cambridge: Cambridge University Press, 1996.
Keller, Catherine. *On the Mystery: Discerning Divinity in Process*. Minneapolis: Fortress Press, 2008.
Keller, Catherine, and Laurel Schneider, eds. *Polydoxy: Theology of Multiplicity and Relation*. New York: Routledge, 2010.
King, Martin Luther, Jr. "Our Struggle." In *A Testament of Hope: The Essential Writings and Speeches of Martin Luther King, Jr.* New York: Harper Collins, 1991.
Lowe, Mary Elise. "Gay, Lesbian, and Queer Theologies: Origins, Contributions, and Challenges." *Dialog* 48.1 (March 2009): 49–61.
Lowe, Walter. *Theology and Difference: The Wound of Reason*. Bloomington: Indiana University Press, 1993.
Lundberg, Matthew. "Echoes of Barth in Jon Sobrino's Critique of Natural Theology: A Dialogue in the Context of Post-Colonial Theology." In *Theology as Conversation: The Significance of Dialogue in Historical and Contemporary Theology*. Grand Rapids, MI: William B. Eerdmans, 2009.
Massey, James. "A Review of Dalit Theology." In *Dalit and Minjung Theologies: A Dialogue*. Bangalore: South Asia Theological Research Institute, 2006.
McAuliffe, Patricia. *Fundamental Ethics: A Liberationist Approach*. Washington, DC: Georgetown University Press, 1993.
McIntosh, Peggy. "White Privilege: Unpacking the Invisible Knapsack." *Peace and Freedom* (July/August 1989).
Milbank, John. *Theology and Social Theory: Beyond Secular Reason*. 2nd edition. Oxford, UK: Malden, MA: Wiley-Blackwell, 2006.
Milbank, John, Graham Ward, and Catherine Pickstock. *Radical Orthodoxy: A New Theology*. London: Routledge, 1999.
Miles, Margaret R. *The Word Made Flesh: A History of Christian Thought*. Malden, MA: Wiley Blackwell, 2004.
Naas, Michael. *Miracle and Machine: Jacques Derrida and the Two Sources of Religion, Science, and Media*. New York: Fordham University Press, 2012.
Nirmal, A. P. "Doing Theology from a Dalit Perspective." In *A Reader in Dalit Theology*. Madras: Gurukul Lutheran Theological College, 1990.
———. "Towards a Christian Dalit Theology." In *A Reader in Dalit Theology*. Madras: Gurukul Lutheran Theological College, 1990.
Olthuis, James H., ed. *Religion with/out Religion: The Prayers and Tears of John D. Caputo*. London; New York: Routledge, 2001.
Ott, Kate M. "Feminism and Justice: Who We Are, What We Do." In *Faith, Feminism, and Scholarship: The Next Generation*, edited by Melanie L. Harris and Kate M. Ott. New York: Palgrave Macmillan, 2011.
Pears, Angie. *Doing Contextual Theology*. London: Routledge, 2010.
Percy, Walker. *Love in the Ruins*. New York: Avon, 1971.
Petralla, Ivan. *Beyond Liberation Theology: A Polemic*. London: SCM Press, 2008.
Rappaport, Herman. *Later Derrida: Reading the Recent Work*. New York: Routledge, 2003.
Raschke, Carl A. *Force of God: Political Theology and the Crisis of Liberal Democracy*. NewYork: Columbia University Press, 2015.
Rasmussen, Joel D. S., Judith Wolfe, and Johannes Zachhuber. *The Oxford Handbook of Nineteenth-Century Christian Thought*. Oxford: Oxford University Press, 2017.
Recinos, Harold J., ed. *Wading Through Many Voices: Toward a Theology of Public Conversation*. Lanham, MD: Rowman & Littlefield, 2011.

Rieger, Joerg, ed. *Opting for the Margins: Postmodernity and Liberation in Christian Theology*. New York: Oxford University Press, 2003.

Riggs, Marcia. "Escaping the Polarity of Race versus Gender and Ethnicity." In *Wading through Many Voices: Toward a Theology of Public Conversation*. Edited by Harold J. Recinos. Lanham, MD: Rowman & Littlefield, 2011.

Rubenstein, Mary-Jane. "Dionysius, Derrida, and the Critique of 'Ontotheology.'" *Modern Theology* 24, no. 4 (2008).

———. *Strange Wonder: The Closure of Metaphysics and the Opening of Awe*. New York: Columbia University Press, 2008.

———. "Unknow Thyself: Apophaticism, Deconstruction, and Theology after Ontotheology." *Modern Theology* 19, no. 3 (July 2003).

Russell, Letty M. "Postcolonial Challenges and the Practice of Hospitality." In *A Just & True Love: Feminism at the Frontiers of Theological Ethics: Essays in Honor of Margaret A. Farley*, edited by Maura A. Ryan and Brian F. Linnane, 109–34. Notre Dame: University of Notre Dame Press, 2007.

Schneider, Laurel C. *Beyond Monotheism: A Theology of Multiplicity*. Milton Park, Abingdon, Oxon; New York: Routledge, 2008.

———. "Homosexuality, Queer Theory, and Christian Theology." *Religious Studies Review* 26, no. 1 (January 2000): 3–12.

Selvanayagam, Israel. "Waters of Life and Indian Cups: Protestant Attempts at Theologizing in India." In *Christian Theology in Asia*, edited by Sebastian C. H. Kim. Cambridge, UK; New York: Cambridge University Press, 2008.

Shore-Goss, Robert E. "Gay and Lesbian Liberation Theologies." In *Liberation Theologies in the United States: An Introduction*, edited by Stacey M. Floyd-Thomas and Anthony B. Pinn. New York; London: New York University Press, 2010.

———. "The Holy Spirit as Mischief-Maker." In *Queering Christianity: Finding a Place at the Table for LGBTQI Christians*, edited by Robert E. Shore-Goss. Santa Barbara: Praeger, 2013.

Smith, Andrea. "Heteropatriarchy and the Three Pillars of White Supremacy: Rethinking Women of Color Organizing." In *Color of Violence: The INCITE! Anthology*. Edited by INCITE! Women of Color Against Violence. Cambridge, MA: South End Press, 2006.

Smith, James K. A. *Jacques Derrida: Live Theory*. Annotated edition. New York; London: Bloomsbury Academic, 2005.

Sobrino, Jon. *Jesus the Liberator: A Historical-Theological Reading of Jesus of Nazareth*. Maryknoll, NY: Orbis Books, 1993.

———. *No Salvation Outside the Poor: Prophetic-Utopian Essays*. Maryknoll, NY: Orbis Books, 2008.

Spivak, Gayatri. "Subaltern Studies: Deconstructing Historiography." In *The Spivak Reader: Selected Works of Gayatri Spivak*, edited by Donna Landry and Gerald Maclean. New York: Routledge, 1996.

Stuart, Elizabeth. *Gay and Lesbian Theologies: Repetitions with Critical Difference*. Burlington, VT: Ashgate, 2003.

Sullivan, Nikki. *A Critical Introduction to Queer Theory*. New York: NYU Press, 2003.

Tatum, Beverly. *Why Are All the Black Kids Sitting Together in the Cafeteria? And Other Conversations about Race*. Twentieth Anniversary Edition. New York: Basic Books, 2017.

Taylor, Mark C. *Erring: A Postmodern A/theology*. Chicago: University Of Chicago Press, 1987.

Tertullian and T. Herbert Bindley. *Tertullian on the Testimony of the Soul and on the "Prescription" of Heretics*. Early Church Classics. London: SCPK, 1914.

Thandeka. *Learning to Be White: Money, Race and God in America*. Bloomsbury Academic, 2000.

Tonstad, Linn Marie. "The Limits of Inclusion: Queer Theology and Its Others." *Theology and Sexuality* 21, no. 1 (2015).

Townes, Emilie M. *Womanist Ethics and the Cultural Production of Evil*. New York: Palgrave Macmillan, 2006.

Trimiew, Darryl M. "Ethics." In *Handbook of U.S. Theologies of Liberation*, edited by Miguel A. De La Torre. St. Louis, MO: Chalice Press, 2004.

Uwujaren, Jarune, and Jamie Utt. "Why Our Feminism Must Be Intersectional (And 3 Ways to Practice It)." www.everydayfeminism.com/2015/01/why-our-feminism-must-be-intersectional/.

Volf, Miroslav. *Exclusion and Embrace: A Theological Exploration of Identity, Otherness, and Reconciliation*. Nashville, TN: Abingdon, 1996.

Ward, Graham. *Barth, Derrida and the Language of Theology*. Cambridge: Cambridge University Press, 1995.

Webster, John C. B. "From Indian Church to Indian Theology: An Attempt at Theological Construction." In *A Reader in Dalit Theology*. Madras: Gurukul Lutheran Theological College, 1990.

Welch, Sharon D. "Dancing with Chaos: Reflections on Power, Contingency, and Social Change." In *Liberation Theologies, Postmodernity and the Americas*. Edited by David Batstone et al. London: Routledge, 1997.

West, Traci C. *Disruptive Christian Ethics: When Racism and Women's Lives Matter*. Louisville, KY: Westminster John Knox Press, 2006.

———. "Is a Womanist a Black Feminist? Marking the Distinctions and Defying Them." In *Deeper Shades of Purple: Womanism in Religion and Society*. New York: NYU Press, 2006.

Williams, Delores S. *Sisters in the Wilderness Challenge of Womanist God-Talk*. New York: Orbis Books, 1995.

Index

Alcoff, Linda, 131
Althaus-Reid, Marcella, 104–105
Altizer, Thomas, 19
Armour, Ellen T., 37n11
Augustine, 20, 170–172, 193–197
apophatic theology, 4–5, 24–25, 164–167, 170–172, 176, 185, 194–202

Baldwin, James, 148
Ball, LaVar, 215–223
Barth, Karl: on nineteenth century, 185–187; on divine decision as truly divine, 182–183, 190–191, 193–201; on Jesus Christ as subject and object of divine decision, 190–196; on impossibility and necessity, 183, 193, 201–203, 225; and natural theology, 165, 187–189; and patriarchy, 205–206; on political power, 187–188; on revelation, 184, 189–192; on theology as human enterprise, 182, 193, 199–202; on theology's proper object, 182, 184–185, 190–191
Bennington, Geoffrey, 44, 73n52
Black Entertainment Television, 221
black lives matter, 141–142, 221
Boesel, Chris, 12n4, 13n13, 13n24, 73n57, 163–164, 178n29, 185, 206
Boff, Leonardo, 85–87
Brunner, Emil, 184, 188–189
Buber, Martin, 1, 3

Calvin, John, 10, 157–158, 170–171, 191–197
Cannon, Katie G., 101–102
Caputo, John D.: critique of strong theology, 28, 159, 166–175, 194, 197, 224; on decision, 28–34, 71; on Derrida and religion, 7, 17, 19–28; on impossibility, 7, 20, 23–25, 27–28, 35–36, 42, 45, 66; on justice, 20, 23–28, 31, 35–36, 57; on problem of exclusivity, 7, 17, 19, 20–21, 25–28, 36, 41, 49, 65–66, 77, 110–111; and radical hermeneutics, 18–19; on religion without religion, 19–23, 26–27, 167; and theology of perhaps, 19, 28–32, 172–174, 197, 225; and *tout autre*, 21, 24, 26, 28, 33, 167; and weak theology, 19, 27–28, 42, 166–172, 175, 194, 197, 225
Carter, J. Kameron, 13n13, 13n15, 177n17
Charlamagne Tha God, 217–222
Cheng, Patrick, 91–92
Clarke, Sathianathan, 105–107
Cone, James, 37n5, 87–90, 98, 109, 113, 142–148, 211, 222
Cowherd, Colin, 215–220
Crenshaw, Kimberlé, 102–103
Critchley, Simon, 38n19
Crockett, Clayton, 37n6, 38n19, 161

De La Torre, Miguel, 108, 153n26

death of God theology, 19
decision: cut and division of, 1–11, 17, 19–27, 42, 48–49, 58–71, 77–80, 90, 119–121, 126–127, 136–138, 148–151, 168, 210–213; discerning difficult, 2–4, 7, 32, 51, 53–56, 59, 68, 77, 120, 126, 134, 152, 212–213, 222; exigency of, 59, 69, 142–143, 151, 211; and exposure, 12, 29, 69, 213; as inescapable, 3, 9, 41, 63, 78–79, 120, 150, 184, 223. *See also* divine decision; exclusion; indecision; justice; privilege
deconstruction: of absolute purity, 53; of metaphysics, 43–44; and method, 2, 6, 61, 63, 67, 73n65; and morality, 63–64; and the gift, 44, 46. *See also* deconstructive; Jacques Derrida
deconstructive: aporia, 7–8, 17, 19, 33, 41–50, 54–60, 63, 65–67, 77, 124, 159, 201–203, 223; critique/affirmation, 50–51; impossibility/inescapability, 2, 7–8, 10–11, 41–70, 159, 162, 175–177, 181–184; *pharmakon*, 43–44, 121–125, 142, 164, 175, 201, 210–211; supplement, 44, 122–124, 125; trace, 43–44. *See also* deconstruction; Jacques Derrida
Derrida, Jacques: on apophatic, 4–5, 21–22, 24–25, 166, 176, 198; on apocalyptic, 21–22, 24, 66; on decision, 58–60, 120; on divinanimality, 213; and *il n'y a pas de hors-texte*, 8, 55; on incalculability of justice, 51–52, 57; on law/justice, 56–57; on messianic, 21–24, 35–36, 45, 50–51, 66–67, 167; on metaphysics of presence, 23, 44, 122, 125; on *mysterium tremendum*, 46, 157, 173; on religion, 19–22, 45; on police, 53–55; on responsibility, 45–48, 49, 61–64; on speech/writing, 43–44, 121–125; and violence, 52–53, 68, 175. *See also* deconstruction; deconstructive
divine decision: avoidance of, 2, 10–11, 157–160, 168–170, 172–177, 202, 203; exclusivity of, 6, 10, 80–90, 158–160, 162–164, 168–169, 203–204, 224; and human mastery over divinity, 10, 158–159, 163–174, 185, 189, 194–203, 205–206; as preferential option, 8, 78–81, 83–96, 105–107, 119, 143; inclusion of, 2, 10–11, 158, 181–184, 193, 201–202, 203–205, 224–225; as predestination, 10, 80, 157–158, 159
Douglas, Kelly Brown, 102, 165, 170–171, 191–195

Ernst-Habib, Margit, 13n23, 159
essentialism, 103, 105–107
exclusion, problem of: contemporary consensus about, 1–6, 10, 25, 48, 64–66, 77–78, 162–163; in Christian tradition, 1, 5–6, 80, 160–163; strategic, 79, 81, 97, 113n3, 138, 141. *See also* John D. Caputo; decision; divine decision; justice; liberation theology

feminist, 100, 102–103, 109, 115n71, 149, 151, 159, 217
Foucault, Michel, 103
Feuerbach, Ludwig, 184, 186, 190

Gramsci, Antonio, 106
Goss, Robert, 92–93, 98
Gutiérrez, Gustavo, 13n19, 82–85, 87, 93, 97–98, 113

Hägglund, Martin, 1, 41, 65–68, 70, 163
Hart, Kevin, 37n11
Hart, Trevor, 206n5, 206n8
Hegelian, 6, 26, 163, 186
Hunsinger, George, 199, 206n7, 207n15
hybridity, 8, 78, 103–104, 143

Ignatius of Antioch, 160
identity politics, 99, 105, 111–113, 135. *See also* hybridity; intersectionality
inclusion. *See* decision; problem of exclusion
indecision: as decision for status quo, 81, 85–86, 89, 90, 127–132, 222; deconstruction of, 17, 30, 49, 56, 60, 79, 211; devil of, 3, 4; illusion of, 2–3, 8–9, 12, 70, 121, 126–133, 144, 148, 223; as injustice, 59, 78–79, 120–121, 132, 150, 151–152. *See also* decision; privilege; undecidability
injustice. *See* problem of exclusion; indecision; justice; liberation theology

Index

intersectionality, 8–9, 78, 80, 93, 99–105, 109, 119, 135, 141, 148–149, 150, 151–152
Irenaeus of Lyons, 160
Isasi-Díaz, Ada Maria, 12n3, 131–132, 177n19
Islamophobia, 214

James, Lebron, 221
Jantzen, Grace, 114n36
Jones, Serene, 116n87
Judaism, 5–6, 13n13, 20, 26, 162
justice, 1–2; Caputo on, 20–28, 31, 35–36; and decision, 8–9, 11, 51, 120, 127–129, 136–139, 140–146, 149–152, 213–214, 222; Derrida on, 43, 45, 50–51, 51–52, 54, 56–60; and particularity, 96, 138–139, 150–151; and preference, 8–9, 78–99, 105–113, 124, 127–129, 136–142; and religion, 19, 20, 24, 25, 35; and solidarity, 90–93, 97, 99, 105–113, 134–136, 222–223. *See also* divine decision; problem of exclusion; indecision; liberation theology

Kaepernick, Colin, 221
Kant, Immanuel, 5–6, 162–163, 185–186
Keller, Catherine, 13n24, 18, 177n3, 177n11, 178n53, 208n80, 208n83
Kierkegaard, Søren, 47, 59, 69, 73n52
King, Martin Luther, Jr., 147–148, 151

Lacan, Jacques, 103
Leahy, Kristine, 215–223
liberation theology: critiques of, 8, 78, 98–113, 119; dalit, 94–96, 105–106, 119, 151; death of, 99, 108, 119; black, 87–90, 98, 100–101, 109, 133, 142–148, 151; gay and lesbian, 90–93; Latin American, 82–87, 140, 151; problem of exclusion and, 8–9, 78–80, 83, 87–88, 91, 95–113, 121, 127–128. *See also* divine decision; justice
Lowe, Walter, 18, 37n11, 61
lynching, 37n5, 147–148, 219–220, 222

Macbeth, 4
Malcolm X, 220

Marion, Jean-Luc, 37n7
Marxist, 50, 85, 104
masculinity, 103, 205, 222
McAuliffe, Patricia, 127–128, 130–132
McIntosh, Peggy, 146
#metoo, 217, 221
Milbank, John, 37n10
minjung , 97
mujerista, 97, 108–109, 131

Naas, Michael, 38n19
Nancy, Jean-Luc, 37n7
negative theology. *See* apophatic theology
Niebuhr, Reinhold, 147–148

ontotheology, 38n42, 166, 224–225
orthodoxy/heresy, 160–162
Ott, Kate, 109–110, 139

patriarchy, 98, 100, 104, 135, 205–206, 214. *See also* feminist; masculinity
Pears, Angie, 13n20, 99, 150–151
Percy, Walker, 209–211
Petrella, Ivan, 107–108, 151
Pickstock, Catherine, 37n10
police brutality, 54, 56, 72n36, 221
postcolonial theory, 78, 103, 104
predestination. *See* divine decision
privilege, 8–9, 79, 88, 101–106, 110, 120–121, 130, 133, 144–149, 221, 223; as distortion, 8, 11–12, 70, 121, 126–127, 147–152, 211; power and, 2, 8–9, 11–12, 70, 87, 108, 110, 121–129, 133, 136–138, 145–152, 158, 212–217, 222–224

queer theory, 78, 90–93, 98, 104–105

racism, 87–90, 99, 108, 110, 112, 129–131, 134–135, 142–148, 164–165, 214, 218–223
Radical Orthodoxy, 19
Raschke, Carl A., 38n19, 38n20
Rasmussen, Joel D.S., 207n10
Rieger, Joerg, 111
Riggs, Marcia, 112
Rubenstein, Mary-Jane, 68–69, 166, 208n58
Russell, Letty, 164–165

Saussure, Ferdinand de, 43
#sayhername, 221
Schleiermacher, Friedrich, 184, 186
Schneider, Laurel, 91, 177n11, 177n12
Sobrino, Jon, 86–87, 140–141, 165
Smith, Andrea, 135–136
Smith, James K.A., 38n19
Spivak, Gayatri, 113n3
Stuart, Elizabeth, 114n36, 116n95

Tatum, Beverly, 129–131, 136, 146, 214
Taylor, Mark C., 19
Tertullian, 160–161
Thandeka, 108, 146
Till, Emmett, 147, 219–220
Tonstad, Linn Marie, 115n67
Townes, Emilie, 3–4, 149–150
Trump, Donald, 221

undecidability, 2–3, 28, 30, 32–36, 53, 58, 142, 157–158, 168–169, 205, 225; alternative reading of, 4, 41, 45, 56–60, 65–71; deconstructing, 2–3, 4–8, 11–12, 17–18, 56, 65, 71, 79, 213, 223–225; as in/decision, 3, 7, 19, 42, 45, 56, 60, 70, 71, 77, 120, 126, 142, 149–150, 157–158, 162, 174–176, 181–184, 210–212; and justice, 58, 60, 79, 142, 149. *See also* decision; Jacques Derrida; divine decision; indecision
universal/particular, 5–6, 87, 96, 97–98, 112, 141, 144–145

Vattimo, Gianni, 37n7
Volf, Miroslav, 12n2, 177n18

Walker, Alice, 102
Ward, Graham, 37n10, 37n11
#webelieverher, 217, 221
Welch, Sharon D., 112
West, Traci, 134–135, 136–137
white supremacy, 112, 129–131, 135–136, 145, 165, 222
Whitlock, Jason, 219–220, 222
Williams, Delores S., 99–101, 102
Williams, Serena, 220
womanist, 99–103, 109, 133, 151; and black feminist, 102, 134–135

Zachhuber, Johannes, 207n10

About the Author

Michael Oliver is a departmental lecturer in the faculty of theology and religion at the University of Oxford, UK. He holds a PhD in theological and philosophical studies in religion from Drew University, with a concentration in women's, gender, and sexuality studies.

www.ingramcontent.com/pod-product-compliance
Lightning Source LLC
Chambersburg PA
CBHW050902300426
44111CB00010B/1343